ENCOUNTERS

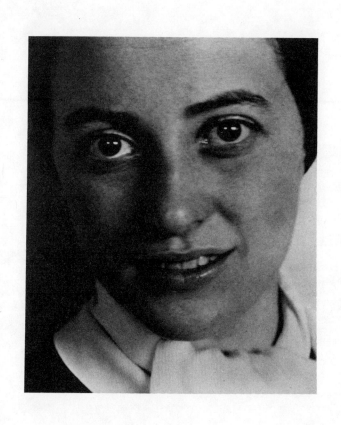

DOROTHY NORMAN

ENCOUNTERS

A MEMOIR

A HELEN AND KURT WOLFF BOOK

HARCOURT BRACE JOVANOVICH, PUBLISHERS

San Diego   New York   London

HBJ

Library of Congress Cataloging in Publication Data
Norman, Dorothy, 1905–
   Encounters.
   "A Helen and Kurt Wolff book."
   1. Norman, Dorothy, 1905–   .   2. United States—
Biography.   I. Title.
CT275.N694A36   1984   973.9'092'4   85-5869
ISBN 0-15-128792-9

Designed by Dalia Hartman

Printed in the United States of America

First edition

A B C D E

To Edward   my first love

Religion is something infinitely simple, ingenuous. It is not knowledge, not content of feeling (for all content is admitted from the start, where a man comes to terms with life), it is not duty and not renunciation, it is not restriction: but in the infinite extent of the universe it is a direction of the heart. However a man may proceed, wandering to right or to left, and stumble and fall and get up, and do wrong here and suffer wrong there, and here be mistreated and over there himself miswish and mistreat and misunderstand: all this passes into the great religions and upholds and enriches in them the God that is their center.

Rainer Maria Rilke

ACKNOWLEDGMENTS

My thanks to the Alfred Stieglitz Archive in the Collection of American Literature, the Beinecke Rare Book and Manuscript Library, Yale University, for gracious permission to publish letters by Alfred Stieglitz to Dorothy Norman and occasional letters by Dorothy Norman to Alfred Stieglitz. My warmest thanks for permission to print their letters to Max Lerner, Lewis Mumford, and Mai-mai Sze; also to the late Honorable Dorothy Brett, Indira Gandhi, Henry Miller, Jawaharlal Nehru, and Ignazio Silone. My gratitude to Rama Coomaraswamy for permission to publish letters from Ananda K. Coomaraswamy; to Ajit Hutheesing for the letter from Krishna Hutheesing; to Pavel Litvinov for those from Ivy Litvinov; to John Marin, Jr. for those from John Marin; to Florence Williams for the letter from William Carlos Williams; to Ellen Wright for those from Richard Wright.

With thanks to the *New York Post* for permission to reprint the Dorothy Norman column of June 17, 1946; to W. W. Norton and Co., New York, for the Rainer Maria Rilke epigraph from *Letters of Rainer Maria Rilke, 1910–1926*; to Princeton University Press for a passage from Mai-mai Sze's *The Tao of Painting*.

Credits for photographs are acknowledged with appreciation: James Abbe (46), courtesy Washburn Gallery; Eric Kroll (24, 25); Mary Lescaze, photographer unknown, by permission of Lee Lescaze (16); Arnold Newman © (frontispiece); *New York Daily Mirror* (27).

Photographs by Alfred Stieglitz (8, 9, 10, 11, 13, 20, 21, 52, jacket front); Edward Weston (48), Mary Lee Leatherbee (57), Gottscho-Schleisner (32, 33), and Dorothy Norman are from the Dorothy Norman Collection.

Special thanks to Andrew E. Norman for voluntarily writing his memories of Stieglitz and the Gaston Lachaise Torso at An American Place.

With deepest gratitude to Elinor Weis for her valuable suggestions and tireless assistance in preparing the manuscript. With added thanks to Ethel Bob for her careful assistance in connection with the photographs, and other aspects of the book.

ENCOUNTERS

1

Born in Philadelphia, 1905. First it moves slowly, then fast—like a miracle. Almost all I know without being told is the torment of being walked to school by the baker's daughter. Marta lives over her father's shop. Our house is larger, on a broader street. No one explains it, but it means I can't walk to school alone. Marta can. Why?

Even in warm weather, Mother insists I wear a hat. Because Marta doesn't wear one, I refuse to. Is she poorer? Why do some people have more than others?

Blood rushes to my hatless head and I feel unaccustomed anger. Mother mentions it later as the time I wouldn't wear a hat—my first act of defiance. As though for no reason. I am ashamed before Marta, ashamed of being protected. I feel guilty, too, of harming Mother's nerves by saying my initial No. I have no notion what might happen if I walked to school unattended, nor do I know whether Marta cares about what I do or do not wear. I understand beyond words that if you ask questions you will hurt someone or be hurt. And you never receive a proper answer. Everything is something that I don't understand and you dare not talk about. I want to know everything. How do you find out?

Strangest of all is that, despite my concern for Marta, I feel there is a certain rightness and dignity about wearing a hat, even when it is warm.

I was born on Diamond Street near Fairmount Park. But the neighborhood changed. "Changed" meant going down, so we moved to a larger house on North Broad Street.

How had my father, Louis Stecker, done it? He had less formal education in all his life than I had by the time I rebelled against walking to school wearing a hat. He came to the United States from Austria, alone and penniless, in his teens; got a job without speaking English; soon brought his relatives from Europe. He supported them and, after his marriage, some of my mother's family and still others.

Slowly I become aware that thousands of young people—unsung, unsure, fumbling their way—have been crowding to America, devoutly committed to building a better life than they had abroad. And don't we children feel superior in a rush, with our proper grammar and pronunciation?

I have a Fräulein whose English is no more perfect than Father's, but that's a different matter because she is supposed to speak German and teach it to me. I have no interest in correcting her English but, with Father, I want very much to tell him whenever he makes the slightest error. I sense, though, that that would be considered brazen.

Between the time Father leaves home in the morning and returns tired and late for dinner, he goes to a big, mysterious, gloomy building he owns called a factory. In it thousands of dresses are made by machine. Motors whir and men and women carry around odd-looking pieces of material to be fitted together. Father looks different from those around him. He is quiet with people, doesn't boss them. Each time I'm taken to visit, I want to leave as soon as possible. The dresses—not like those my mother and her friends wear—are more elaborate; some are even beaded. I can't understand why anyone would buy them or why Father has them made.

Father is trim and fit, stands straight. You know just what he's thinking, and if anyone is vulgar or noisy, he looks pained. He wants to be proud of us—my two older brothers, Jack and Bob, and me. He speaks a great deal about loving us and working hard so we can have everything he was deprived of. I don't know what "deprived" means and I can't see that I've done anything to deserve what I'm given. Most of the time I'm uncomfortable and constrained. I rarely speak. Father never acts as though he wants to be thanked, but I find it rude not to show my gratitude. I don't know how. And I feel a vague sense of impatience.

We have poor relatives to whom we give our old clothes. Doing this is just as embarrassing and demeaning as being walked to school by Marta. What a dreadful way of insulting someone, rather than being kind, I think. But you can't just throw things away either, or be mean if you have more than others. Like everything else, it is puzzling and distressing.

Mother was born in Philadelphia, in Germantown. Her parents came from the outskirts of Berlin, arrived in the United States before the Civil War. Grandfather fought in it and received a wound that caused his untimely death.

By the time I know Mother's stately, straight-backed mother, she is a widow rocking in her chair, reading the Old Testament. She never smiles. My grandmother speaks cultivated North German, as does Mother. They frown upon any other. Their sense of superiority annoys me, yet I like making well-enunciated sounds myself, and the more I hear inferior accents, the more I respect the way Mother and Grandmother roll their German meticulously off their upper palates.

They instruct me often and solemnly, "Remember you are Jewish." Both admonish me to be quieter, more polite than others. "Never be loud." Father also says to speak softly and be polite. "Be a fine and generous person." But he never mentions doing things for a special reason. I love him for that.

Mother and I visit Grandmother on Saturday afternoons; she gives me the same advice each week: "Never wear glasses and never marry anyone who isn't Jewish." Father tells me to "treat" any friend with whom I have lunch or ice cream, and never let others pay for anything. It sounds kind and generous, but makes things difficult. Of course, be generous. But how can you always pay without seeming preposterous? I haven't earned the money Father gives me to spend and I become so self-conscious about always treating that, if I lose a battle to do so, I feel I've committed some unspeakable, stingy crime. I'm miserable and afraid, too, that Father will find out.

I like to go shopping with Father rather than Mother. Our tastes are similar and much simpler than hers. I can't understand why she complains about our extravagance, since what we buy is plain. Father never discusses how much a dress or sweater, hat or purse costs. Mother's objections always confuse me if I buy something with Father, or don't want to buy anything when I go out with her.

Will it be forever impossible to have one uncomplicated, clear experience that isn't embarrassing or nerve-racking?

We own an automobile, and since cars are big and complicated, a man is hired to drive it. Gradually I become aware that other "chauffeurs" wear uniforms. Since I dislike attracting attention—not many people we know have cars—I bend my head down, hoping no one will see me. Still, if we have a driver, he should wear a special kind of suit and politely call me Miss Dorothy, the way any properly trained chauffeur would do. He should open the car door and close it with an air of decorum. I decide that Father must dislike ostentation as much as I do, and that our "chauffeur" doubtless does additional jobs for him at his factory. Still, our driver remains a problem for me. He never looks entirely neat, nor does he have the manner of the usual chauffeur. I hide my face for one reason and blush for an opposite one.

Rumors spread about the possibility of the United States entering the war; it's considered wise not to speak German. So my German vocabulary remains that of a child of ten. Having anything German in your background makes people nervous. But war or no war, our family is moving up. I pretend not to notice but cannot help it. Fräulein must leave; a mademoiselle is engaged.

Mademoiselle didn't live in the house, as Fräulein had, but came twice a week after school to teach me French. She took me to one of Sarah Bernhardt's farewell performances. Mademoiselle claimed to know Madame Bernhardt, which may or may not have been true, but box seats were reserved for us, and I rigidly clasped a bouquet that became hot in my hand and wilted. I was instructed to present it to the celebrated star backstage, and to recite something for her I had learned by heart. I disliked memorizing—especially poetry in a language I didn't understand—and I was frightened. Scenes from Edmond Rostand's *L'Aiglon* were performed, and a short war play.

I was interested in neither the plays nor the actors. I sat too near and was terrified. We went backstage and Madame Bernhardt bent over to kiss me. I hoped I would faint but I didn't know how. She had only one leg; her hair was dyed bright carrot-color; she wore a great deal of garish makeup on her face, which was so wrinkled I thought she must die. Her soiled, shredded shirt was largely covered with red paint supposed to look like blood.

Mademoiselle told me what a lucky girl I was. To be sure, I never before had sat in a box or met an illustrious actress. It took me days to get over the horror and shock of what I witnessed under those glaring lights.

Most of the children's books I read come in series—about Dotty Dimple, Elsie Dinsmore, Grace Harlowe, Molly Brown, Betty Wales; about Little Women and Little Men. Each story in turn holds my interest for a while—except Elsie Dinsmore—but always before I've finished any series, I can't look at one more word in it.

I cry so hard over Oliver Twist, my tears make enormous stains on the large green plush chair in our library. If you smooth the plush one way, the tears don't show too much, but when you smooth it the other way, the effect is alarming. One day Mother enters the room while I'm reading *David Copperfield*. I'm as frightened she'll see the new stream of tears ruining the chair as I am embarrassed to be found weeping. After that I always read in my own room and resent any interruptions.

1915. A children's picnic, in the country. I become blissfully aware of flowers in a field. It's spring. There are violets. Violets! "You may pick them if you wish." If I wish! I rush, bend down, pluck the fragile, cool stems. And look up. Confusion again. Thrice the amount of blossoms sag in my warm, excited hand as in that of any other girl.

I run from one to another, blushing, offering some of my flowers so as to feel more comfortable—the sole gesture I can think to make. What's wrong? I have such a profusion only because I love them.

At the time I didn't realize flowers could be bought. I imagined that sensitive people possessed them by way of some fitting though mysterious logic. We have no garden and when Mother first takes me to a florist's shop, I'm amazed to hear her ask about prices and place an order. Flowers are expensive, she explains; she buys them only if we're having guests. Then we also use fine linens with lace, special china, and silver. This seems dishonest.

Sometimes a florist hands me a single flower, with a smile. Most often a red rose. I'm told, "Your brown eyes are so *large*." I stand speechless because of the magnificent flower pinned at my shoulder, but dislike being told about my eyes. Afterward Mother warns me not to be misled by flattery. I must believe neither florists nor other shopkeepers who say they admire my eyes or that I'm pretty. Their sole interest, I'm assured, is in keeping her as a customer.

We plant a rose bush in our back yard; its leaves fade almost at once. A catalpa tree comes up by itself, radiant in the spring. Year after year I save and plant every cherry and peach pit I can retrieve; I visualize the miraculous blossoms and fruit that will appear momentarily. To my despair, not a single seed takes root.

On Saturdays and high holidays the family goes to a Reform Jewish temple. The building is ugly, the music dull. Mother looks virtuous, prim, pious; she is neatly dressed but never overdressed. Father is clearly bored, as am I. Jack and Bob fidget. I hear nothing that inspires: the rabbi speaks endlessly against such irreligious activities as playing golf on the sabbath. Sunday school supposedly informs us about Judaism, but I remember none of its lessons even the following day. I vow never to attend temple unless forced to by Mother.

Our house on Broad Street is two doors from Dropsie College—devoted to Hebraic studies—and an Orthodox Jewish synagogue, Mikveh Israel. My parents and all their friends, Reform Jews, are less strict and ritualistic; for them the two buildings are objects of ridicule.

In the autumn my brothers insisted on my going to a celebration of Sukkoth at Mikveh Israel. On the synagogue's grounds and on those of Dropsie College, I witnessed the only lovely sight I ever saw in our neighborhood. Strung from the top of a booth, called a *sukkah*, that was partly open to the sky, were shining red cranberries and yellow tomatoes. The sides were decorated with fresh greens, wildflowers, cornstalks, clusters of vegetables and fruit, and an overflowing cornucopia. I found nothing anywhere during the Thanksgiving season to compare with the *sukkah*'s glory. Children who lived nearby crowded into the synagogue grounds. On two evenings fruit, cake, and wine were served. I had the impression—perhaps mistaken—that many came because of the refreshments. This seemed indecent, like ringing doorbells greedily at Halloween.

At ten I heard my first opera, because Father advertised in the program. He received two free tickets that he and Mother had no interest in using, so one of my brothers was made to escort me on Tuesday evenings, whenever New York's Metropolitan Opera Company performed in Philadelphia. Both Jack and Bob disliked their assignment, but at least they could divide it.

Enrico Caruso's voice in *Pagliacci* so astonished me that I couldn't believe he was a human being like myself. I heard the word "virtuoso" for the first time, used to describe him, but I found it not sufficiently extravagant. Geraldine Farrar in *Carmen* was the most glorious of all women—even more splendid than the movie star Norma Talmadge. I was told Farrar sang false notes but refused to believe it. After I noticed the flaws myself, I still rushed to defend her.

In a solo performance Anna Pavlova danced with such magic that a dying swan became for me the most romantic of images.

Because of the sad, long lane of automobile showrooms that opens near our house, we move to an apartment on Spruce Street, close to the Academy of Music.

If you don't subscribe by the season to Philadelphia Orchestra concerts—which my family does not—you have a hard time obtaining single tickets; the seats are always sold out. I, who have no knowledge of music and play the piano abominably—I take lessons, but to no avail—find myself even more enthralled by symphonic music than by opera.

A friend, Louise Weyl—the same age as I am, but a fine pianist—attends the Friday concerts. She is the first person I know whose family subscribes. I look upon her as extremely knowledgeable, yet she confesses that when, at twelve, she first was taken to Academy concerts, she was unprepared to understand the music. Her primary interest was to see whether anyone present was either younger or smaller than herself!

On Friday afternoons I rush to the Academy and look for elderly ladies who step from limousines or walk toward the building in groups. They sit in boxes, and if a friend is absent, they bring back her unused ticket, to be sold for the Orchestra's Pension Fund. I plead, I beg to buy one of the cherished bits of cardboard before they reach the ticket window. Now and then an imposing dowager places an arm upon my shoulder and says, to my amazement, "You have such beautiful big brown eyes, my dear. You must come and sit with us in our box. No, child, we wouldn't hear of your paying for your seat!" And I am swept along into fairyland.

The conductor, Leopold Stokowski, is the most impressive figure I have ever seen. He so fascinates me that I would gladly watch him without hearing a note of music. Even to observe his back is electrifying: the tall, imposing figure; the subtle way he moves his long slender hands; the gold-crowned head —alert, poised like that of some glorious bird. When Stokowski faces the audience with aloof grandeur to acknowledge applause, my eyes fill with tears.

I am moved not only by his superb classical programs but by the first modern music I hear. I revel in Stravinsky's *Petrouchka, Firebird, Fireworks.* How, I wonder, can people be shocked by them? I am excited by Moussorgsky, his depth and dissonances. I would be happy to listen to Tchaikovsky's *Nutcracker,* Rimsky-Korsakov's *Snow Maiden,* and *Petrouchka* for hours on end. They rush about in my head day and night; there's no way to stop them.

The first time I dared utter a critical musical judgment was when Stokowski conducted his own arrangement of Bach's *Passacaglia and Fugue in C Minor.* "The harps," I lamented shyly, "are too sentimental, too theatrical. So is the entire performance." I was astonished that everyone with whom I spoke agreed. Yet I blushed, realizing how easy it was to criticize genius.

One Friday afternoon Stokowski stopped abruptly after conducting only a few bars of music. The audience hadn't settled down between his entrance and the raising of his baton. He wheeled about, glared, turned back to the orchestra, and signaled to begin again.

He interrupted still other concerts: the audience had applauded after separate movements of a symphony, failing to reserve its appreciation until the end. Stokowski rapped his baton sharply, faced the audience, gave a short lecture—the accent at its most beguiling—and no one present made the same error again. Another time he tapped for attention as a reprimand to those who habitually created a disturbance by leaving early to catch trains for the suburbs.

8

The audience was roughly divided between the furious, who resented Stokowski's "lectures"—they ranted endlessly against him—and his admirers, who were enchanted by whatever he dared to do. Like it or not, his refusal to compromise, the respect and discipline he generated, swiftly altered the audience's behavior. This rapid transformation made me feel that now, at last, we were functioning correctly within a great tradition.

The orchestra played better for Stokowski than for anyone else. At concerts in other American cities, I discovered, the musical public responded with far less sensitivity and decorum than did Philadelphians.

At thirteen I'm sent to Camp Accomac in Maine for the summer months. The melancholy of evening taps. Spirited singing around an aromatic, crackling campfire under brilliant moon and stars. Waking to watch the sunrise in the awesome intimacy of the out-of-doors. Writing letters on gleaming birchbark, until we're told it destroys the trees.

The excitement of being in a bunkhouse with girls my own age. They come from cities whose names I have only read, but now distant places seem real and close. Intelligent, well-bred girls with whom I can have endless discussions about books, dreams, fears. I develop crushes on handsome older campers and counselors. My spirits rise in direct proportion to how often during a day I see them.

Accomac—strict and well run—has compelling qualities to which I respond. No moment of the day is wasted. The necessity of having excellent form in everything we do is beautifully satisfying, just as was speaking German for Grandmother and Mother. Landing a canoe perfectly—parallel to a float, without touching it—is a goal glorious for its own sake. I become obsessed with sports and good sportsmanship, with trying to attain perfection in tennis, basketball, hockey, swimming, diving. But especially in tennis.

The head of the camp, Miss Corinne Arnold, looks to neither right nor left when she walks through a room full of people, yet notices everything. What does it matter that she is large, that her dresses are without style or loveliness, that her face is in no way memorable? The restraint, the quiet dignity of the woman—her awareness—arouse my loyalty, admiration, adoration. In a low, firm voice she reads aloud Edith Wharton's *Ethan Frome*, a book different from and more tragic, more relentless, than any I have yet known.

Miss Arnold speaks to us about Accomac's ideals; about truth, generosity, being a good loser. To be silent when you win is as important as to lack bitterness in defeat.

I am unable to look upon my experience at camp in merely personal terms. Miss Arnold's goals open up new vistas and I'm never the same again. I find it difficult to sleep, I'm so busy thinking about how I must live. I come to believe the virtues she extols can contribute not only to the well-being of a single life, but to that of a community—even an entire civilization. I dream of a universe in which everyone will be honorable, well-disposed toward his neighbor and capable of doing a first-rate job.

Accomac friends describe with elation boarding schools they attend in winter. They are just like camp, except that you study; the teachers are good, the sports excellent. You have a sense of independence, the way you do at Accomac, because you're away from home and with girls from all over the country.

I listen almost with disbelief. Back in Philadelphia, I rebel more than ever against the dreary public school I attend. Our books are tedious and soiled; the teachers—unlike the counselors at camp—uninspiring; the buildings, hideous. The treeless, paved yards in which we play are harsh and intimidating. Everything seems tawdry. I learn nothing I long to know. The spirit of camp, its beauty and high standards, are totally lacking.

I study every boarding school advertisement I come upon. The ones that sound most tempting describe schools in New England. By what seems coincidence, the camp counselors I have most admired are from New England; the simple farmhouses and landscapes I have loved in Maine symbolize New England for me, too. Everything I read and hear about the region contributes to my exalted vision of it.

Excellent private day schools are located in Philadelphia, but they are anti-Semitic. The few Jewish girls who go to them pretend not to be Jewish. How contemptible. One private school does take a limited number of Jews, but is called "dummies' retreat." All I can do is keep on dreaming of idyllic boarding schools in New England.

During vacations I'm invited to other cities—Baltimore, New York, Boston—to visit camp friends. Away from home, I feel the same excitement I do at camp—as though I've taken a further leap into a most desirable vastness; I am surer, despite my shyness.

The world is so large. It beckons and I want to move out into it. At home I feel confined. I try to be polite, but I become more and more silent, tense, restless. Why remain in a narrow circle? Why not experience all you can? How else are you to grow? What I must do seems obvious: go away to a good college-preparatory school and then to college—in New England.

I explain my plans to Mother and Father, who are horrified. I'm too young to leave home and mustn't think of going to college. I'm too serious already; I should go to more parties, make more friends in Philadelphia, meet more boys, and have a good time!

Have a good time! Don't they understand anything? Why should anyone who wants a better education be thwarted? Father works so hard for us, yet both he and Mother raise objections at the first sign of my reaching out for a richer, fuller life. If I were told boarding school and college were too expensive, I could accept it. But Jack and Bob are being sent to college, which means little to them. What irony!

I raise such a fuss about not learning anything, the family can listen no longer. Because the daughters of two of their friends are going to school in Washington, they agree that I may, too. I'm torn by the decision and cry at night because Fairmont is not in New England, but at least I am to set forth into new territory.

Fairmont is not at all what I have dreamed about, nor is it organized primarily to prepare girls for college. I achieve high marks without trying; the courses are too easy, and—with one exception, English—uniformly dull.

Our Saturday afternoon sightseeing trips instruct me far more than do classes. We make the rounds of Washington, some of which, we are told, is superbly planned; but much is sordid. Except for the White House, which I find splendid, only Mount Vernon and the Smithsonian Institution have significance for me. We see everything too swiftly. We walk in, through, out. People explain things, but I never feel satisfied and we never dare ask questions. Afterward we say dutifully, "Yes, we've seen it," and in a way we have.

I begin to make notes about every place we visit on little scraps of paper, in small notebooks and large ones, on anything I can find, and keep them carefully.

The entire school attended Warren G. Harding's Inauguration on March 4, 1921. Everyone, I recorded, was fascinated by the amplifiers; it was their first important public appearance, but because of their blare we couldn't understand a word being said. A classmate and I were chosen to be ushers for the President, the Vice President, and their wives, who came as guests of honor to the Senior Class Play given in the Fairmont gymnasium on April Fool's Day.

Mrs. Harding invited us aboard the Presidential yacht, the *Mayflower*, and to the White House for tea. We saw the china "somebody" had used. Mrs. Harding wore dowdy clothes; the much-publicized shade of blue she favored struck me as insipid, especially when used for a machine-made, imitation lace dress. (My eye had been trained by the fine handmade laces Mother brought back from Europe each summer—the sole objects about which her taste and mine agreed.)

The only political speech I heard by an American leader was delivered at an afternoon "May Day Party in honor of the Vice President of the United States," Calvin Coolidge. The festivity took place at the National Press Club post of the American Legion at the Marine Barracks. Coolidge was a lean and colorless man whose words were without meaning for me. I wrote down that as we listened to him struggle through a speech, we were unkind and giggled. He awakened me to the fact that all public officials were not necessarily awesome. I understood, too, the vaguely humorous things people repeated about Coolidge behind his back. We were told he so seldom said anything that when he did open his mouth, a moth flew out. Asked his opinion of sin, he replied he was "agin it."

(The first time I became even faintly aware of politics was during a parade in Philadelphia when Woodrow Wilson and Charles Evans Hughes were competing for the Presidency in 1916. I stood in a crowd on Broad Street and was told President Wilson wanted to keep us out of war. People screamed in favor of one candidate or the other. I raised my voice fervently for Wilson. That we entered the war after he was elected didn't strike me as his fault. At least he tried to keep us out. How could anyone favor going to war?)

After a year at Fairmont, while I was at camp and Mother and Father were in Europe, I took matters into my own hands and applied for admission to the Mary C. Wheeler School in Providence, Rhode Island. I had heard about it from the one exceptional teacher in Washington, who praised its excellent college-preparatory courses and assured me it was by no means just a "finishing" school. A twenty-five-dollar deposit was required and I asked Miss Arnold to advance it from the emergency money left for me.

A few days later I was summoned to her room and became perplexed by the first stern look I had ever received from her. She showed me a letter from Miss Wheeler's, inquiring politely if I were Jewish. She explained there was a directory that listed camps as Christian or Jewish. Accomac was Jewish.

"You mustn't consider going to an anti-Semitic school," Miss Arnold stated firmly. "No one would write to a Christian camp, asking if an applicant were Christian. You can be certain Miss Wheeler's is prejudiced." I was shocked.

"But can't you just reply," I pleaded, "and say I'm Jewish? Last year, when Mother applied to Fairmont, she simply informed the headmaster we were Jewish and we had no trouble at all. I was accepted at once." Miss Arnold was so taken aback by my reply that she wrote as I suggested.

A formal correspondence followed. Miss Wheeler's took note of my application but stated that no vacancy existed. I asked to have my name placed on the waiting list. Toward the end of August I became unnerved and wrote again, requesting an interview after camp, before my parents returned from Europe. To my amazement, the head of the school agreed to see me. I stayed with a friend in Boston and arranged for a counselor who lived in Providence to chaperone me.

Miss Mary Helena Dey was imposing and soft-spoken. We eyed each other with unmistakable curiosity. She assured me again that the class was full and suggested, logically, that since there were so many other good schools, I apply elsewhere. I explained I had selected Miss Wheeler's because of the recommendation of my English teacher in Washington. "But," countered Miss Dey, "your headmaster at Fairmont has written a glowing letter about you and I have had a similar note from the head of your camp. It's late now. Why not go back to Washington for your senior year, since you're doing so well there?"

I knew I mustn't move my eyes a fraction of an inch. To do so might break some imagined thread to which I clung. I tried as best I could to put into words why going to a New England school was so important to me. My reasons must have sounded preposterous. How could I possibly make Miss Dey understand my strange obsession, based as it was on scattered reading in Emerson, Thoreau, Miss Alcott, and Hawthorne; on the dignity of a few counselors; on the beauty of Maine; and on the atmosphere of Boston and Cambridge, as experienced during two brief visits to a camp friend?

I said no, I didn't want to return to Washington; I must come to New England. The silence that enveloped us was frightening. I was wasting Miss Dey's time. And then, there it was! She told me, with simplicity, that even if her school did have a place for me, there was the matter of my being Jewish. Except for the daughter of a college classmate of hers, no Jews had ever been accepted. I must understand, too, that everyone must attend church on Sundays. I replied I didn't mind that at all. I had gone to a Presbyterian church in Washington the previous year. Since it didn't specially interest me, perhaps I could try a different sect—Unitarian or Congregational. I hastily added, in order not to seem insulting, "I don't know much about Judaism either." I pointed out that I wanted to choose my own religion; that I was anxious to examine as many as possible; that I didn't see why anyone should have to inherit a faith.

Miss Dey's expression didn't change. What was she thinking? She promised to keep in touch with me. The interview was at an end. I walked out into a void with a heavy heart. How could I explain to my parents what I had done? How could I get into any other good New England school at so late a date?

I received a courteous telegram on September 9, 1921: I VERY MUCH REGRET THAT NO VACANCY HAS OCCURRED MAKING IT IMPOSSIBLE AT THIS TIME TO ASSURE YOU OF A PLACE IN THE SCHOOL FOR THE COMING YEAR / MARY HELENA DEY / MISS WHEELER'S SCHOOL. In spite of my disappointment, for some unaccountable reason, I still felt certain I would be accepted.

My parents returned from Europe and were aghast at my actions. I was informed that young girls didn't enter themselves in schools on their own, nor did they go to see headmistresses unattended. I replied dutifully, "A lovely counselor from camp chaperoned me." A letter from Fairmont asked whether I was returning. How to answer?

On September 17, less than a week before school was to begin, a second wire arrived from Providence. I was terrified to open the envelope. The message read: VERY HAPPY TO OFFER YOU VACANCY PLEASE TELEGRAPH WHETHER YOU STILL WISH TO COME / M.H. DEY / SENDER REQUESTS REPLY.

Wth delirious joy I telegraphed back: HAPPY TO ACCEPT VACANCY.

The trees and shrubs at Miss Wheeler's look neither as full nor as lively a green as they did a month before. (I noticed then that the red-brick buildings lacked distinction.) A chill in the air makes me feel lonely and a bit frightened. I am only sixteen, a new girl and a senior. It may be difficult to fit in.

But—New England! The thought of it cheers me as the door opens and a sense of warmth envelops me. The late afternoon autumn sun slants through a window. I am delighted by a copper bowl filled with richly hued dahlias, and a pewter vase of bittersweet, Japanese lanterns, and pine boughs. Miss Dey is cordial in her welcome. I like the look of the girls—intelligent, aware, restrained in manner.

My roommate, Audrey L., is also a senior and a new girl—we are the only two. She is tall, lanky, simply dressed, has a quick sense of humor. We at once agree about which girls and teachers seem particularly attractive, and which most ghastly. Our taste in books, drama, music, clothes is much the same. We are delighted with each other.

In our room the first night, we express our happiness at rooming together and whisper—which is forbidden—after the "lights out" bell. Suddenly Audrey sits bolt upright in bed and lowers her voice even further: "Which church are you going to?" Startled, I reply, "I don't know yet. No one has told me where I am to go." A curious answer, I think. A knock on the door, a voice of authority: "You must not whisper. You must go to sleep." Then silence.

"Listen," Audrey whispers tensely from under her covers. "You mustn't tell anyone—not *anyone*. Swear it." "I swear it." "I'm half Jewish. But you mustn't tell *anyone*." "I promise." I'm thunderstruck. What in heaven's name does she mean, "Don't tell *anyone*?"

As Audrey speaks, I realize I must behave about being Jewish exactly as I have in the past. She is strengthening, without knowing it, my ever-present hatred of pretense. More than that: to be dishonest—even in silence—about being Jewish is unthinkable, because of the blind stupidity of anti-Semitism. You can't just go around all day declaring you are Jewish, but you can say it at appropriate times.

Audrey doesn't ask, but I make a point of telling her: "I'm Jewish." I don't want to continue the conversation. I feel a strange wave of coldness. I'm certain she does, too, since I hold her secret, even though I won't break my promise.

The next day I can't go on actively disliking Audrey, but our first spontaneous excitement and pleasure have been destroyed.

Miss Yarborough, our English teacher, is brilliant, extraordinary. But we are expected to absorb the entire history of English literature from *Beowulf* to the nineteenth century. (It would seem all courses end with the nineteenth century.) We must read too much, too fast.

We never pause to consider the meanings of the books we read. We date things, talk about the differences in form and style used in one period or another—that is all. I quickly become impatient and perturbed.

On my own, I read contemporary writing omnivorously, compulsively, even though the pressure of work is far greater than at previous schools. I order a copy of the Sunday *New York Times* each week to follow the New York theater news. Current drama, novels, poetry have little to do with our discussions in English class, or with the compositions we must write. (I make a note about my longing for books and plays without conventional plots; for an end to the making of black-and-white judgments.)

One day as I was leaving class, after everyone else had departed, Miss

Yarborough reentered the room. Her eyes were wet with tears. She shook her head sadly. "Youth is cruel, Dorothy." Her unexpected confidence, spoken from the distant heights of maturity, lifted me out of girlhood for the moment. My answer, "I know," was presumptuous, since I did not know. But then, in a split second, I did.

Must one forever wear a mask? I love New Englanders because they are reserved and well-bred. Yet here am I, ecstatic because someone has dared to reveal emotion.

At Miss Yarborough's next class, I cannot take my eyes from her now accessible and handsome face. She is large, has glowing gray-green eyes; a straight, classically perfect nose. Her heavy long gray hair is streaked with white, parted in the middle, pulled back in a large bun. If she is seated and all you can see is her noble head, she is majestic. But as she rises, she becomes a stout, nondescript figure. I stare at her face, as I stare at all that fascinates me.

Miss Yarborough asks me to visit her in her room. We have long talks about books. Our conversations become more important than anything else at school. English class comes tremendously alive. My writing has a new flow and freedom. My marks soar. One of my poems—not a very good one—is printed in the school magazine, *The Quill*. Others are singled out and read aloud. Strange that a revelation of one person's hurt should liberate another, should become so mysterious and powerful a stimulus.

By a curious twist of fate, my geometry teacher—mathematics is my worst subject—is so outstanding that my College Board entrance examination mark in math equals that for English. Happily, Miss Dixon's love of the theater is as great as mine. After class we discuss Clemence Dane's *Will Shakespeare* and other plays of the season, with far more sense of involvement than anyone expresses about anything in English class.

European history is absorbing, but again we go too fast and must read too much. Virgil is a trial, and I have no gift for speaking French. Nonetheless, Miss Wheeler's satisfies something in me not easily explained. My year there fosters a yearning for an even wider world and ever greater knowledge —for the arts, for music, painting, ideas. Except for the experience with Audrey, nothing disagreeable occurs about the "Jewish problem." I continue to behave as I have at Fairmont or anywhere else. I tell those with whom I become friendly that I'm Jewish, just to keep everything clear. The reply is always the same: "What has that to do with anything?" Friendships develop or not, according to the soundness of their basis. I have no more desire to be confined by an all-Christian society than by an all-Jewish one. I seek a life without such restrictions. I feel absurd announcing what I am, since I don't really know what being Jewish means. But I can't help doing it.

My year at Miss Wheeler's goes well; I continue to feel less shy and more secure. I plan to enter Smith College and am accepted. Our Wheeler Senior Year Book facetiously declares that I came to Providence to play tennis; that I'm seen always carrying a book of contemporary writing; that it hears a voice of the future recite "modern verse" attributed to me:

> *The trees are waring* [sic]
> *The cat is under the trees.*
> *Behold, she purrs!*
> *Behold the sky is green!*
> *My soul moaneth to liberty.*
> *Liberty! Cat!*

I get little out of Smith, but still love being away from Philadelphia. All the courses I take are required; none is of interest to me. My English class is lamentable. I read books of my own choice avidly, but mainly I want to get on with life.

Just before final exams, in the midst of a freshman tennis tournament in which I'm doing well, I have a severe attack of appendicitis. I am rushed to the Infirmary, then home to be operated on, and miss my examinations.

Mother and Father refuse to permit me to return to Smith. They feel the Infirmary has handled my illness badly; above all, they are glad to have any excuse to keep me in Philadelphia. They continue to consider me too serious; I know they want to make certain I marry. We go to Europe for the summer and I am kept there, in spite of my complaints, until October, after Smith has opened. I feel desperate. All I can do at so late a date is attend the University of Pennsylvania, in Philadelphia, as a day student. Few departments are open to women. My only choice is to enroll in the School of Education, although I have no intention of becoming a teacher. Again I must take required subjects.

The Philadelphia Orchestra, the Widener and Johnson Collections of Art, a few museums, camp friends, and the William Allen Bookshop are my salvation. At the last I receive most of my education—from Mr. Allen and the volumes on his shelves. One after another I place secondhand Loeb Classical Library books inside the bulky, dull texts—tomes about the history, theory, and practice of education—that I hold on my lap during class.

I also conceal contemporary writing as I sit in the large, stuffy halls in which professors drone through the same lectures they have given in previous years and will repeat in years to come. We can buy cards telling us the salient points to note in the volumes we are supposed to study; also cards providing answers to last year's examinations. We learn through the grapevine that quizzes each year are identical. We can't help but get high marks.

After the beginning of the second year, I can't go on taking courses without meaning for me. I sign up instead for subjects about which I care, without getting credit, and I give up the idea of receiving a degree.

A stroke of luck: I have free hours at just the right time to enter the first classes available to college students at the Barnes Foundation in Merion, Pennsylvania. I have no idea what the Foundation is, but the catalogue description of the courses strikes a responsive chord. As I walk through the new and beautiful building designed by Paul Cret, I am overwhelmed by the wonder of what I am told is "modern art." A professor directs us to stand in front of a particular picture. We must not walk around or look at anything else until instructed about how to view it. I'm so intimidated by the rigid procedure that, for a time, I obey. I soon learn, however, to gauge the way in which the professor fixes his eyes upon each of us in turn. His gaze passes beyond me; I shoot a swift glance at whatever painting is to my immediate right or left, before he can reach my eyes again. My carefully timed and "bootlegged" peering permits me to observe at my own pace far more during a lecture than we are allowed to "study" in a single afternoon. This proves a superb method of learning to identify artists and to "see" without benefit of explanation. The repetition of words relating to line, form, space, color is of no importance to me. How can such matters compare to the grandeur of the work before us?

I find it impossible to care about how the curve of an arm follows the shape of a teacup's handle; how the line of a curtain is related to that of a tablecloth; how shadows are made in blue now, rather than black or gray. Renoir's marvelous love of woman—natural, full-blown—and his flowers and children are, to me, most moving. How direct he is! How can one make the world an equally fair and exultant place?

The tenderness and passion of Van Gogh intensify my response to nature, to the sorrowful, the ecstatic. Like those of Picasso, Matisse's figures—stripped of all artifice—become a portrait of my own inner struggle against every counterforce of pretense and clutter. The subtle lack of rigidity, the ambiguity of Cézanne fascinate me, as do the dissonances of Stravinsky. "You are like a gazelle," Gertrude D. whispers as my eyes dart at the pictures.

Against the walls stand early Pennsylvania Dutch painted chests—simple, colorful—which I am told Dr. Barnes loves. They make my heart leap. I never question their being in the same rooms with a small, unadorned Van Gogh house, the sun blazing overhead; with a primitive Rousseau forest or stark African carvings. (We are admonished to notice how the sculptures' chins, the curve of their breasts, the roundness of bellies and knees correspond to the shape of toes!)

Whenever Dr. Barnes enters the room during a class, I imagine every-one else trembles as I do. He is a tall, portly, seemingly gruff individual who makes decisive and often derogatory remarks either about some painting on the wall against which he seems to bear a grudge, or about some famous art expert who, in his view, is totally ignorant. One day he speaks irately against a Thomas Benton, explaining that it is hung as an example of bad painting. He detests every official in any nearby art institution.

Signs of something explosive—revolutionary—in the world outside move onto my horizon. In my immediate surroundings I feel a stranger. At the Barnes Foundation I say to myself with joy, "I have come home."

Yes, I have "come home," but in spite of my love for the arts, I remain troubled about being protected while others are not. I must do something for those less fortunate, but so little time remains each day after my classes.

I find an hour during which I read to eager children at the public library. I am clumsy at it. I want to communicate the magic of the words before me, but am too self-conscious and shy to dramatize them. I go to work instead at a settlement house in a distressing slum area in South Philadelphia. Father insists on sending me in our automobile—for me, an infuriating and deeply embarrassing gesture.

I read to young boys and girls, but am bewildered by how to handle them. They are wild and destructive, tearing up the treasured childhood books I have brought on my first visit. I wish someone would help me deal with the situation, but no one does. The children resent everyone who comes near. Some way must exist to break down their resistance. But how?

My pitifully tiny acts of good will fail to satisfy me or to be of real value to anyone. For the present I must concentrate on my own education; later, I may be able to work for others more skillfully and in some significant way.

I immerse myself in a sociology course, to learn about the many wrongs in the world and how they may be set right. Crime statistics and theories of criminology are the primary topics discussed; they strike me as cold and abstract. But then we are assigned to read the *Survey* magazine and, like the Barnes Foundation, it brings life alive.

The *Survey*, the country's leading liberal periodical, deals in forthright and humane fashion with our most serious social problems. The dilemmas to be resolved are formidable. Reading about them for the first time is a staggering experience.

My mother and her friends work for charities once or twice a week, when not playing bridge or shopping, but I have never heard them discuss what I learn now. The difference between the intense compassion of a Van Gogh painting and the tepid etchings on our walls parallels the vast discrepancy between the stark portrayals in the *Survey* and what those around me do to alleviate society's ills.

I know no great social reformers, just as I know no artists. But the *Survey* makes me long to become involved in the fields it discusses, just as I want to help Van Goghs not yet recognized. The clear and blistering articles of such outstanding idealists as Lincoln Steffens, Patrick Geddes, and Jacob Riis move me deeply. I have been totally unaware of the evils of child labor; of the torturous conditions under which young children perform arduous tasks. I haven't realized how many people are out of work and hungry, how many lack adequate clothing, shelter, medical care.

I read still other sociological publications that shock me and arouse my concern. After the war, business conditions weren't good; I often heard Father speak of how, in view of the way wages were going up, before long he wouldn't be able to run his business. He is such a good man and works so hard. Everything worries him, even the weather—if it's bad, people don't shop. But up to now, I've been unaware of labor's point of view.

I learn of strikebreaking for the first time—of industrial diseases, starvation wages, corrupt politics, depressed classes, class war, the dire need for relief. Much of what I absorb becomes blurred, but I receive a clear overall message. I must pay more attention to it, and prepare myself more diligently to be of use.

The Barnes Foundation. Music, literature, beauty—the arts. And now the world's social problems. Always, as new vistas open before me, I become increasingly impatient with the frustrating aspects of my own constricted, ineffectual life, yet I feel wildly excited. If only I could move out into the world more forcefully; if only I knew someone with whom I could share my ecstasies and my growing pains.

For a short time at camp, boarding school, and Smith, I succeeded in entering other landscapes, in forming warm relationships with those of different backgrounds, of wider vision. But in Philadelphia I associate only with members of families my parents know and I refuse to be caught up in the life I see around me: bridge and mah-jongg and petty gossip. Mother insists on joining friends or accepting invitations to play cards every evening. Father, tired at the end of the day, cares nothing for such pastimes. Mother wants to go for a drive when Father does not. He prefers to spend his spare time in the country playing golf. Arguments flare up, nerves are frayed, digestions suffer. No one discusses anything of importance. I feel more and more pent up, restless, trapped.

2

I am invited to dances in Philadelphia and New York during the Christmas holidays. I both want and don't want to accept. On the whole, parties are boring, but New York is not. I shall see boys and girls from the same circle— the most select Jewish families of both cities—but there will be new faces and I confess I like being included. A few moments even at dances satisfy, although the enchantment swiftly dissolves. Emptiness. But I dream of a large love—I who am virginal and still painfully shy with boys.

The subject of sex is mysterious and frightening to me. I hunger to know about everything else, yet avoid learning about it. Several boys who attract me invite me to go out with them; Paul D. is the most stimulating. He is tall, beautifully built, handsome, with gray-blue eyes that are brooding, haunting. He is brilliant and well-read. But the moment we're alone in his car he tries to kiss me. It doesn't feel right. Nothing warrants our kissing— nothing about it is inevitable. My refusals spoil our meetings. The moment we part I regret having said no. I have fantasies about letting him kiss me, and hug my pillow when I go home to bed. I write a poem about my con- flicting emotions. Whenever we have a date I'm happy. I love to talk with him. But then he tries to kiss me and I feel tormented and afraid.

My withdrawals make me wonder whether some inner signal is pro- tecting me from a less than total relationship. I am full of love, but it has nowhere to go. Nothing can touch me, because nothing deeply touches me. What is it people feel, I worry, when they are sure enough to marry? And if they are so certain, how can anything ever go wrong afterward?

The first New York Christmas party—1924—time for midnight supper. Bill S. approaches and asks whether he may sit with my escort, Robert Josephy, and me. A brown-eyed, brown-haired boy crosses the room to greet Bill, who introduces Edward Norman and asks him to join us. Edward looks directly into my eyes when we meet and his handshake is firm. His brow is high, his lips full and soft. "God," he exclaims, "how I hate these parties!" I've never heard anyone say just what I feel. I look at him in amazement. For a split second I experience a sense of exalted relief: "I hate them, too." "Imagine," he continues, "spending your life doing nothing but this." I want to shout "Imagine!" but fear I'll sound like an inane parrot.

When dancing resumed after supper, Edward cut in, but we soon sat down to talk, as though under a spell. His voice, words, face had a touching quality. He sat and stood very straight. Who was he? I asked what he did. "I work for the *Survey* magazine." Was it possible that I should meet someone associated with the *Survey*? With fervor I explained that I had been reading the publication in my sociology class—that it brought alive for me many of the social problems I had just discovered and yearned to help rectify.

Edward described the Consumers' Cooperative movement, which he was trying to write about for the *Survey*. I didn't understand what the movement was, but his enthusiasm and knowledge enthralled me. *Who is he?* As we parted, he took down my phone number. A dreadful pang: perhaps he wouldn't call. The next day he phoned and asked me to lunch.

Further coincidence: he speaks with reverence of Harvard and Cambridge, of New England. As I relate even the briefest of anecdotes or listen to Edward, all I can think of is the wonder of meeting him. The books, music, places we love in common take on new dimensions. Our dreams are the same.

Edward lowers his voice. "You are lovely. May I come to see you in Philadelphia?" I murmur a subdued "Yes," but am elated.

Within a matter of days he arrives, bearing a gift—a handsome dark-brown, leather-bound, gold-tooled edition of Erasmus's *Praise of Folly*. He talks to me about Erasmus and the great historical significance of the book. Who *is* this young man, indeed?

Edward is soon to be twenty-five. He wants to use himself well for the public good, since he feels his family already has enough money. "Why," he asks, "should I waste my energy and life making more? My needs are few. Above all, I want to devote myself to the work of the Cooperative League."

"Oh, darling, dear one," he says without transition, "beautiful one, we must get married at once. At once! You are the answer to everything I've ever looked for. Angel!" Edward kisses me passionately, holds me close, and I don't withdraw. I trust him completely: "I love you, too." Three more meetings and fourteen intense letters later, we consider ourselves engaged. I'm sure every vision of life I have had is on the verge of realization. Out of nowhere, as in a fairy tale.

Our parents are troubled by our decision to marry—mine because we've known each other so short a time and I'm only nineteen. My father worries that Edward is too high-strung and isn't earning his living, but is dependent upon his father. The Normans object for similar reasons, but also because my parents aren't fashionable enough. They believe only three New York families are worthy of their son: the Warburgs, Lehmans, and Lewisohns.

The Normans, Edward laments, are snobbish. They don't know my parents and haven't met me. A battle ensues. Edward assures me that my credentials, as recited to the Normans by mutual friends, are unassailable. My parents take me to Florida and Cuba to remove me from Edward's presence and put a stop to our marriage plans.

Edward has told me that, while at Harvard, he became partly paralyzed. He believes his constantly strained relationship with his parents was the cause. It was diagnosed as "sleeping sickness." But he recovered and now looks strong and well.

Edward is so gentle with me, so loving and ardent, I can scarcely believe him when he describes the rages he gets into with his parents and the hysteria from which he has suffered. I feel, as does he, that once he is freed from the domination of his family, his major problems will disappear, including a vagueness he displays at times, when he can't remember people's names or work well. I have nothing but sympathy for him and faith in him, he is so sincere, idealistic, and full of goodness.

He writes a letter I receive just as I return home from the South.

For days I have been in the most unsettled state of mind—an indescribable vague condition—where I couldn't concentrate on anything or formulate any expression. And I'm still in the midst of it. I just am not self-confident any more nor do I have a feeling of security. What it all means I can't say, but it's awful. Discontent, says Emerson, is want of self-reliance. Mr. B. of the *Survey* says it's due to "dispersed thinking," and while I admit the possibility of my case being due to either of those two reasons, I think strain or tension has something to do with it. I get so I want to blow up, and always have gotten that way after spending any considerable time home in New York. I've been able to concentrate on nothing, and since my article published February 15 which I wrote in December I haven't done a thing. I hate to be taking myself so seriously, as it only makes matters worse, but I have a feeling that taking it seriously now a bit may enable me to get away from the silly kind of taking things seriously the people around me do. I mean I have to get a hold on myself.

However, I did get some wonderful thrills from your letters. I realize my smallness and unworthiness of—I'm ashamed to write it—your faith. Please, dear, don't fail to let yourself realize that few people, and certainly not me, are worthy of inspiring any faith in a woman like you.

I feel better even after writing this to you.

I am startled by the turn of events but cannot accept the fact that anything serious is wrong; I want only to rush to Edward, to comfort and reassure him. A short time after, another letter arrives: "I snapped out of myself enough to go to see a psychiatrist. The Editor of the *Survey* wanted me to. Of course I'll have to talk with him a few more times before he can make suggestions to straighten me out."

The next day:

The Doctor I am seeing feels that my not standing on my own feet is a large part of the cause of my mental unrest and vagueness. I wonder how you feel on this. Do you think of me as a man—man enough for you? I know I have had a large part in making myself what I am—in outlook and ideals, but that's about as far as it goes. I'm not living them much, nor getting nearer to. And I'm not my own master.

But the Doctor didn't have to tell me all that—I knew it anyway. What I'm worried about is that being held in all the time is breaking me, dulling me, killing my interest, my intensity, and my spontaneity. A spring compressed for long enough loses its elasticity and when released will not rebound to its free shape.

This was the first time I'd known anyone who had gone to a psychiatrist. I had read some Freud—his interpretations of dreams and theories of the unconscious. But, I wondered, can psychiatrists "straighten out" people so quickly?

Edward tells me of progress and setbacks, yet I'm certain he will win out. A further letter: "I'm on the crest—really and truly now—I'll be a new man next time you see me—no more vagueness or troubled, distraught mind."

The following day:

Now, dear, all practical obstacles have been removed. It's only a question of time till we are able to do whatever we want. And at the same time I am recovering. So really, dearest, there's nothing to worry about. I can see nothing real in the way to prevent us from living a wonderful life, seeing glory everywhere through one another.

But then Edward writes that more problems have arisen about our marrying:

I'm in despair. I don't know what's happening. All I know is I'm clashing seriously with the family. I am so confused I can't tell what their attitude is—whether they're unalterably opposed, or whether they just want time to get used to the idea to approve, or whether they'll approve provided certain conditions are satisfactory. But whatever their attitude, it's not sympathetic and open and kind—it's cautious and crafty and calculating—and totally unrelated to our spirit in the matter. Dear, I don't know what the outcome will be. I can't for the life of me allow you to be considered in that material way—with a price, as it were. All I know is that you're the finest thing that ever came into my life, and I want you irrespective of any conditions.

If my family gave their consent provided only I am content, all would be well. But they won't. They are not thinking of how I feel, but how they will feel. They are thinking of what your folks are like and how they'll like being connected to them. Honestly, that's the whole trouble. You'd be all right provided all my folks expect of "in-laws" is all right. And I can't let you be considered that way. Please, darling, don't misunderstand what I am saying. I'm in the most awful agony.

Well, if my folks don't agree yours most likely won't, and where'll we be then. Then, we could take the bull by the horns and get married anyway, which you probably won't do. And there we are. Do you wonder that life looks black to me?

I'm all at sea—I'm distracted as a fool. I don't work at all any more.

A week later:

I have the most awful feeling that the "world" is pressing in upon our lovely almost-achieved seclusion, and we will have to be very much aware of ourselves to protect it. It was so lovely to have our relationship our private affair, but now it isn't any more. The family have taken it up. They are going to "approve"—but they want to know you, they think we should wait—"not be hasty"—and they ask me questions about you. And I hate to answer them—everything I feel and love about you is so precious, I hate to express it to anyone. Darling, we may—for the sake of what I don't know, harmony, I suppose—have to let them into our affairs a little, but we'll never achieve our kind of happiness unless we keep it in mind to not open ourselves too much and to close ourselves up at once at the first opportunity—i.e. the day we are married.

I'm so frightened this evening at the way things are going—for though our marriage may be accepted our lives may be so trespassed upon that all our dreams will be lost. Oh, I wish we could run away to some far, far away place. We may have to.

P.S. If Mother should ask you over by any chance, will you please come?

Ten days later the clouds lift:

> Today I've worked hard on my real job, and felt great doing so. Maybe soon I'll be calm and definite enough to write again on my own hook instead of just editing and getting information.
>
> It's a good feeling to be able to devote yourself to work without distraction and a feeling of instability. Gee, we'll have a great time when we get to it—we'll be so alive and so full of vitality. Life ought to mean a lot to us and we ought to mean a lot to one another.

Each time Edward says everything will be fine, I am certain it will be. When he asks me to cast aside all doubt, I do so at once and without reservation. I love this beautiful, idealistic boy-man with all my heart and soul.

The Normans finally said they wanted to meet my parents, and then me. We appeared separately at the Norman apartment. Father Norman was tall, dignified, erect. He had a fine head, an impressive mustache and goatee. His portrait would look well in any exclusive men's club. Mother Norman was smaller, stouter, a bit florid; she didn't really listen when you talked. Both made me feel they liked me, and I wanted to hug them because they were Edward's parents, but we were all too reserved.

At last the Normans and my parents agreed we could marry. The next day Mr. Norman asked me to come to see him alone. He begged me to consider the fact that Edward was not totally stable, that he had been ill, that he had been out of college for a year. I said I knew. The fresh warning not to marry Edward only convinced me the more that our love would resolve all difficulties. Mr. Norman shook his head sadly.

Later Edward telephoned. Could we meet? When he appeared, his face was lovely as always, but his eyes had a broken, splintered look I hadn't seen before. He kneeled. "Angel, I cannot marry you. I am not worthy of you. My father is right. Your father is right. Oh, darling, don't marry me." He buried his face in my lap and wept. It was as though he were saying, "Don't marry me," and at the same time, "Oh please, please do." I bent over and as he raised his head to kiss me softly, the first and only serious doubt I had felt about him stabbed and suffused me. In a rush I felt young, terribly, terribly young. I knew so little. "I don't question you or our love," I whispered. Edward and I both got up. He took me in his arms, held me close, and my certainty returned. My body relaxed. His doubt also passed. It was as though we had gone through a perilous storm and survived intact. We looked at each other with new certainty and an even deeper love.

Edward feels at peace once more, and harmony is achieved between him and his father. The psychiatrist says Edward is now fine and need not see him again. Mr. Norman agrees to give Edward sufficient money so we can marry and Edward can continue with the work he has chosen. But then, within a few days, everything his parents do arouses Edward's anger all over again.

Just a month before our wedding in June, he sends a dejected letter:

> Mother asked me how you'd like a big diamond bracelet and it was a devil of a job to show her that it would—more than most anything she could give you or do to you—start our life off with a handicap. You couldn't sell it and you couldn't not wear it, and wearing it would cut you off from your real self in that it would be a barrier to people who might give you opportunities or the kind of friendships you want. It might interfere with their having any confidence in your sincerity, integrity or intelligent consistency.

June 10, 1925. My parents' apartment. Only immediate members of both families have been invited to our wedding. The service is brief and simple. I refuse to wear a veil or accept an engagement ring. A thin golden wedding band seems beautiful to me and I happily agree to wear it.

Just before the ceremony the Normans say they want to present me with a wedding gift and ask me to choose between a string of pearls and ten thousand dollars. I am nonplussed. I had hoped they understood my aversion to jewels. And how embarrassing it would be to say, "I prefer ten thousand dollars." I explain as politely as I can that I wouldn't wear the pearls and, if presented with the money, I'd give it away. As I say, "Thank you so much for your kindness," I feel as though I were drowning.

"But we want you to have the pearls, Dot," Mrs. Norman persists, "and we can get more for ten thousand dollars in Europe than we can here. So we'll bring them to you after our summer trip." A painful silence follows. "Don't force her," Edward volunteers. I want to fly into his arms. "Mother," he repeats, "don't get the pearls if Dot doesn't want them." How clearly I understand his difficulties.

Finally the moment comes for Edward to place the tiny gold band on my finger. He kisses me and we look at each other with love and longing to get away.

3

Greenwich, Connecticut: the Pick-wick Arms Inn. Confetti floats from our bags, from our clothes, as we step from the car. Embarrassment. And then the extraordinary moment of registering. The shock, the challenge of being out in the world—the mysterious, newborn world. On our own. No one to blame or ask.

Edward had lost his temper on our drive from Philadelphia; a police-man stopped him for speeding. I supposed him overwrought, tired, excited, but found myself withdrawing. The tantrum deflated my exalted feeling for the moment more than I'd have been willing to admit.

We reach our room and Edward says at once, "Quickly—undress." He does not caress me. "Did your father tell you everything?" I hesitate a moment and say a vague "Yes." It had been agreed that, in view of my innocence, virginity, and ignorance, my father would tell me the facts of life. In my room two days before, he had sat down and said only, "My dear, when-ever your husband asks you to come to him, you must always go, willingly." How determined and anxious he looked. I had no clue to why he spoke as he did. He explained nothing.

Now, I don't know what to do except follow my father's advice. *Edward and I are married. I love him. I am his wife. This is an irrevocable fact. Until death do us part.* (I have always wept at the subtle beauty of wedding ceremonies.)

I was awkward as I undressed. Edward pulled me toward him on the bed. He pressed against me and pushed my legs apart. I was too small. His attempt to enter was excruciatingly painful. I tried not to scream. "My God," he said, "your father didn't tell you anything!" He became enraged and I wept. He forced and forced. I lay sobbing, shaken, in agonizing pain. The bed is covered with blood. "Oh, darling!" I tried to make the words audible, but they disappeared into my tears. I clenched my teeth. Edward satisfied himself swiftly and fell asleep.

I understand what has happened without really understanding. What must he think of me? My mother has always told me not to ask others about sex. In due time, she assured me, she would explain everything. She never did. All she has said was that I mustn't cheapen myself by letting boys kiss me. "You will be like a soiled towel if you do." Her warning filled me with dismay, but also with fear of becoming tarnished. Other boys and girls kissed. The girls weren't soiled. I had remained virginal because I was trained to believe this was expected of any properly brought-up girl who didn't want to "throw herself to the dogs." But I had no comprehension of what not being a virgin entailed.

I have read many of the great classics, seen many of the world's most superb dramas, have thrilled to them, discussed them, felt I understood them. Now I discover I have lived in an unreal world. Is it possible that love and marriage are like this for everyone? They can't be. What has gone wrong? Why has no one written about what I am experiencing?

I cannot stop weeping. I feel that Edward, for his part, would gladly send me back to my parents; I would be secretly relieved to send him back to his. Then, as I lie shaking and smarting, I watch him as he sleeps. A great wave of tenderness sweeps over me. I want to reach out and assure him that everything will be all right. I want to clasp his hand, but fear I shall wake him. He turns over, scowls, and continues to sleep. My sobs well up beyond control. They can help nothing.

––––––––––––

Sunspots in the sky. The days have been uncomfortable, exhausting, hot. I hadn't minded. But now, in the morning, after a short, troubled sleep, I feel stifled. Edward is calm and sweet, asks forgiveness for having been harsh. I apologize, too, for having been unknowing. I explain that it's because I've been so athletic that my body is taut and thin, that I'm so small. "Everything will be all right," I whisper. I feel normal, even though I have no idea what being normal means. I can't be unique. "I know," Edward replies gently. He takes my hand and kisses me; I am comforted. What is he feeling? For the first time I don't know, and have no idea how I can say with such assurance that everything will be all right.

We drive to secluded Lake Mohonk for a few days, to trees that shade us from the too torrid sun and from the world. We ride and play tennis; laugh at playing croquet, at our poison ivy, at the pagodas around the lake—so many we can't count them; at the sweet questions of the elderly, reserved, proper guests. Time and patience will be required to resolve our plight. Mainly we try to ignore it, but each time we're together in our room, I feel an undercurrent of confusion and sorrow. I vow we shall not be defeated. We write exalted postcards to our families about our blissful honeymoon, and in many ways it is.

For the next six weeks we attend Harvard Summer School. I am as eager as Edward to spend time in Cambridge. He had written before our marriage, begging me to get a taste of it with him

> while it is still a bit like it was when I was there. Dearest, to you it's only an institution but to me it's the inspiration that in a way gave me life, the life that counts, and as you're the stimulus that's going to keep me living that life, it is the stimulus that started me. And because it means so much to me I love it, and I love you so much I'd like to bind the two of you together a little.

Arriving in Cambridge was like entering paradise. I chose a course in philosophy, about which I had long wanted to know more. My only previous instruction in the subject was made inaudible by a professor who muttered in a large, airless classroom with atrocious acoustics. This time I could hear, but was tormented by a too-rapid presentation of a highly complex assortment of terms, names, ideas: syllogisms, Sophists, Epicureans, Stoics, Socrates, Plato, Aristotle, Anaximander, Anaxagoras, Pythagoras, Heraclitus, Empedocles, Parmenides, Xenophanes. I wasn't clear about how much could be learned in a brief summer-school course, but felt critical about the superficial presentation. I took astronomy, too, and Edward studied horticulture. To a limited extent the six weeks were instructive. We were in love and full of curiosity; we read voraciously.

We rented a student's small apartment. Although I had never cooked, I was eager to try. I considered it stuffy and bourgeois to consult a cookbook, being certain I could figure everything out for myself. After experimenting a while, I was ready to invite two guests for dinner. Louis, the Normans' butler, who had come to Boston on his vacation, knocked at our door to say hello. We welcomed him heartily. He discovered I had put no bicarbonate of soda in the peas to make them greener and hadn't thoroughly singed the broilers; he threw up his hands in despair and departed. We laughed, the guests arrived, and I proudly served dinner.

I had planned the meal so I would have to interrupt the proceedings as little as possible, though I must remove the soup before serving the main course, and then clear the table properly before dessert. I felt relieved that I got up only twice, but Edward looked at me, puzzled. "Why," he asked sharply, "do you keep jumping up?"

"Darling," I called out after lunch one day, "listen to this. Isn't it extraordinary? According to Kepler, the shape of a planet's orbit around the sun is an ellipse, not a circle. At a certain point a planet speeds up—" Edward interrupted in a rage: "Who told you such nonsense?" "But, dear one, I'm reading it. In a scientific book." "Who told you to read it?" The voice rasped in anger. "Darling, our professor, of course, Dr. Shapley—for the astronomy class tonight. Look!" I picked up an orange, a tennis ball, and my tennis racquet, lying nearby. "Look, dear. It's amazing. Look—the ellipse, the sun, the earth." Edward grabbed the racquet in a fury and hurled it across the room. This was the first time such a scene had occurred. I was silenced and terrified.

35

No prelude had prepared me for the sudden outburst. "Bunny," I cried out, but stopped, frozen. Edward's eyes blazed. "I'm going with you tonight and take your damn Harlow Shapley and thrash him."

What could have brought on this harangue? Edward had behaved this way to his parents. He had flared up at me on a few occasions since our marriage, but never like this. I had seen Dr. Shapley only in a crowded room and hadn't even spoken to him. What could Edward possibly hold against him? Edward and I had been married only a few weeks. Nothing had come between us. I felt nothing could.

The day seemed endless. We were both tense, speechless. In silence we walked through the streets of Cambridge. We reached class; I could hear my heart. What was going to happen? How could I escape? I dared look neither at Edward nor at Dr. Shapley. To my amazement and relief, Edward wheeled around and quietly left the room.

I barely heard Dr. Shapley's talk about Kepler. My excitement had vanished. Blushing, I felt hot, miserable. Edward, beside himself with shame, was at the apartment when I returned after class. He couldn't do enough to please me. I assured him I understood and all would be well. "Darling," he pleaded, "you must stop me if I get out of hand. Don't you understand?" But how could I, since his tirades came out of nowhere? There was never a split second during which I could so much as get my breath. I had no wish to add ugliness to violence. Whenever Edward lost his temper, I became too frightened to speak, to move. His parents and the policeman were figures of authority to him. Because they encroached on his illusory freedom, he wanted to strike out against them. But with me?

I put on the mask that appeared on such occasions—the mask to give the impression I wasn't troubled, and to hasten the return of loveliness to life. Yet the mask frightened me. It represented a dishonesty and I feared it was transparent. But our marriage had to win out. It had to.

We enjoy Cape Cod on weekends and decide to spend our summers in Woods Hole. Another family explosion. Edward's mother, Lottie, berates us: "You're very foolish young people. Why do you go to a place where you know no one? In Westchester we all have many friends. Why not go there? If you have children, you'll want them to be well established in a community where they are known and respected. Don't lose contact with those who are close to you. You'll regret it, if you do."

We shudder. The Cape attracts us: Edward loves to sail. I have boarding-school friends in various towns, and Dr. James Warbasse, the head of the Cooperative League, lives in Woods Hole during the summer months. We don't need to discuss with anyone our mutual desire to summer there, or to move out into the world. We already have left our restrictive existence behind us. If problems are to be faced, we shall deal with them on our own.

Edward remains the most intelligent, knowledgeable, beautiful young person I have met; I could have married no one else. He appears to know about everything worth knowing. He explains clearly how New York State could be transformed into a vast and beautiful park system; how interstate authorities could protect the natural grandeur of the land and use its resources without corruption or profit. He has enlightened and definite ideas about how the world can be made better in every respect, from doing away with billboards and ads on highways, to establishing a United Europe. The League of Nations has been a failure; a better organization should be created. There must be effective customs unions and an end to divisive nationalisms. He astonishes me by knowing all about history, geological formations, geography—about how the weather works, how one wind follows another and why.

He gives me Lewis Mumford's recently published *Sticks and Stones*, the first visionary book of the kind I have read. It makes me see in a startling new way the origin and significance of the beautifully planned New England villages through which we drive; their finely proportioned buildings, their great elms planted and nursed with patience by farsighted early settlers. Mumford sharpens my awareness of the complexity of New England's fine traditions, so many of them vanished in our heedless, headlong contemporary civilization. "We've gained so much," I burst out to Edward, "but haven't we lost more?" We search for clues to how closely knit, planned, yet inspiring communities might flower today.

We pore over Le Corbusier's *Towards a New Architecture*—Edward has bought the French edition—and dream of how the look of the present-day world could be transformed at every level. Modern architects seem the most satisfying of all contemporary innovators. My horizon expands, my yearning to live a useful, meaningful life is intensified to an almost unbearable degree.

Our return to New York marked our entrance into reality. We had not yet chosen an apartment. All we owned was my trousseau and assorted wedding gifts; also an old pewter mug, a whaler's harpoon for poking fires, and a brass and wooden bedwarmer we bought on the Cape. My father was to give us our furniture. Since the Normans were still in Europe, we stayed in their Park Avenue apartment.

As we walk through its rooms, with a sense of shock I count twenty-two. The Normans have six servants and a chauffeur. Edward tells me with mingled laughter and embarrassment that there was a footman, too, until a year ago. (Now I understand his consternation when I "jumped up" while serving dinner in Cambridge.)

A huge entrance hall. The floor is marble—a vast expanse of large black and white squares. Cold. An enormous ballroom. Gilt chairs against the walls. The drawing room, formal, used only for special occasions. Leather-bound books, mainly sets. Tapestry-covered chairs and sofa, stiff. A fine antique Oriental rug. My parents have one also, as do many of their friends. I have come to dislike such rugs with an irrational intensity. They are the very opposite of the kind we want in our own apartment. Edward says the family usually gathers in the small study.

The more I see of the Norman apartment, the more I long for primitive, or equally simple, stark modern furniture. Above all, I hope we'll spend as little as possible, so Edward can be independent.

Edward has told me his father was a founder of Sears, Roebuck, but sold his interest in the firm and retired many years ago. Sears, Roebuck, I know, is a large mail-order company, but this signifies nothing to me. (People assume Edward is "a Sears, Roebuck heir," which he is not.) Father Norman is unostentatious, seems modest, and is too well-bred to give any hint of his status, if that is the correct word.

Edward and I walk about in the Normans' empty palace like two lost children—two young, tender shoots reaching out to lead a clean, clear, simple life in which we can believe. But how are we to escape being placed in a false position? Will we not be living under the shadow of a double standard, since Edward's father does have money—money on which, I presume, we are to live?

I know we must move on and out of these too large, ill-fitting rooms. We have enough faith and vitality to make our life together turn out well—of that I'm certain. Even so, I feel bewildered and uneasy. I feel guilt about not earning my own way, and a certain discomfort about Edward's not earning his, but my trust in him sustains me. Living in the gigantic apartment is unsettling. So is moving out into limbo.

Edward and I have no idea how much a sensible apartment should cost, but finally we rent one he feels is within our means. The first piece of furniture we select is an old, heavy, severe primitive Italian table, long and narrow. "It's so noble," I say happily when it's delivered.

I know nothing about the price of anything. I was given an allowance at college. Otherwise my parents have paid for my needs without stint. My father, who considers it vulgar, has conditioned me not to discuss money.

We have lived well, but in no way on the scale the Normans do. I astonish myself at times because I'm so ignorant about practical matters, but ignorant I am. I never ask Edward how much money we have, any more than I have ever questioned my father. Discussion of material possessions having been taboo at home, for me it continues to be so. I believe my reticence is helpful to Edward, who is trying to come to terms with his new situation as an adult, but I am left in the dark about many aspects of our life.

I feel confused about the amount I can spend, not by what I like. I need to know where I stand and how I should handle problems, but remain shy and silent about money and want to make no demands. I realize that I should face reality more forcefully and that my very simplicity, in being so soothing to Edward, may be keeping him from developing as he should. I'm unable to alter my conduct and don't really want to. I look forward to establishing the way of life Edward and I have discussed with such passionate concern.

The Normans returned from Europe. A number of relatives gathered in their small study to welcome them and to receive coming-home gifts. An aunt asked me in an aside, "You and Edward don't play bridge, do you?" "No." "Well, what will you do when you grow older?"

Finally all the presents had been handed out and unwrapped; Mother Norman disappeared into her bedroom and came back holding up a string of pearls. A collective gasp—an awed one. I cowered in my chair and was aghast. The pearls were dangled before me. I said tensely, "Thank you so much but, as you know, I said I couldn't accept them." An even louder gasp—of disbelief. Edward and I looked at each other with love—and despair.

Mother Norman said sweetly, "Someday, Dot, you'll change your mind." I replied, as politely as I could, "Oh, thank you again. But no, oh no, I won't!"

Edward goes to work for the Cooperative League under the stewardship of its founder, Dr. James Warbasse. At last I understand what he wrote to me with such ardor:

> Cooperation, in marketing agricultural produce, but especially in buying—consumers' cooperation it is called—is a big thing, the most important idea I know of, in that it is feasible and practical and appeals to human nature just as it is, without education or modification, and requires no government reform or aid except to be left alone, and has in it the power to remake the world—the material world especially, and the spiritual world indirectly as a result—into the kind of a world we'd all like to live in. And to get it started does not take inordinate vision—in fact requires but the commonest kind of self-interest. Few people—in the U.S.—understand what it means, and there is a lot to be done in publicity and education.

I love Edward for the warmth of his point of view. Consumers' Cooperatives sound sensible to me in avoiding the pitfalls of both working for profit and government control. We aren't attracted by Communism; any system other than democracy seems ominous. Soviet Russia, for all its slogans, appears cruel and repressive. We remain rebels, reformers at heart, but not revolutionaries.

After looking into New York's social welfare organizations, I decide to work for the American Civil Liberties Union. Roger Baldwin, director of the A.C.L.U., becomes my first "boss." His face is sensitive, mobile, lean, New England. I identify him with the Founding Fathers—with a composite portrait of them. He speaks of the current Bible Belt–Scopes-antievolution case, of the cruel suspense of the still unresolved Sacco-Vanzetti trial. He possesses the knowledge and authority of one so deeply involved in the goal he fights for that he becomes a living symbol of it, the very voice of democratic freedom.

During the war he was sentenced to a year in prison as a conscientious objector. I have heard only of war heroes, never of heroic opponents of war. Now he is such a figure for me; I feel I can trust him with my life, even though I don't always totally agree with him.

The work of the Civil Liberties Union represents a poetic endeavor in which I feel privileged to share. How extraordinary to be involved in the battle to protect freedom—especially the concepts guaranteed in the Bill of Rights. Freedom of speech and the press. Freedom of religion. Freedom of assembly. The words form a life-giving litany.

My first assignment is to do research for a book by the playwright Sidney Howard, *Professional Patriots*. I have been unaware that, in the postwar period, reactionary forces have been persecuting those considered even vaguely radical. I am sent to interview the first extreme right-wingers I have ever met. They show me a U.S. map flagged at what they call danger points. In such areas, they announce firmly, cluster Bolsheviks, Anarchists, and other questionable characters—all in America's Northwest. "Here in centers of radicalism we find numerous cases of goiter." The absurdity of the correlation momentarily escapes me.

The second thing I am asked to do is interview an American Communist (I have never met one) who writes about the interpretation of dreams. He is involved in a civil liberties case the Union is investigating. I am sent to speak to him in his apartment. His wife, born abroad, has been trying to take out her citizenship papers. "She refused to pledge allegiance to or salute your goddam flag. She's a pacifist. What did they expect her to do?"

I've never heard such hatred for the United States, or encountered such passionate and uninvited personal advances. I feel fortunate to escape unscathed.

A third and extended task involves reading newspapers from all over the United States each day and marking those articles that refer to the abridgment of civil liberties. I must examine the precise nature of the abrogations. I can imagine no more welcome education or more profound challenge.

Starry-eyed, Edward and I take an evening course in philosophy at the New School for Social Research. Edward already has attended lectures there and describes the school's general program with enthusiasm. I respond at once.

The school is located in a splendid complex of old-fashioned houses far west on Twenty-third Street. On the shelves and tables of an inviting, informal bookshop—where we meet and talk with other students before and after class —I see writings by the most progressive political and social scientists. Some have been or are now teaching at the New School, among them Charles Beard, James Harvey Robinson, and Thorstein Veblen. Edward tells me that most of the original faculty—the school was founded only a short time ago—rebelled against the lack of academic freedom, especially during the war, in many of the country's best-known, established colleges. Alvin Johnson, the head of the school, has proudly made it the first broad-based, adult-education institution in New York, with the aim of providing fresh insights into current social problems.

As I listen to Horace Kallen, a disciple of William James, lecture on "Dominant Ideals of Western Civilization," I feel at last I am hearing something of value about philosophy. Kallen makes the point that the various ideals that have prevailed throughout history have been compensatory—a hypothesis totally new to me. I had thought of philosophical ideals as absolutes, abstractions. I thrill to the list of books Kallen, in his soft, highly cultivated voice, tells us to read. As he lectures, the lilt and quality of his voice are mesmerizing. I can't move my eyes away, lest I miss a single syllable. His selections range from Plato's *Republic* to the *Communist Manifesto*; from the Book of Job (which Kallen views as a Greek tragedy) to Bergson's *Creative Evolution*; from Saint Augustine's *City of God* to Nietzsche's *Will to Power*.

———

At the New School we meet the Arthur Holdens, with whom we become fast friends and co-workers. Their bearing is aristocratic and reserved, but they are dynamos of energy. Miriam's first love is setting the record straight about the vital role women have played in history, a role so largely ignored. Her second passion is fighting against racial persecution. Arthur's major commitment is to architecture—to seeing that better public housing is provided.

The Holdens describe the New York Urban League, its excellent work and motto, "Opportunity, not alms, for the Negro." They ask us to join its board, of which Arthur becomes chairman and Edward treasurer. I am also invited to work for the American Jewish Committee, which fights anti-Semitism; Edward is already a member. I decide, however, to accept only the Holdens' invitation, believing I should work in behalf of those even more discriminated against than Jews.

Tucked somewhere in the back of my mind is the memory of a Negro child I scarcely knew at public school in Philadelphia. I was ten. Our teacher had just told us about monotheism and polytheism, and added that Judaism was monotheistic. I hadn't known the word, but it aroused a responsive chord. When we were asked to raise our hands in favor of the belief we preferred, I chose one God with enthusiasm. In the cloakroom after class, the Negro girl called out to me in a harsh voice, "You dirty Jew!" A shy and quiet child, I was dazed and hurt, but mentioned the incident to no one. I sensed dimly that a Negro child must have problems I couldn't even imagine. Now, as an adult, I realized with new clarity that discrimination is indivisible, and that helping any beleaguered group automatically affects all who are oppressed.

Edward and I attend the International Consumers' Cooperative Summer School in Manchester, England, in 1926, and travel. Our trip is totally different from two earlier journeys abroad with my parents. Then, we made the Grand Tour of resorts: Le Touquet, Aix-les-Bains, Saint-Moritz, Biarritz, the Lido. We went to London, Paris, Lausanne, Zurich, Amsterdam, Antwerp. The lists are long. A new, luxurious world had opened before me. Vast Cunard liners—the *Berengaria*, *Aquitania*, *Mauretania*. Great museums, cathe-

drals, monuments, palaces, tombs, public buildings. Opera, theater, ballet—
Diaghilev. The finest hotels—Claridge's, the Meurice, a dozen Excelsiors. And
the shopping! Tailored suits from O'Rossen; dresses—soft, simple, cut on the
bias—from Vionnet; Chanel No. 5 perfume; shoes from Peal's; leather marvels
from Asprey; stationery from Cassegrain. But expensive resorts and objects
quickly ceased to tempt me .

Now in Manchester Edward and I visit every cooperative store and factory in sight; most are nondescript. We discuss consumers' cooperatives with
colleagues from all over Britain and the continent. The factories we see are
primitive and ill-organized, and turn out unattractive products. We listen to
wordy seminars that make my eyes close.

The movement's influence is far more widespread abroad than at home.
Many who attend the summer school hold important positions in their organizations. Everyone is serious, but few have the grace of humor or an aesthetic
sense. I criticize myself constantly for noticing and being irritated by these
shortcomings.

It rains every day. Umbrellas, umbrellas. The dampness seeps into my
bones. I feel spoiled, unreal, as though seeing everything from the outside.
I'm sympathetic, don't complain, but feel remote, which worries me. Edward
cares so. Yet I cannot believe Consumers' Cooperation—or any other panacea
—will solve all the world's problems.

Rochdale. The cooperative movement was born here. As we stand at
respectful attention in the rain beside the graves of its founders, listening to
tributes, our tireless guide pulls at our coats and mutters, "C'mon, c'mon. We
must be getting on. Back to tea. C'mon, c'mon—we'll be late." He repeats the
ritual every afternoon, wherever we are. Each day there is high tea—too
strong brews, salty hams, heavy breads—and then in the evening tedious
banquets in factories with overcooked meats. Brussels sprouts, Brussels sprouts,
Brussels sprouts, watery potatoes, tasteless "sweets." Speeches are endless. I
often stand next to a rebellious soul who, each time "God Save the King" is
sung, utters an explosive "Tripe!" I feel more tired every day. The food dis-
agrees with me, my throat hurts, and I fear I'll burst out laughing at the wrong
moment.

As soon as the summer school is over, Edward and I set forth on a modest tour, staying at small, uncomfortable hotels and visiting cooperatives wherever we go.

Nuremberg. A mammoth National Socialist meeting is in progress. The men moving through the streets have grown too stout for their uniforms. Their necks, indeed their entire bodies, seem distended. They drink quantities of beer and gorge themselves in crowded, noisy restaurants. Even their helmets seem too small for their heads. Riding up and down in the closely packed elevator of our hotel, the obese men stare and leer. Each behaves exactly like the others, as though all were members of some homogeneous group, subject to an unspoken directing force.

Edward and I have an overwhelming urge to leave Nuremberg at once. In Munich the same coarse group conformity confronts us. We visit an enormous *Bierstube*, the Hofbräuhaus, where men assemble and fill their mugs, then sit at heavy wooden tables that seem a mile long. The building is cheerless and glowering. I detest beer and order a lemonade. My glass is set before me; everyone at our table leans forward to gaze at what I, an alien monstrosity, have perpetrated. Edward and I burst into uncontrollable laughter.

We are young and slender. Everyone else is large and older. I am the only woman present. The men, as they peer at me, are at once comic and ominous. This bizarre and disturbing experience brings Edward and me closer than ever.

Berlin is hard and cold, so different from London and Paris. Was it always this way, or did the war badly affect all of Germany? Strange: although my mother's parents came from the environs of Berlin, I feel no curiosity about their birthplace—no nostalgia or sense of roots. Neither did my parents express any interest in their European background during our travels together.

Vienna: the saddest city I have seen. An empire collapsed. Here I am even more aware of the cruel, savage aftermath of war than at Verdun, only now, instead of confronting gravestones and ruins, we witness the bitter reality of live human misery, of inflation and poverty. A grayness pervades the atmosphere. Vienna is almost a ghost city. I ache for the Austrians.

The museums we visit are breathtaking: we spend hours at the Albertina, where polite attendants take out hundreds of great drawings from immaculate, long, thin drawers and place them before us for our delectation. The Prater, like other romantic images I have harbored, is drained of wonder. From the past, the Schönbrunn Palace strikes us as distasteful and ugly. In contrast, we find the clean-cut lines, the functional quality of the modern housing for workers outstanding and heartening, but are told little more will be built—it's too expensve. Innovators in the arts are leaving the city. But theater and music—in Vienna and Salzburg—are overwhelming. All theaters should be red and gold.

My father was born in Austria some fifty years ago, but again I am devoid of any sense of ancestral connection.

We must be in Italy by a certain date to chaperone Edward's sister, Ruth Alice, and a friend of hers at the Lido. They are about to set off for Tripoli as guests of wealthy Italians who, we discover to our horror, are ardent supporters of Mussolini.

On my previous visits to the Lido with my parents, I wasn't conscious of the Fascists' rise to power in 1922. By now Edward and I have read much about Il Duce and his Black Shirts, his sinister use of dictatorial power and reign of terror. Brutal suppression of striking workers, persecution of intellectuals, murder—the list of abominations grows daily.

The Lido is more popular than ever. People swim, idle, dance. But this time *carabinieri* in black uniforms walk around two by two, silent but menacing. Only our afternoon journeys to the wonders of Venice relieve our uneasiness. We warn Ruth Alice and her friend that their prospective hosts are Fascist supporters; they laugh at us and appear to know nothing about the situation in Italy. They prattle gaily, "We hear their mansion is fabulous—simply fabulous." We leave the Lido the moment they do.

After our return to New York, we lunch at the Normans' with Edward's cousin Katherine and her Italian husband, the composer Italo Montemezzi. They express wild enthusiasm for Mussolini, even repeating the cliché that he's made the trains run on time. Edward and I argue passionately against Fascism and feel ourselves, as so often, estranged from the family.

The Normans invite us to the revival of Italo's opera *L'Amore dei Tre Re*, at the Metropolitan Opera House. I confide to Italo it was the first opera I ever heard, in Philadelphia, when I was ten, whereupon he becomes especially attentive. Yet nothing makes me agree with him about Mussolini.

The correspondence between the Normans' reactionary political attitudes and their admiration for conservative works of art is as logical as it is disturbing. It accounts for much of the discomfort Edward and I feel in their presence. We disagree not only about Mussolini but about domestic politics as well. Although I'm not yet old enough to vote, Edward and I consider ourselves Democrats; Lottie and Aaron are Republicans.

The family disdainfully labels "liberal"—even "radical"—the lectures and meetings we attend in the evenings. Our choices of plays, operas, and concerts are in direct opposition to those our close relatives enjoy. The conventional musical or superficial drawing-room comedies to which they invite us make us suffer; we never can take them to the dramas or concerts we prefer.

In all fields, Edward and I automatically gravitate to art that is breaking new ground. In music, concerts performed by the International Composers Guild, arranged by Edgard Varèse and Carlos Salzedo, are the most advanced and satisfying. The Guild presents Schönberg, Hindemith, Ernest Bloch—names new to me—and also the first performance of Stravinsky's haunting *Les Noces*. Varèse's own music, influenced by sounds heard all around us in the contemporary world, turns its back on traditional Western harmony and melody. His work explodes before an audience unprepared and at first hostile. But its grandeur and conviction give it an immediate classic ring. The League of Composers is more catholic in its choice of modern music than the Guild, but we follow both with an exalted sense of involvement. To be in New York—to be exposed to the best of the past as well as of today—is exhilarating.

The first labor dinner we attend, shortly after our marriage, is held under the auspices of the Brotherhood of Sleeping Car Porters; it is a dramatic experience for me. Never before have I participated in so large an interracial event. At another "liberal" dinner, Clarence Darrow argues brilliantly against Prohibition. To my amazement, he says simply to break the law as much as you can—only so will it be repealed, only so are absurd laws ever eliminated! At a Civil Liberties Union annual dinner, we hear a strange and disturbing report by my beloved special hero, Roger Baldwin. Currently under a suspended jail sentence of six months for reading the Constitution from the steps of the County Courthouse of Paterson, New Jersey, he has just returned from California, where he found much bitterness and widespread persecution of radical and minority elements. He comments with irony that prejudices once expressed about race and religion are now marshaled against unions.

We remain close to a few childhood friends, but see a growing number of associates from the Cooperative League, Civil Liberties Union, New School, Urban League, and the *Survey*. On weekends we walk, climb Bear Mountain, visit High Tor, and drive to West Point—all places of extraordinary beauty. We take simple picnic lunches. The conversation is stimulating; those with whom we hike are dedicated and full of delight. In the winter we ski, if possible, in Van Cortlandt or even Central Park. Relaxed and together, both Edward and I love the out-of-doors and enjoy walking and sports.

At the same time that our circle of friends is widening in New York, it increases during the summer months at Woods Hole. Many acquaintances from there become part of our winter life in New York.

My musical talent is small, but I sang alto happily in the Smith College choir, conducted by Ivan Gorokhoff. Now, by another splendid New England coincidence, he turns out to be the director of the Woods Hole Choral Club, which I join. The woman who introduces me to the club suggests at summer's end that I look into the Adesdi Chorus in New York, conducted by Margarete Dessoff. Her chorus is a fine one; to my delight we sing early music by Vittoria, Palestrina, Aichinger—music that has something of the archaic quality of Stravinsky and Varèse.

An Adesdi member urges me to join the Women's City Club. Ten years before, a number of public-spirited women had started this nonpartisan organization, which fights for the causes I want to support: better housing, public education, health services, improved courts, fuller employment. The club's work is carried out by committees; I serve on one concerned with the city's courts, about which I know nothing. (For reasons I'm unable to fathom, the Urban League also puts me on a court committee.) I am asked by the W.C.C. to look into a situation in the Women's Court.

The building is gloomy; the proceedings lack dignity. I expected a court-room to be orderly, but the impression I get is one of people wandering about aimlessly. The club has been told detectives approach prostitutes on the city's streets and arrest them as though they had done the soliciting. The men gain promotions and salary increases in direct proportion to the number of women they turn in. As I hear the evidence given, within a matter of moments it becomes clear that the charges are flimsy. No witnesses are called—I'm watching a miserable frame-up. The judge is quick to detect the charade.

I report to the club that our information is correct. We communicate our findings to other civic groups and the press, so that the greatest possible pressure may be put on the city to reform corrupt procedures. When I think about how minor my own role is in bringing about needed social change, I feel dispirited and discouraged. Yet as I view the accomplishment of a single organization such as the Women's City Club, in cooperation with other like-minded groups, in the course of a single year, I am astonished and heartened. But now even my limited social work must come to a temporary halt: we're going to have a baby in November.

For some time after our marriage, I didn't feel ready to bear a child. Also, I was at first frightened by the idea of bringing one into so unjust a world. My father had said to me, "You must have children—don't postpone it." Within a year, neither because of his advice nor because of sexual excitement, but because of what I can only call an overwhelming life force, I beg Edward, "We must have a baby. Now—now. We must!" Miraculously, we do.

During pregnancy I often feel afraid, which I'm sure is normal. Not to know whether the baby will be perfectly formed is agonizing. Labor is long and painful. But then, why did no one tell me about the ecstasy of gazing for the first time upon a healthy, newborn infant—our own! Of holding it, hearing its startling cry, touching its velvety skin—tiny curled toes and fingers—and nursing it. The miracle of the appearance of milk. I am transfigured and cannot wait to share my wonder with friends who have had children—each will understand and approach me with new eyes, with a welcoming gesture of recognition. Later, however, I am astonished when everyone acts in an everyday manner. No one looks at me as I had expected. Strange.

Since knowledge about birth control has given us such extraordinary freedom, I feel others should have the same access to it. The more I read about Margaret Sanger and the widespread opposition to her fight to disseminate birth control information, the more I want to help. I telephone and make an appointment to meet and talk with her. She is intense, has a sweet, open face and blondish hair, somewhat frizzy; she is completely feminine and focused. She asks me to be on one of her committees.

A few of us who work for the Urban League decide it is of utmost importance that a birth control clinic be set up in Harlem. During a meeting Miriam Holden and I have with Mrs. Sanger about the proposed clinic, the telephone rings. Mrs. Sanger is told the police have raided her Clinical Research Bureau and seized its confidential records. That this should happen to such a center, operating within the law, is insupportable. So is placing Mrs. Sanger in the false position of seeming to break her promise that all information at the clinic will be kept secret.

We frantically call lawyers committed to fighting for civil liberties. Morris Ernst agrees to take the case. He establishes with brilliant skill the principle that a physician's advice to a patient is a private matter and not subject to public scrutiny or arbitrary interference; he wins this historically important case.

Our first child, Nancy, was born in November 1927. Not long after the birth of our son, Andrew, Margaret Sanger telephoned. She explained that a widely read newspaper wanted to contrast in interviews a young woman with two children and a mother with numerous offspring. She begged me to talk to the sympathetic reporter and to be photographed with Nancy and Andrew, "because they are so lovely. It will be helpful to the movement." Who could resist?

A friendly young woman from the *New York Journal* came to our apartment, admired the children, and asked whether I considered two the ideal number. It was the first time anyone had interviewed me. I was shy, but spoke as forcefully as possible. "I have no such presumptuous notion, nor would I dare mention any number as ideal. I can't speak for others and have no idea now whether we shall have more children or not. However, I do favor birth control information being made available to everyone. Those who don't want it need not use it." The next day's paper quoted me: "Two children make an ideal family." I was stunned. The article continued: "The pretty young society matron smiled at her babies and directed the maid to pick up their toys"—the last words a further fabrication.

The other mother interviewed was quoted: "I wouldn't take a million dollars for one of my children. Birth control? I don't know what you talk about!" Under Nancy and Andrew's picture the caption read: "Mrs. Norman's Two Children" and next to the photograph of the large family: "The Other Side."

After hours of effort, I located the woman with six children; she told me she, too, was entirely misquoted. I called the *Journal* to complain about the double distortion. No one listened. I wrote a blistering letter, only a tiny part of which was printed on the back page of the next day's edition. With tears of anguish I showed the interview to Edward, who said firmly, "You must never speak to the yellow press again." I gladly obeyed.

4

After I became pregnant, my doctor insisted that I cut down on activities and give up my job at the A.C.L.U. His order saved me from feeling guilty about having time to do other things. "Other things" consisted mainly of visiting as many art exhibitions as possible.

I had made myself stay away from galleries since coming to New York, so I could concentrate on my marriage and work. My desire to see more painting and sculpture had not abated, but little good contemporary French art was on view. As for significant American art, none seemed to exist. Were all great artists dead, or living in France?

One day I tear a list of exhibits from an art magazine. While making the rounds, I enter a small, shabby room called The Intimate Gallery, at 489 Park Avenue. On its dark walls, covered with white cheesecloth, are brilliant watercolors, modest rectangles of paper transformed as though by magic.

A New England mountainside zigzags with the swift, vibrant, sure strokes of a master. Buildings, seascapes explode, give the feeling of being syncopated, yet classic. The pictures are unmistakably of today. One painting's rich autumnal burnt orange-red, subtle greens, black with a touch of muted blue—I long for it! I decipher a signature: Marin. Who is he? If I had even a little money or if Edward agreed, could I buy the picture? What would it cost? Perhaps not too much, since I have never heard of the artist. In my insanely romantic way, I hope Marin is alive and an American, even though his name sounds French.

The man in charge is talking to other visitors. Too shy to interrupt, I go away frustrated and sad. Yet I want to—I must—see the Marins again. I cannot resist going back to the little room. There, to my relief, the pictures are still on the walls, as extraordinary as before.

The same man is talking again. How am I ever to find out about the painting I love most? Finally there is a lull and I ask about the picture. "It has been acquired." That is all the man will tell me and he goes ahead with his conversation. In other galleries, the moment you show interest in a painting, attendants fall all over themselves. If a work you like has been bought, you are shown something else with utmost haste. This time I leave The Intimate Gallery confused and a bit irritated.

Because the Marins continue to haunt me, I return once more. To my disappointment, an exhibition by another painter has been hung, and the man is addressing a young woman. Upset, I pick up a circular lying on a shelf:

The Intimate Gallery is dedicated primarily to an Idea and is an American Room. It is used more particularly for the intimate study of Seven Americans: John Marin, Georgia O'Keeffe, Arthur G. Dove, Marsden Hartley, Paul Strand, Alfred Stieglitz, Number Seven (six + X). [X is the unknown possible.]

It is in The Intimate Gallery only that the complete evolution and the more important examples of these American workers can be seen and studied.

The Intimate Gallery is a Direct Point of Contact between Public and Artist. It is the Artist's Room. It is a Room with but One Standard. Alfred Stieglitz has volunteered his services and is its directing Spirit.

The Intimate Gallery is not a Business nor is it a "Social" Function. The Intimate Gallery competes with no one nor with anything.

As I glance at the statement, I am filled with curiosity. I have never heard of Alfred Stieglitz nor seen work by any of the artists listed, except Marin.

The young woman is questioning the man about the meaning of a particular picture. "Do you ask what the wind means?" he replies. His voice has a peculiar, penetrating resonance. "You might as well ask what life means." The girl doesn't answer. The man: "If an artist could explain his work in words, he wouldn't have had to create it. And remember, your attitude toward a picture may alter, but the picture itself won't."

The voice rivets my attention. I notice the man's face for the first time. The lips are finely drawn, as though carved; the eyes are deep-set, dark, piercing. The hair and mustache are gray, bristling. Someone enters the room and says, "Hello, Stieglitz," so at least the mystery of his identity is solved.

All my life I have been waiting for someone to answer my own questions. Now a stranger, Mr. Stieglitz, in refusing to reply to the girl, makes the first satisfying statement I have heard about art. He refuses to pin down—to limit—any of the reasons why art is important. I bless him for it. Especially so because of the depth of his eyes, the quality of his voice, his uncompromising attitude. The encounter seems absurdly slight, yet within a split second an inner music soars.

Edward and I were invited to dinner by the first American artist we had met, Bertram Hartman, and his wife, Gusta. With them were Paul and Rebecca Strand. Mr. Strand was reserved, had small, chiseled features. She was classically handsome and dressed with classic simplicity. He was a photographer and later showed us his prints. Unaware that photographs of such quality existed, I was startled by their striking beauty. Mr. Strand placed strong lamps at proper angles so that the most powerful light was focused on details, sharpness, modeling. He waited just too long, for my rhythm, before showing the next picture, but I was so amazed by his technical achievement that I exclaimed innocently, "How did you get such fantastic effects? What kind of a camera do you use?" Paul Strand glared at me and replied haughtily, "It is *not* the camera." I blushed and was silenced.

I visit The Intimate Gallery again, as much to listen to Mr. Stieglitz as to see paintings. Sometimes he addresses me directly, clearly, without having any idea who I am. At other times I pretend to look at pictures but instead pay attention to what he is saying to others in his unique way. After leaving, I write down what I have heard:

"We protect one another only by telling each other the truth."

"I am not interested in people's claims—only in what they do. The act came first and then the word."

"If an artist has a sufficiently deep feeling, the seemingly impossible will happen. He will find a form through which to create what he must, even if it means death."

"The world of our dreams is more real than the world that exists."

"All art, like all love, is rooted in heartache."

"Without equality of respect there can be no true relationship."

"No man can be satisfied within himself unless he satisfies the woman he loves."

"To say what you really feel and see, not what you are supposed to feel and see."

"To do the best job of which you are capable, then to reach for a point even beyond that."

"To be in love is to wish to possess. To love is to seek release for the other."

One day I am the only visitor; Mr. Stieglitz shows me an issue of the loveliest periodical I have seen, *Camera Work*. It is large; the text is beautifully printed on heavy paper. On many of its pages, photographs in sepia tones are tipped in, printed on fine tissue. I am afraid to handle the copy for fear of harming it. To my surprise, Mr. Stieglitz tells me he published it from 1902 to 1917, and that his earlier gallery, 291, was the first to introduce modern art to America, beginning in 1908—and not Dr. Barnes, as I had imagined.

We are interrupted by the entrance of a young man who is introduced as Kalonyme, an art critic for the *New York Times*. Apparently Mr. Stieglitz and his intimates are called by their last names and each of them refers to the little gallery as the Room.

Because Kalonyme falls quickly silent, which makes me self-conscious, I search for something to say. I ask whether Stieglitz knows a man named Paul Strand. He smiles and says yes. I tell what happened when I met Strand and saw his photographs. As I speak, a dim recollection haunts me: I feel I have seen the name Strand printed somewhere. To my horror, it may well have been on the little circular I carried away from the Room earlier, without having read it too carefully. I feel I have fallen into some nameless trap, but continue uneasily, confessing my embarrassment at Strand's, then burst out laughing. Stieglitz is amused. Kalonyme bristles, gazes at me coldly: "You wouldn't ask Eugene O'Neill the kind of pen he uses." "No," I reply, flabbergasted, "Certainly not." I wish I hadn't spoken.

Stieglitz says nothing, goes to a black box, and takes out a mounted photograph. He places it on a shelf before me, in ordinary daylight. I don't quite understand what I'm being shown, nor do I know who has made it. As the picture becomes clearer to me, I make out a small black-and-white cloud formation. At its tip is a tiny disc of light toward which the dark part of the cloud reaches. The photograph is not at all sensational, nor does it resemble anything I have seen before. Stieglitz remains silent and shows me another print related to the first, but in no way identical. I feel certain the photographs are by Stieglitz himself and ask no questions. Now, instead of being saddened and humiliated, as I was at Strand's, I exult at having seen something extraordinary.

After the summer months and the birth of Nancy, I go to the Room once more. Stieglitz is alone, looking far into space. He asks if I am married, if the marriage is emotionally satisfying. I'm so full of questions of my own, his questions startle me. "Yes, I'm in love with my husband and we have a new baby." "Is your sexual relationship good?" Talking about such matters is of vital importance, in spite of my inability to be totally honest.

Stieglitz inquires, "Do you have enough milk to nurse your child?" Gently, impersonally, he barely brushes my coat with the tip of a finger over one of my breasts, and as swiftly removes it. "No." Our eyes do not meet. Again, I'm neither affronted nor self-conscious.

Why has no one ever asked me the questions Stieglitz does? I know I can speak freely, openly, to this man about anything, everything. I soon discover that for years he has had the same effect on others.

Try as I will not to go to the Room, I go. As I drive or walk down Park Avenue, I look dumbly at the windows of Room 303; by some magic, they may tell me if Stieglitz is there.

I make valiant efforts to space my visits. I can wait three days at most before returning. With expectations of I don't know what, I open the door and glance around the nondescript room. For the moment, the paintings on the walls do not hold my attention. Stieglitz sits relaxed in his dilapidated chair. I observe carefully the figure before me, clad in a not specially well-cut black and white tweed suit, a grayish, heavy cashmere knitted vest, a white shirt and black tie. His slightly untidy hair looks as though the wind has blown it. Every move is a natural one. His words pour forth like a torrent. No rhetorical flourishes heighten his simply spoken sentences. He does not lecture or theorize. I can't say after I leave that he has explained anything. But, without doubt, his vision is changing something in me I cannot yet define.

Why, in the Room, do I feel a great stillness? A sweet quiet envelops me. Yet I am so excited and filled with such curiosity that I can barely move, barely speak. Finally I contain myself no longer. I write a breathless letter:

[April 17, 1928]

I know it is awfully young of me to do this. But it's rather a formal, cold world on the whole—so why, when something lovely and warm comes along, shouldn't I *tell* the creator of it? (This protected method of a letter and this introduction are not the methods I'd like to use with which to tell you all this, but I know you so slightly that I'm coward enough to protect myself with them.)

Obviously enough—it's just this—I have a very difficult time keeping away from 303! And when I do come I love the work you're doing so, I feel so jolly about everything all the way thru' me that I *have* to write and thank you for it.

But here is the irony: I don't come in as much as I want to because, after all, it is your place for a purpose and just because I love the purpose and I feel this warm bond there is no earthly reason why you should want me to come in for any other reason than to view the pictures—or perhaps to buy them. And when I do want to buy them—I can't!

At the base of it all is the fact that I would love to help you with what you are doing. I instinctively feel pulled toward doing that. I should like to devote a lot of time to it.

I feel real sentiment so seldom that I hate to be afraid of telling of it—and yet rather than be laughed at, I inhibit it mostly. I must tell it or burst—and if the hearer has no need of it I suppose he laughs. This is a unique little episode in my experience—so I don't know quite how to describe it to you. I hope you'll understand all the things I'm not saying —because I mean them all so very deeply!

Perhaps I should be ascetic and unselfish about the whole thing and view it impersonally. I should just thank you for being and let it go at that! But the whole thing is too personal a need and joy to me. I want to incorporate knowing you into my life—and I want to feel that once in a while when I feel just like it that I can come in and enjoy the whole thing with you—just because—and further that if you do want any help—I'm just aching to give it. I love what you're doing. I *feel* it, and I'd love to help.

In case you don't know which "who" I am—I was in this a.m., I like the White Lily, the Island, the Lachaise Bronze—and quite a few others.

Dorothy S. Norman

As I sign the letter, I realize Stieglitz has never asked my name.

After mailing the outburst, I am so upset I go to the Room at once. There I behave in a most impersonal, restrained fashion, trying to conceal what I have done. I ask Stieglitz questions about how his activities have evolved and, taking out a notebook, write down his answers. "Do you mind my doing this?" I add hesitantly. "I want to write about you. I'm not sure I can do it. I'd like to start with an article, but of course I've never published anything."

Stieglitz responds by giving me copies of *Camera Work* to take home. No longer am I afraid to touch them. The beauty of the photographs and the aliveness of the articles fascinate and excite me. But most astounding are the dates of the early exhibitions Stieglitz held at his Photo-Secession Galleries at 291 Fifth Avenue. As I turn the pages I read a tale of high adventure. The list of "firsts" in America is astounding: Rodin's drawings and Matisse, 1908 —three years after I was born. Cézanne's watercolors and Picasso, 1911. Alfred Maurer and Marin, 1909. Arthur Dove and Marsden Hartley, 1910. *Camera Work* was the first to accept Gertrude Stein's writing for publication, in 1912; 291 was the first to exhibit both Georgia O'Keeffe's work and Strand's photographs in 1916. Francis Picabia, 1913—the year of the famous Armory Show, which I've never heard of but which Stieglitz describes to me. The primitive African sculpture I saw at Barnes was exhibited at 291 as art for the first time in America as long ago as 1914—the same year Stieglitz held Constantin Brancusi's initial one-man show in America.

He takes out a large, thin publication, 291, issued in 1915–16. It was a precursor of European Dadaism, about which I must learn more.

As long ago as the 1890s, Stieglitz was making, battling for, buying, showing, and reproducing the most advanced photographs of the period. He fought to have first-rate photographs recognized on the same basis as other already established art forms. After he won over 150 prizes for his photographs, he opposed holding competitions, finding them meaningless.

He tells me, "In 1900 I met and admired the work of a young American photographer, Edward Steichen. Five years later, we founded the Photo-Secession Galleries. From the beginning we planned to show not only photographs but also work in other media, breaking new ground. Steichen, who lived in Paris, introduced me to paintings by important European and American artists—many of whom we exhibited for the first time in this country."

To my relief and joy, Stieglitz answered my letter. His penmanship was itself a work of art; I had never seen such distinguished writing. Its bold black strokes were almost chilling in their beauty.

> Don't be afraid of being a nuisance. Ask all the questions you like—come whenever you feel the need. There is more literature I can give you. Also what I wrote (not very much). Naturally I'm interested in what you want to do. And I hope you'll do it. I feel you can. Forget all about Inferiority of all kinds. With me all people can be themselves—if they so choose. And if they choose otherwise I know the consequences. The Room is ready.

Again I wrote of my desire to help:

> I might park as a handyman to answer the phone, shut the door—hang the pictures—make order out of chaos among the what-nots—or I might

see whether long-hand would be possible as a means of taking the place of short-hand— Now any of these things I'd like to do— All of them will strike you as undoubtedly absurd—

Stieglitz permits me to look through black box after black box of his photographs. And then, to my surprise, he gives me a print, a delicate picture of clouds—one of the series he calls "Equivalents."

I am awed. His photographs, as he states, are a portrayal of his basic philosophy of life. "I have communicated with greatest clarity in my *Songs of the Sky*. In reality my photographs are not of sky, or clouds, but of life. Art is rooted in life and life believes in life." He writes to me: "My photographs and I are one. The Room and I are one. Each relationship has an indefinable difference. No two moments are alike."

The forms in the Equivalent he gives me are in part crisp in their definition, in part most subtly modeled. The thrust of the image is reserved, reverent, yet erotic. There is nothing vague or sentimental about it. The work of no other American artist today touches me with equal intensity.

To capture Stieglitz in words, as I have hoped to do, is difficult. With others, you ask a simple question and receive a direct reply. With Stieglitz you hear why he cannot answer. He may recount an anecdote to prove the impossibility of explaining why he prefers pictures to words. But while he is talking you learn something you didn't ask about that may be more important.

I listen to Stieglitz, read about him, watch him function, look at his photographs, talk with him, and begin to fathom that he represents an approach to life I have been seeking in the world around me but had not found. I understand why the art he has fostered, without fanfare or pretension, satisfies me. Like some great force of nature, he has attracted to him and helped generate much of the most vital and life-enhancing work of our time. In his own prints he creates images that arouse me deeply, churning up depths that, even while they astonish, I know have only been waiting to be lifted into new awareness.

I conclude that no single article will suffice; I shall have to write a book, which will take a long time to do. I want to put together bits and pieces as they emerge and make a significant whole of them later. I have so much to learn. I need time to be clear even about what I mean by saying Stieglitz is changing my perspective on many aspects of life, or that he is clarifying for me many vague and only partly formulated thoughts.

At a party Edward and I attended at the Hartmans in 1928 I met John Marin for the first time. His face had deep wrinkles that looked as though they had been formed as much by laughter as by peering at the sheets of paper on which he painted. His twinkle made me smile. Throughout the evening, whenever we looked at each other, we simply laughed at nothing in particular. Someone told me his wife put a bowl over his head and cut his hair along the edge. Thus it was as long as the bowl was deep, and his bangs served only to intensify his amused expression. The face was sensitive, somewhat craggy. Marin had the look of an outdoor man. The mobile, ever-changing features evoked a sense of grandeur, as did his pictures. The quality of his silence made speaking seem unnecessary. My eyes kept returning to watch him when he wasn't looking.

The sculptor Gaston Lachaise, also at the party, is a monumental figure, impressive and handsome. There is no laughter in his dark, deep eyes. His recent exhibition at the Room should have prepared me for his brooding look. Because I couldn't buy the Marin I wanted, I acquired instead a small Lachaise: a nude of great dignity and classic reserve, standing with out-stretched arms. The modeling is full, sensuous, subtle. Observing Lachaise's face, I understand the depth of love that inspires his work. At the Room a short time later, Stieglitz introduces me to Madame Lachaise. Lachaise joins us and we have a warm, friendly talk. They invite Edward and me to dinner.

I bought my Lachaise with a birthday gift from Edward's father—at the moment, the only sum of money I could call my own. Mr. Norman, like other members of the family, believes one should either acquire established art that is a good investment, or help unrecognized artists who are poor—the latter being considered an acceptable act of charity. To buy the work of a living artist simply because you love it is in another category—one that is frowned upon even if the artist is in need.

I confess my act to Father Norman, knowing he will disapprove. From a puritanical point of view it must strike him as self-indulgent. Had I bought a mink coat or pearls—both of which I have frequently refused—I would be considered sensible. (One relative berates me, "You owe it to your husband to have a mink coat.")

At the Lachaises, we describe my difficulties with the family about buying art. Madame Lachaise looks at me quizzically. "My dear," she says serenely, "rest assured that if I were offered an ermine wrap or a Matisse, I'd choose the ermine wrap." Knowing the Lachaises have little money, I smile (which I'm supposed to do), but find Madame Lachaise's remark unsettling.

Not long after the sculpture was delivered to our apartment, Edward's sister and her husband stayed with us overnight. We went our separate ways after dinner; on our return we found crumpled newspaper raffishly placed around the reverently fashioned figure. I felt outraged.

Exhibitions at the Room are beautifully presented and of uniformly high quality. In rapid succession I meet the artists shown there. The paintings of Georgia O'Keeffe—Stieglitz's wife—attract a large and enthusiastic audience. I respond to two small pictures: a subtly painted white shell and a delicate white flower.

O'Keeffe's appearance is striking. She is dressed in black with a touch of white, just as Stieglitz told me she was at their first meeting. His photographs of her are remarkable portrayals of her beauty.

She asks why I don't work for the Woman's Party and drop all other "nonsense." My answer: "Other causes interest me more." Clearly the subject is dear to her heart. Someday, I explain, I may work for the party, but so far I can't look upon any such single cause as all-important. The Civil Liberties Union includes in its action the fight to gain equal rights for everyone. Meanwhile I'm learning more about being a woman, beyond and including "women's rights." I can act only when I'm ready.

O'Keeffe refuses to be called Mrs. Stieglitz, which mystifies me. I completely favor emancipation for women but, because of my temperament, cannot be a Lucy Stoner and use my maiden name. But I respect O'Keeffe's point of view.

Arthur Dove, who is not well, lives in the country and seldom comes to the Room. At our first meeting I'm struck by his dignity. A gracious man, he gains my sympathy at once. His paintings are striking. I respect him greatly for having been the first abstract painter in the United States—as far back as 1910—and for having given up a successful career as a commercial artist to lead the hazardous life of a "pure" one. He has written of his own art that, like modern art itself, it has tried to eliminate nonessentials. Stieglitz has said of Dove: "His painting is true to itself, which means true to time."

Marsden Hartley's rather stolid bearing scarcely prepares me for his forceful paintings and elegant literary style. Perhaps his electric blue eyes should have done so. He gives the impression of being offhand, slightly superior, essentially bored, which is deceptive. At times his gaze is beseeching; his shoulders shrug if someone makes a particularly tactless or insensitive remark. He has a habit that amuses me: he leans toward me confidentially and whispers about a nearby shop where one can buy extraordinary old buttons made of bones, shells, and other incredible materials; some are most beautifully decorated. After a while I listen more seriously as he tells me where one can find bits and pieces of rare, ancient Coptic textiles, and mentions Baron Corvo, whom I absolutely must read. I understand Hartley's heraldic paintings and his love of the romantic better after our conversations. His wanderings about town in quest of the marvelous are lonely. I never see him with anyone else on the street. He rarely smiles, but if he likes you he chuckles in a reassuring way. He comes to the Room often; wherever Stieglitz is, he admits, is home to him.

Charles Demuth—as debonair and subtle as his watercolors and writings—is delightfully witty. I long to live with one of his pictures, but his work is out of reach. At first I have no knowledge he is diabetic and quite ill. Despite his infrequent shows at the Room, Demuth belongs there.

Most of the artists Stieglitz has shown over the years have encountered serious economic problems. I don't understand for some time how the Room operates financially. Stieglitz accepts no commissions; his own photographs are not for sale. He makes no attempt to "sell" the art he exhibits, as my own experience has proved. The Room does not advertise. "Those who really need what is here will find it." The Intimate Gallery is not listed in the phone book, nor is it a business. "You can acquire art here, but we don't sell it. There is a difference."

If an artist has a good year, Stieglitz deducts a certain percentage from his earnings for rent and overhead. Should the year be a poor one, by mutual agreement a larger share of the others' funds is used for expenses. When times are difficult for everyone, Stieglitz helps with his limited means or tries to raise money.

He does not look upon such arrangements as having anything to do with charity. He clarifies his position for me in a letter:

> Before all else I have no sentimental ideas about charity. I personally have never accepted the idea "charity" as it is practiced and understood by people generally. But that's my private affair. To me charity is a degrading influence. I know that our system demands it. But I don't accept the system. To take an artist's work and give money for it in the name of charity makes my blood boil. I have been fighting that for years. I'd like to hang the artists who accept in that spirit. I never gave anyone any charity.
>
> Please don't imagine I have much, if any, sympathy with the wailing artist. I dislike him. I have never heard Marin or O'Keeffe or Dove wail. Marin and Dove have certainly been up against it hard for long stretches. Dove still is.

While most people try to buy art at the lowest possible price, Stieglitz seeks the highest possible amount for the living artist. He writes me in 1928: "Remember the artist is not a business man. Business and art are not bed-fellows. The trouble today is that art dealers are turning art into big business —making the whole thing another Wall Street. Naturally in such an atmosphere the true artists can't exist." I watch and listen as visitors hear Stieglitz speak out in this way and are moved, bored, or offended.

He is incensed at the suggestion he has put Marin or O'Keeffe "on the map."

I'm not making a map, nor *helping* Marin or O'Keeffe, nor anyone. Marin represents positive development—creative—to me. So does O'Keeffe. I like to live with the results. And I like to share the living with anyone wishing to share it.

As for offending possible customers, I don't recognize the idea "customer" in the Room. I don't want to hurt anyone's feelings, so undoubtedly hurt many. You have heard me say over and over again I'd much prefer to have the Room exist without anything for sale. You see, my own work is not for sale.

Although I hoped to help Stieglitz, I couldn't figure out how to do it. A hundred dollars was left over from my birthday gift; I sent it to him. A first, minor, tentative step, but not at all the aid I had in mind. The sum—more than enough to pay for the *Camera Works* I had bought—was far too limited. Stieglitz had told me he would keep none of the money for himself. In order to understand how he functioned, I asked how he intended to use it. His reply:

I keep no records. No books. No inventories. No insurance. The hundred dollars will go in a fund that is used for many purposes, all of them constructive. Rent and printing bills are paid. Many artists—not necessarily painters or sculptors—are given the opportunity to work. One very brilliant man received quite a sum of money to be able to spend time in a European sanitarium to see whether his eyes could be saved. This is not charity. The man has done much for artists although he has no money himself. I look upon him as a co-worker, as a force needed in America. Another white soul, tubercular, penniless, proud, needed a year in Europe—six hundred dollars. A writer and painter. I knew of it—the man was given the opportunity. This is not charity. These people are under no obligation to me or to anyone else. Anymore than you are, in taking my energy and time to satisfy something in yourself. For that's all anyone can do.

Now how can I tell you who or what will receive your particular hundred dollars? No hundred dollars will ever have been put to better use. But if you feel any charity about it, I'll return the money to you at once.

I was elated; Stieglitz had reacted against the very attitudes I found so troubling in the family's approach to charity for artists.

Arguments about the "objective," the "subjective," and similar theoretical matters always discouraged me. Sensing that Stieglitz might be equally impatient with them, I asked him. He wrote a short note:

8/28/28

You ask me about Objectivity and Subjectivity. I had years of such discussions at "291"— Some of the discussions led to "action"—most of them were just academic twaddle. I don't care whether something living is subjective or objective— All I ask is for the *livingness*. The rest of it I'll leave to the discussionists.

They'll find everything but the Quick of the moment—Object—or what-you-will.

Greetings—

The first letters Stieglitz and I wrote to one another led swiftly to more frequent ones. A day without receiving a magnificent envelope was a day lost.

The need to go to the Room became obsessive. The Barnes Foundation came alive for me through its pictures; The Intimate Gallery was doubly vital because of Stieglitz, as well as the painters and writers who appeared day by day.

Paul Rosenfeld's *Port of New York* reveals much about Stieglitz, as do Waldo Frank's *Time Exposures*, *Salvos*, and *Our America*. Within a brief period, both authors walk into the little room. Rosenfeld is sandy-haired, somewhat heavy, and moves with the self-consciousness of a timid man. He makes me feel unbearably shy because he is so shy himself. But his writing is courageous, perceptive, generous in spirit.

As my reticence in his presence disappears, I find it unexpectedly rewarding to share our thoughts about all the arts. Rosenfeld is, for me, the finest living critic of modern music, but he is more than that. His writings about literature, the plastic arts, and dance are equally wide-ranging and sensitive. Possessed—like Stieglitz—of only limited means, he is selfless in helping those in whom he believes. (Even to the point of surreptitiously placing money in the pocket of a hungry young poet whose umbrella he shares on a rainy night.)

Rosenfeld's intuition and knowledge are a source of joy; with increasing frequency we discuss the books we read, the plays we see, the concerts we hear. We so often agree that I am surprised by his attitude toward Stravinsky's neoclassicism. For me, the tragic grandeur of *Oedipus* alone—a composition Rosenfeld attacks—would keep Stravinsky in the first rank of composers.

I am astonished at disagreeing with Rosenfeld at all, I so admire him. He arouses such a maternal, protective attitude that I find myself defending him even if at odds with what he writes or says. His courtly manner is disarming. I argue with those who complain he overwrites, and feel compassion for him when he bursts into the Room to ask Stieglitz, as though his very life depends upon it, "How would you define the creative moment?" To which Stieglitz replies, "I wouldn't."

While reading Rosenfeld's erudite, perceptive articles, I have no inkling of his miserable and humiliating childhood until his autobiographical novel, *Boy in the Sun*, is published. At school he was taunted for being a Jew; he hadn't known that he was one or that anti-Semitism was widespread. At home he asked fearfully if he was the only Jew in the world.

Rosenfeld and Frank, though friends, couldn't be more different in temperament, yet both are ardent champions of young, unrecognized talent. Warm and outgoing, Frank at once puts me at ease. His keen insights and fine intellect, clearly evidenced in his writings, are exhilarating. Rosenfeld is more poetic, modest, his critical essays more penetrating. But Frank's wider, more philosophical range of vision accounts for his interest in Spinoza and the Upanishads.

The next time Frank appeared at the Room, he offered to walk me home and asked whether he might come up to the apartment to continue our talk. I liked his enthusiasm and intelligent eyes. On entering our living room, his somewhat flirtatious look changed drastically. With immediate and shocking hostility he picked up from a table Joyce's *Ulysses*—he had spotted it at once—and like a spoiled child hurled it under the piano. (It was the single gift I had requested from my parents on their 1925 trip to Europe.) I ignored his action and offered him tea. He moved toward the bookshelves, discovering his volumes of criticism. "You don't have a very good library, I see."

I understand at once the reason for his complaint. Edward insisted on organizing our books strictly according to subject matter, beginning with pure science, then the applied sciences, philosophy, history, *belles-lettres*, novels, poetry. Since Frank was also the author of novels, his work was not all in one place, which I pointed out to him. Blushing, he found a number of his writings in separate sections and looked enormously pleased, whereupon his opinion of our library improved. But it took me time to recover from this strange experience.

Although born in Europe, Edgard Varèse strikes me as the most impressive and original of "living American" composers. After we are introduced at the Room, he tells me that, following his arrival in New York in 1915, he went straight to 291 at the suggestion of Marcel Duchamp. It became the only place in New York in which he felt at home.

I laugh heartily as he imitates soporific ladies swooning at symphony concerts, soothed by stringed instruments playing—in his opinion—senti-mental nineteenth-century music. He mimics Toscanini's martial gestures, suggesting that even his powerful conducting puts adoring females to sleep. Varèse's huge shoulders shrug; his face becomes diabolically contorted. Words of disgust sputter as he expresses anguish over the current state of music. For me the quality of his own work gives him the authority to do this; it makes me feel a partisan of his.

The originality of his music at first shocks and repels most of his audi-ence. But his revolutionary use of everyday sounds in the world around us and his electronic music soon establish him as America's foremost composer. His influence becomes world-wide.

Varèse tells how he met the wife of an elderly musician who conducts only classical opera. She said, "Mr. Varèse, I understand you detest all music that isn't modern." He replied, "That's absurd. To mention just one composer I admire—Monteverdi." The wife, sweetly: "We call him just Verdi."

Varèse's wife, Louise, looks fragile standing next to his strapping figure. Crisp and witty, she possesses a biting intelligence. She is translating *Eloges* by the French poet Saint-John Perse (Alexis Saint-Léger Léger), which I read for the first time. Edward and I become friends with the Varèses and see them often. At their apartment on Sullivan Street, which has a noble character, Varèse cooks the best veal parmigiana I have ever tasted.

One day a stoutish woman with straight, graying, bobbed hair sat talking to Stieglitz as I entered the Room. She wore a felt hat and a simple, ill-fitting tailored suit. Her cheeks were round and rosy; her manner gentle, courteous. She carried a huge ear trumpet that looked as though it were made of tin. Stieglitz introduced the Honorable Dorothy Brett, but I moved away so they could speak to each other with as much privacy as the smallish Room afforded.

Brett's accent was British, she was very deaf, and when she held up her enormous trumpet to hear Stieglitz, she beamed at me shyly as though to imply, "It's awfully funny, isn't it?" Someone interrupted their conversation and Brett hurriedly told Stieglitz she would return the following day. I rose to bid her goodbye, but she somehow wafted me along with her. We smiled at each other sympathetically in the elevator going down; reaching the front steps on Park Avenue, we sat over to one side and talked for hours. I felt I had known her always.

Brett tells me something of her life; although much that she recounts is sad, we laugh a good deal. Her grandfather was created Viscount Esher by Queen Victoria. "I had the most dreadful childhood. I was sent to dancing class at Windsor Castle when Victoria was still Queen. I was terribly shy, felt ugly, and was so frightened, I decided to become deaf so I wouldn't have to hear what people said."

Brett's pale brown eyes seem to grow more enormous as she stares at me with horror and then laughs mischievously, as though widening her gaze will make everything she says more believable. "No wonder I have always been a rebel. I went to the Slade School of Art and have painted ever since."

Katherine Mansfield was a close friend. "I must tell you about our first meeting—you'll understand. We were seated next to each other at a large luncheon—absolutely silent, like two terrified children. Katherine made tight little wads of the inside of rolls, hid them in her hand, and passed them to me under the table. We stifled our laughter and became friends for life."

The talk moves to D. H. Lawrence, who clearly is the major figure in Brett's life. Bits and pieces of conversations that have taken place recently at the Room come back to me. Brett's appearing at the gallery fits into a larger framework. Friends of Lawrence have been trying to persuade Stieglitz to exhibit both his paintings and those by Brett. Letters from Lawrence express fear Stieglitz is being bothered. Stieglitz has given serious consideration to showing Lawrence, whose writing he admires, but decides it would be a mistake. Such an exhibit could be misinterpreted as a desire to present the sensational, in which he has no interest. Brett surely will be disappointed, for now her paintings won't be shown either. She doesn't mention her own work, but expresses joy at having met Stieglitz, even briefly. I sense they have established an immediate rapport.

Although Brett is not precisely a member of the Bloomsbury group and is by no means enthusiastic about all so labeled, she has been closer to them than anyone else I have met. As she describes Virginia Woolf, Middleton Murry, Roger Fry, Clive and Vanessa Bell, Lytton Strachey, Carrington, much of my reading by and about them takes on new life. Brett is the first person I hear mention the name Ottoline Morrell.

I find Brett a delight; we meet often. I tell her how much Lawrence's *Lady Chatterley's Lover* has meant to me. It has just been privately printed in Italy. Stieglitz, who received some of the first copies, has given me one. He greatly respects the book, as do almost all who frequent the Room. Except Kalonyme. "You don't really mean that this ridiculous book has opened anyone's eyes to anything," he fumes. "In France it would simply be laughed at. You might think the English and Americans have never before known the facts of life. What rubbish!"

I protest. "Clearly, *Lady Chatterley* is not great literature. It's over-simplified, but it does place poetic stress on most women's hunger for greater sexual fulfillment." I say, too, that I find the way in which Lawrence has used four-letter words healthy, liberating. Kalonyme shrugs.

Barring the book from the mails as obscene, I feel, represents a serious blow to a free press, as does the banning of Joyce's *Ulysses*. Also upsetting is the fact that a pirated edition of *Lady Chatterley* has appeared, for which Lawrence receives no royalties. To my knowledge, Stieglitz is the only one in the United States making a strong effort to halt the sale of the edition.

One day I enter the Room and find only Stieglitz, who motions me to sit far away from him. He smiles. "Out of danger." I had thought he was teasing when he said this before, but now he sounds as if he meant it. A tense silence. We look at each other intently, deeply. I hesitate to speak. I'm so young, my words will sound absurd. I whisper across the space, "I want to say something to you." "Say it." The voice is gentle, encouraging. I remain miserably silent. "Say it," he repeats. "I can't." "Say it." A huge effort; I feel almost strangled. "I love you." His face softens, his eyes glisten. His voice grows even more tender, his expression more intimate. "I know—come here." He reaches out his hand. "We do," he says and brings a new world into existence. He adds, "I've wanted to do this for a long time." He kisses me as I have never dreamed a kiss could be. I am another person in another body. Footsteps outside the door—we move apart. I look studiously at the nearest picture; Stieglitz sits down quietly.

Stieglitz—much older than I—has a youthfulness, vigor, and sense of fullness about life unlike anyone I have known. His experience and wisdom are qualities of a mature man, but not of a father; I have no daughterly feelings toward him.

I am bewildered, exalted, tormented. Our mutual declaration is so surprising. Stieglitz is married and so am I—for good. I love Edward, as Stieglitz does O'Keeffe. But our relationship is different. We must be in touch in person, by letter, by phone at every possible moment. No day is complete without communication, contact, repetition of the magic words that join us.

Immediately after I leave, I receive letters from Stieglitz entirely different from earlier ones:

I know you love my spirit in my work as I love the spirit in whatever you do— It is ever lovely, beautiful. And I love it not because you do the work but because you are *One* thing all the way through, always. . . .

But Dorothy, Loved One, when you feel like saying something you must *never* hold back—never.—

I don't analyze.— You and I see pictures—hear music—feel things —as you know, very similarly— We are *one*.— Every day proves it *more and more to be true*. Dorothy, do you have any idea how much I W Y.—

From Lake George:

We are of one spirit, of one everything— Oneness—Onlyness—sacredness rules us both—fills us, every fibre of us. Yes—I was at Peace within. And I counted the days when we'd see each other again—look into each other's eyes—see each other's mouths—touch each other's hands—each glorified by the long long insufferable separation.

Dorothy, it is really incredible the depth of that feeling— So full of Wonder Everlasting—the satisfaction complete that there is one other human being in the world who feels exactly as one feels—and who cares exactly as one cares—who knows what love really is—and loves Completely! Dorothy, that is your gift to me—your complete being!!

Your love for me is not merely a woman's love for a man—
It is our spirits that merge—our very souls merge into
an eternal Oneness of Being—
    I know that's True
    And you know that's True
      Dorothy—before God.

Again from Lake George:

You know me— You are the only one who does or ever did—or ever will —completely. That I know. You are my other Self.

There is our own sacred world that we only can destroy or touch. You must remain well—you must—for our common work—for our world— ILY.

Everything is very beautiful, and to keep everything very beautiful that's really one's work if beauty means anything at all to one. But how few really know of it—how many really need it—can't live without it— That edge that gives peace.

I am my own heartache—when one has experienced the absoluteness of $1 + 1 = 1$, the rarity of its occurrences on this Earth and one is powerless as we are—separation becomes unbearable. Why Child that is perhaps the greatest Heartache one can know.

Is it impossible really to know. In the $1 + 1 = 1$ the only actual "release" outside of Death— I know what I crave is the Impossible—ITY all—all—all . . . Dorothy—listen—listen—hear—all of you—hear —*I DO*.

You have no idea what your letters mean to me—have always meant to me. . . .

Yes, the Centers of Centers become one Center. That is ours as long as each lives whatever may happen. How fortunate after all we are to have that. . . .

I have faith in your beauty—your gentleness—your wisdom. . . . You are very young. You are a wife and you are truly a mother. Your life is all ahead of you. . . . I love you as you will never be loved again. And my love for you will bear fruit and the fruits of it will be in your lap.

I L Y— You know it— And it strengthens you—the knowing absolutely. And it will strengthen you more and more as years roll by.

The love of this sensitive, passionate man arouses me to perfect fulfillment. To have a complete erotic experience again and again is breathtaking, almost frightening in its intensity.

In front of others I appear as I have before: shy, workmanlike, a polite young lady. Once in a while, after I leave Stieglitz, my disbelief takes over—to his dismay and my own. He spends much time trying to make me have total faith in the uniqueness and perfection of our love; in spite of all complications every day more fully confirms it.

5

Edward and I continued to spend our summers at Woods Hole on Cape Cod. We drove miles to see and see again salt-box houses, beaches on which Thoreau walked, stark and handsome white meeting houses. We visited local museums and tempting antique shops, where we made our first modest purchases. We listened to tales about whaling; examined scrimshaw work and sailors' logs, peach-bloom Sandwich glass, lovingly made early American furniture. We were worshipful of the reality of New England and shared our aesthetic pleasure with enormous zest and affection.

Emily Wheeler, who lives a few miles from Woods Hole, becomes my closest friend during the summer months. She has lived in, and takes me to visit, the magical town of Concord. The American Revolution and the transcendentalists take on new meaning. I visualize Thoreau, Emerson, Hawthorne, the Alcotts, and the rest walking in and out of their simple, dignified houses. Concord becomes a symbol not only of the Revolution but also of social reform, of the antislavery movement and the idealism of Brook Farm— even though reading Hawthorne's *Blithedale Romance* swiftly shatters much of my positive vision of that experiment.

I write a glowing description of the Wheeler place to Stieglitz:

Emily Wheeler lives far out, all year round. On a farm. Many many flowers—a pond—a lovable little early hug-the-ground house—heirlooms so discreet it takes a while to appreciate them. All is simple, lived in, functioning aesthetically, not antiquely dead. A joyous, colorful kitchen, full of plants. Books around the house—good ones—that have been read. The finest music, that is played—oh, a lovely place.

Mrs. Wheeler and I discuss books, philosophy, art, handwoven fabrics, gardening. I learn a new reserve from being with her, an understanding of the quintessence of good breeding, a buoyant joy in the exquisite details of living. These are not subjects about which we talk. I note her unforced, quiet consideration of others. She creates an atmosphere in which the dignity of each is respected. No attention is called either to shortcomings and blunders or to victories. She is generous, smooths things over, brings out the best in people, effortlessly—just by being. There is no extraneous movement, gesture; no petty conversation, no abrasive sound. For me, Mrs. Wheeler is the best of New England.

Coomaraswamy. Ananda Coomaraswamy. Ananda K. Coomaraswamy. Nothing extraordinary about the syllables in themselves, but linked together they cast a spell. They appeared on the jacket of a book I bought in 1929: *The Dance of Shiva*. I knew nothing about author, title, or the Indian art reproduced, but read it at once.

Coomaraswamy is an Indian art historian, a strict traditionalist. The Hindu way of life, he writes, is based "on a sense of unity, the recognition of which is the highest freedom." Monotheism, no matter how glorious, has been for me a passive belief about one God, in abstract space. Coomaraswamy's words make a fresh, sharp demand upon me. "The highest freedom"—I had never thought of my attitude toward monotheism in that manner.

When the image of Shiva first appears in the book, I presume I am looking at a sculpture of a tangible Hindu god. Coomaraswamy at once disabuses me of any such limited, literal notion. He writes, "The deepest significance of the dance of Shiva is felt when it is realized that it takes place within the heart and the self. Everywhere is God: that Everywhere is the heart." This is the first time I am made aware that a cosmic, metaphysical vision is in truth an inner one, involving not the mind or some vague term such as soul, but the heart.

Reading Coomaraswamy brings back an instant that mattered to me as a child in a mysterious and haunting way. A rabbi read from the Book of Samuel. My body tensed. I was startled to hear that when Samuel ministered to the Lord before Eli, the Lord called out to him and he replied, "Here am I." But it wasn't the right moment; Samuel must not have been sufficiently ready.

"Here am I" rang in my ears for days. I didn't know why I was so shaken. I wasn't clear about who Eli was, but for a brief time God became real to me; I was exalted and ready to answer his call. I felt I was Samuel—only I wasn't. I hadn't been summoned and had no Eli to guide me.

The "call" that Samuel heard, I now realize, was spoken in his own heart, and was related to Coomaraswamy's description of the Dance of Shiva. We are not always ready. Sometimes we speak or answer too soon. But if the moment is truly right, we know within; then the Dance of Shiva begins afresh, and we need no one to instruct us.

One day Mrs. Wheeler invites me for tea. On her table is *The Dance of Shiva*—the first time I have seen the book out in the world. We discuss it with enthusiasm. Mrs. Wheeler calls across the room to her niece, Margaret Fairbanks, who is visiting her: "Dorothy has been reading *The Dance of Shiva*. She is much excited by it."

Margaret responds warmly, "Come to Boston. I shall show you Indian art and you must come to dinner with Coomaraswamy. He's head of the Museum's Indian department; I'm his assistant. You two must meet."

Extraordinary that, next to a tiny pond deep in the woods of Massachusetts, doors should open upon such unsuspected treasure.

As Edward and I entered the Fairbanks' apartment in Boston, I was exhilarated, shy, and expectant. A tall, lean figure—Coomaraswamy—sat slumped and immobile in an easy chair. Relaxed, formidable, he said not a word. When introduced, I was too awed to speak. My lack of familiarity with Indian art and tradition made it impossible for me to ask questions. I must know far more before I could talk seriously to this venerable man whose pale, bespectacled, olive face reflected his apparent omniscience. He was all of a piece: his tailored gray-green suit—it looked handwoven—was just right for him; his hands were long and sensitive—the hands of an artist.

I realized we represent players on opposing teams. Perhaps he had not so much as heard of my modern art heroes, nor paid them any notice. At least I could speak of them from my own experience. After dinner I worked up courage to ask, "Would you be willing to tell me your opinion of Picasso and Matisse?" Coomaraswamy: "They delude themselves into thinking they are original. They are of no interest whatever. The very term 'modern art' is an absurdity."

"What about contemporary American art?" I ventured, crestfallen. Coomaraswamy did not reply. "Do you happen to know of a photographer named Alfred Stieglitz?" Pause. "Or the paintings of John Marin?" Coomaraswamy, evenly: "Stieglitz? Of course. I admire him greatly. He is the only artist in this country whose work counts." Mystified, I asked why, since Stieglitz used a camera, which was not traditional; nor was Stieglitz himself, in the strict Hindu sense of the word. Coomaraswamy: "Stieglitz's photographs are in the great tradition. In his work, precisely the right values are stressed. His art is absolute, in the same sense that Bach's music is. Stieglitz uses symbols correctly." Bewildered, I inqured, "What do you mean by absolute?" Coomaraswamy: "Even a frog would know that Bach's music is absolute."

I write to Stieglitz about meeting Coomaraswamy and learn that it was he who—with John Lodge, a fellow curator—persuaded the Boston Museum of Fine Arts to acquire some of Stieglitz's prints in 1924. Boston thus became the first major museum in the country to own and exhibit photographs of distinction on the same basis as art in other media. This, ironically, because its traditionalist Curator of Indian Art had taken the initiative.

From a Stieglitz letter: "And you met Coomaraswamy—and in such a perfect manner. When one lives as completely and truly from inside out as you do—why 'miracles' inevitably happen—that's the only way they can happen. It's all so simple—when seen."

My reading Coomaraswamy is related to my coming upon Stieglitz's

Equivalents for the first time—upon his images of the outer world that are, for him, precise portrayals of his inner state. I waited for Stieglitz without knowing, just as I have waited for Coomaraswamy without knowing.

Coomaraswamy comes to New York to lecture; much to my delight, he telephones from Grand Central Station after getting off the Midnight Owl from Boston, early in the morning.

"This is Ananda Coomaraswamy," he says slowly. "I shall come to see you at two o'clock today." The voice of authority has spoken, I am bereft of choice. I say, "Yes, how lovely." I break any appointment that conflicts with his schedule and at two o'clock sharp we embark upon an extended dialogue. The procedure is often repeated and he becomes a most important figure in my life, although to begin with I am not prepared to comprehend the complexity of his arguments—his way of thought.

I am eager to know more about the significance of tradition. Does he believe only in the Hindu tradition? "Not at all. All great traditions are one. All are equal one to the other. Each is right. That is why one cannot be either a convert or a Protestant. Tradition must be purified from within if it becomes decadent; renewal must be constant. The great order in life is achieved only by following the great tradition. Catholicism, Judaism, Hinduism, Islam—all are aspects of it. We behave as we do from our particular vantage point, depending upon where we happen to stand along the river of life."

D.N.: "But then why, if Christ sought to purify Judaism from within, did a new religion arise? Why did the same thing happen when Mohammed became dissatisfied with both Judaism and Christianity? Or when followers of the Buddha seemed to split with traditional Brahmanism?"

A.K.C.: "People forget what the great tradition is. They lose their way."

D.N.: "But how can we be certain we know what the great tradition is—what the right way is?"

A.K.C.: "That is a question upon which we need waste little time, Dorothy. Either one knows or one does not. There exist, after all, the found, the saved, and the lost. The found are those who know the right way of doing things. They are the priests, the seers. The saved—the flock—are those who are able to follow the found. They are those who can learn. They are teachable. As for the lost, not only do they not know the right way, but they cannot be taught. They are the heretics."

D.N.: "Has the great order ever existed? If it has, when? And when did it break down?"

A.K.C.: "It existed in the West during the Middle Ages. It broke down with the disintegration of the Catholic Church."

D.N.: "If a mystic's revelation happens to be identical with the Way—what then?"

A.K.C.: "That is merely coincidental."

This makes me smile. But I am convinced, despite Coomaraswamy, that if the Dance of Shiva takes place in the heart, then revelation about the Way takes place there, too—in the hearts of the wise ones, the seers, the poets—in the beginning and always.

(Mrs. Wheeler tells me Coomaraswamy has said to her, "Dorothy is so beautiful and intelligent. But she has one flaw: she does not believe in Catholicism.")

The door to Indian philosophy and art is first opened to me by reading Coomaraswamy, then flung wide by my being able to talk with him, even though I am puzzled by certain of his views. Often they sound condescending and dogmatic, which they did not when I read his *Dance of Shiva*. Between visits I reread that ever-haunting book. The image of Shiva's Dance becomes clearer to me. Within a circular band of tiny, jagged points of flame—of energy—the figure of Shiva appears, one foot upraised, the other firmly planted on an infant—a demonic figure—symbolizing forgetfulness.

Shiva embodies in his Dance the concept of creation, preservation, destruction. At the point of destruction, when decadence sets in within the world and in ourselves, tradition has been forgotten and creation must be renewed. Shiva destroys the bonds that tie us to an illusory, prideful sense of dualism, to the mistaken notion that we are separate from others, from the cosmos. We must banish from our hearts all incomplete vision, false sense of ego, destructive delusions. Realizing a sense of unity with the universe—with all that is—brings release. Not achieving it leads to desolation, self-destruction, destruction of others. *You would not kill another if you really felt the other to be yourself.*

I asked Coomaraswamy eagerly whether the cycle of Shiva's dance was not indeed the representation of an act of faith.

A.K.C.: "Of course."

D.N.: "Then isn't the relearning of tradition possible for each of us, not just for some? When we talked before, you referred to the 'saved, the found, and the lost.' I don't understand."

He made no specific answer. I had to accept the mysterious way in which Coomaraswamy so often expressed himself. So many of his statements —which at first bothered me—soon challenged. I listened more carefully to him than to almost anyone else.

As Coomaraswamy spoke about the ideals of Gandhi and the curse of British imperialism, I realized that, in spite of my interest in civil liberties, I had paid little attention to the evils of colonial rule. Yet I found it difficult to reconcile Coomaraswamy's written defense of the caste system with Gandhi's championing of India's untouchables.

D.N.: "For me, India's division of society into castes does great injustice to the lowest. You don't agree, do you?"

A.K.C.: "Traditional Hindu society in ideal terms has placed the greatest demand upon the highest caste, the Brahman, the philosopher and educator. This is the opposite of traditional Western doctrine, according to which the King can do no wrong. In India the lowest caste could do no wrong, the highest being punished most heavily, and the lowest remaining free from innumerable forms of self-denial imposed upon the Brahman."

D.N.: "Who decided who was the highest and the lowest?"

A.K.C.: "The assumption in India has been that on the basis of heredity, the most intellectual and spiritual would rule. This is an aristocratic view of life, as opposed to the democratic. In this country you believe in equal opportunity for all. In India we believe in equal opportunity for all within each caste. Each caste—there are more than four—has had collective privileges but also collective responsibilities. You must not overlook the fact that the castes have had to do with duties and vocation; that they are not always strictly adhered to; that they have been self-governing. Individuals have always been tried by their peers. Members of the lowest caste are also artisans and are in no sense outcasts. At times certain artisan castes have been regarded as equals of Brahmans."

D.N.: "An American simply can't accept the caste system, in spite of your description of its complexity and advantages. We have a kind of class system ourselves, but the possibility of moving out of the group into which one is born often exists."

A.K.C.: "That is true in India, too."

D.N.: "I've read your claim that the hereditary division of labor has seemed ideal for India, but it just isn't right for the modern world. Why, if the system was so perfect, did India decline, as you admit it did?"

At another time:

D.N.: "I don't understand what is considered sinful to a Hindu."

A.K.C.: "We do not use the words 'good' and 'evil,' but, rather, 'knowledge' and 'ignorance.'"

There is nothing personal about my relationship with Coomaraswamy. He kisses my hand in greeting—a mere courtly gesture. But one day, to my surprise, as he imprints his kiss, he runs his tongue across my hand. No one has done that before. I pretend nothing out of the ordinary has occurred and proceed with our conversation. The incident, however, causes me to relax in a new way. I speak impersonally about the difficulty young women in America have in making love, since they often develop sexually more slowly than young men. I point out that a young American man seems to have no idea of how to arouse the one he loves to the point of orgasm. I ask whether the same thing is true in India.

Coomaraswamy replies without emotion, "In India we have the book of love, the *Kama-sutra*, which is explicit about the numerous ways of heightening the ecstasy of intercourse. In India, also, yoga is widely practiced so that control is taught, not only of breath but of other faculties as well. Thus, when making love, the man controls himself until he fully arouses the woman and they then come together. We call that '*In Gloria*.'" The Latin expression, applied to India, makes me smile.

The next time Coomaraswamy arrived he was eager to talk about modern Western aesthetics: "American preoccupation with good design—with the mere desire to improve it—is absurd. To have any profound significance, rugs, houses—anything man creates—must have far more to them than just good design. Quality is essential, of course, but all objects must be living symbols of a religious approach to life. They must be fashioned with the gods in mind and in their image. They must face toward the gods, reach toward them, symbolize them."

D.N.: "I agree that our period is impoverished by lack of a religious attitude, yet craftsmen who create modern design are in love with quality and purification of form."

A.K.C.: "In my view, a work of art must be 'made' in the sense that Saint Thomas Aquinas envisioned it—art being the right way of making things, which involves more than simply craft. It must embody the right spirit. We cannot ask only, 'Is your violin properly made?' or 'Is it properly tuned?' *We* must be properly tuned ourselves in every act we perform."

Another day, Coomaraswamy, in a different mood: "I do not believe tradition is a matter of mere copying."

D.N.: "Of course."

A.K.C.: "On the contrary, the vision of beauty is spontaneous and cannot be attained by deliberate effort. The secret of art is found in the self-forgetfulness of the artist—the true artist who says, '*It* did it.'"

He returned to a previous observation: "Just as we cannot think of a rug, a house, or any other artifact in terms of design alone, so we cannot contemplate the right way of living in terms of the individual. We must take into consideration man's relationship to and concept of the community, the gods, the cosmos."

D.N.: "Your saying that is one of your greatest contributions to the modern West."

Coomaraswamy spoke of Gandhi in relationship to art: "He can be looked upon as a moral saint, but not as an aesthetic one. He claims that a woman should not wear a necklace. Were he also an aesthetic saint, he would state instead: 'If a necklace is worn, it should be a *good* one.'"

———

A.K.C.: "If we live fully we will not be in conflict with our age but will be perfectly adapted to the best within it; we shall disappear as egos. We should be so completely in tune with our era that we use available materials without rebelling.

"We should dress in the style or fashion that our time dictates, but in the best taste, so that we disappear as noticeable entities."

D.N.: "Aren't you really saying that the world wants fits, not misfits? The artist today does not prefer acceptance at any price. Often he is called a misfit to begin with, until the world catches up with him."

A.K.C.: "The medievalist automatically made his everyday articles conform to his religious precepts. Today scientific concepts constitute our religion. Our art applies to our religion—to science—to skyscrapers. The generation that has assimilated the theory of relativity naturally creates skyscrapers, which are symptoms of the current appreciation and understanding of relativity."

As I write down Stieglitz's sayings and those of Coomaraswamy, I recognize their differences, but often also the similarity of the two men's philosophies and why the traditionalist admires the photographer. The reverent spirit of Stieglitz's work is in perfect accord with Coomaraswamy's emphasis on the sacred in art. Coomaraswamy's call for a renewal of the life-force, when creativity is in danger of disintegrating, corresponds to Stieglitz's advocacy of the new and fresh in art, which rescues us from the dead hand of the academicians. The knowledge I gain from one man's words helps me to understand the other's. In spite of Coomaraswamy's frequently contradictory views, he—like Stieglitz—is a giant influence in my development: far beyond the usual channels of learning, both contribute greatly to my education.

Gradually but surely the pattern of Edward's and my life shifts. Incidents that seem trifling reflect deeper, often subtle changes. Conflicts mount. Understanding is sometimes easier to attain than accommodation.

If we stay at home in the evenings, organizing and reorganizing books and records, talking, loving—just being—our relationship is peace-giving. But then this, too, mysteriously changes. Edward begins to feel he is missing something and nervously insists we live a more active social life with the very people he has found boring.

We no longer walk along the Hudson and eat simple picnic lunches on Saturdays or Sundays. Instead we drive to Westchester and spend weekends mainly with Edward's sister and her husband, Sylvan Weil, at their large estate in Katonah. It boasts a tennis court, swimming pool, stables, horses, cows, dogs, turkeys, chickens, a pond on which we ice-skate in winter. Edward buys a horse and joins the Goldens Bridge Hunt Club.

Leaving Nancy—still so young—in town for long weekends unnerves me. Suppose she should become ill? The trip is tiring for her; whenever we take her with us, she becomes carsick at Hawthorne Circle. For me, instead of relaxation, the days are full of tension.

Pressures from the Normans increase. Edward's quarrels with his father resume with greater intensity. The constant and heated arguments stem mainly from Edward's not taking responsibility for his own financial affairs.

In my family, resentments are bottled up. We never dare lose our tempers with one another. Hence my special horror when Edward and his father are at odds. My dread of their stormy altercations is second only to my fear that they may physically harm each other.

Edward no longer goes to the Cooperative League every day, but travels throughout the country helping to publicize the movement. He has become intensely interested in newly organized credit unions and their effort to replace commercial lending firms. Yet even these noble activities are not wholly satisfying to him. I write to Stieglitz:

The solving of the what-to-do problem is difficult for Edward. He doesn't want to do nothing naturally because he's too vital—he is not an artist in the usual, craft meaning—he is not interested in charity in the accepted sense. He gets attractive business offers in stupid businesses which I am fighting against because freedom is more important—(and by freedom I mean nothing Utopian). His decision is in the making right now—and much of our living depends on the whole thing. Much can be done with money in freeing others—once we are independent—but in the meantime he will be tired, tense—bound. He will suffer for the myth of doing something.

The Normans urge us to live more extravagantly and at the same time more economically. Edward tells his father we cannot do both and that our expenses inevitably are mounting. He pleads with me to stand up for him, which I do gladly. Edward's motives in not wanting to spend time on making more money are as pure as ever, nor have I any desire to live more elaborately than we do now. Constant accusations poison the atmosphere. At times I serve as a calming influence, but not always. My success decreases as tensions and threats mount, as Edward's failure to take charge of his affairs persists.

No matter how hard we try to economize, demands upon us increase; our own desires become more complex. Could we accomplish as much if we spent less? Is there any valid reason to reduce our expenses? We never sit down to work out logical answers.

If I were to do the cooking and housework, and take care of Nancy, obviously we would save money. But Edward will not permit that. Even though the Normans lecture us about spending less, they would think me mad not to have a nurse and a housekeeper. I am torn about the entire matter, just as I am about going away for weekends. Edward cannot understand my conflict about leaving Nancy in town; he becomes upset if, on the spur of the moment, I am not free to do everything with him he wants me to. And I ask myself if I am temperamentally prepared to live a confined life.

There are problems in Philadelphia. My father, wanting to make certain I would have a measure of independence, gave me an office building as a wedding present. The rent collected was to provide me with a steady income.

While I was growing up, Father told me repeatedly, one must never overextend oneself financially. He spoke of a man he knew who had done just that—the results were fatal. Now I learn he himself has bought too much property on a speculative basis—he has overextended himself. I give my office building—from which I have received no income at all—back to him. It vanishes into nothingness. I have no money of my own and Father is in difficult circumstances—this after all his years of supporting us and helping so many others.

I speak with anguish to Edward about Father's plight; he and Aaron are exceedingly generous and understanding. Aaron lends Father enough money to tide him over a precarious period. He never makes me feel he is being imposed upon or that his kindness is in any way extraordinary. Aaron's delicacy in the matter surprises and touches me. But I am devastated by having to ask for anything—especially for my family.

The irony of the entire situation overwhelms me. My proud father had objected to my marrying a young man who was unstable and had not established himself on a sound financial basis. Edward's parents had objected to my family because it was not sufficiently wealthy or socially prominent. Now my father has had to go to the Normans for help. My sense of humiliation is enormous. I can only guess what Father feels.

Edward and I are living on money gained in a system he is trying to fight. I am disturbed both about not earning my own living and about my father's difficulties. I even feel guilty about wanting to help more and more causes.

Edward and I contribute to charities, also to organizations attempting to change destructive social patterns and protect freedom. But it is Aaron Norman's money that makes possible everything we do.

During the boom Edward at last yields to Aaron's plea that he take more financial responsibility. He doesn't go into business but instead plunges into the stock market, which makes him tense and anxious, even though for a while he is jubilant when his stocks increase in value—on paper. Without knowing anything about the market, I am more pessimistic than Edward. I cannot believe that "trees grow to the sky," especially in this nerve-racking, confusing period.

October 1929: the Wall Street crash. Paper profits disappear. Bankruptcies. Panic. Suicides. The number of unemployed soars.

Edward's illusory gains vanish.

To our astonishment, Father Norman also has suffered severe reverses. We had believed him to be a cautious, farsighted man. We had taken it for granted he was efficiently organized and are amazed to discover that the only records he has of his holdings—some of them unsound—are little slips of paper tucked away in assorted desk drawers and a closet in his study. He has no office and no clear, overall picture of which stocks he owns or of their fluctuations. Stories I have heard about his youth, his career, his accomplishments have been vague and unfocused. Now, as Edward tells me more, the details come alive for me.

Born Aaron Nusbaum in Plattsburg, New York, in 1858, the son of a peddler, he had seven sisters and a strong sense of family. Refusing to marry until all seven had found husbands, he worked successfully throughout his teens for one company after another in the Midwest, finally making his home in Chicago. Ingenious, competent, and industrious, he established a fine reputation among Chicago's leading businessmen.

During the World's Fair of 1893 he was offered any franchise he wanted. His choice, the soft-drink concession, proved extremely profitable. At the Fair's end Aaron looked for other enterprises in which to invest. By chance he heard of a man named Sears, who operated a mail-order business and was in trouble with the postal authorities. Mr. Sears had advertised in farm journals: "Five-Piece Bedroom Suite—$7.59," "Twelve-Piece Dining Room Suite—$11.10." Farmers who read his announcements backed their wagons up to depots to pick up their bargain "suites," but out came small boxes containing sets of doll furniture. In due course some of the recipients made formal complaints against Sears. The matter aroused controversy, even though Mr. Sears had included in his advertisements—in very small type—the word "miniature." A battle ensued between Sears and the Post Office Department.

Hearing this story made Aaron recognize the potential of a properly run mail-order business. The country was opening up and becoming more densely populated, yet in small towns scattered across the land, few stores existed where people could shop. Aaron decided if Sears's enterprise were run in a straightforward, honest manner, it could have a great future.

He met Sears and a document was drawn up, according to which Aaron agreed that the company's inventory and goodwill would be matched with his own $75,000. For this sum he was to be given half interest in the newly reorganized enterprise, which would be run with the utmost integrity.

Aaron's sister, married to Julius Rosenwald, urged that her husband be permitted to put up part of the original investment. Although Aaron agreed, the two men never got along well.

Because Aaron had an extraordinary talent for organization, Sears developed in spectacular fashion. Aaron personally hired the first three thousand employees of the new venture, instituted efficient procedures, and worked at least eighteen hours a day, often seven days a week. In a short time the volume of sales surpassed that of Montgomery Ward, the main competitor.

Shortly after the turn of the century, Aaron decided to retire. He sold his share of Sears to his brother-in-law, thus terminating all association with the business.

Just before the beginning of the war, the family settled in New York. As the result of prejudice against anything German, Edward soon suggested that "Nusbaum" be discarded and a more American name—Norman—be adopted. Aaron agreed.

Aaron never went back into business after his withdrawal from Sears. Instead, he invested in many companies and so, by the time of the 1929 crash, he had opened a number of brokerage accounts. He kept no formal books, but had become a large speculator on margin, and suffered great losses.

On the surface our daily lives changed little immediately after the crash. Edward's losses seemed no more real to me than did his profits. Our general good fortune served as an embarrassment, in view of the disastrous plight of so many others. The affairs of people all around us altered dramatically. The economic situation of the country at large deteriorated rapidly, with terrifying consequences.

The 1932 election campaign centered on the financial crisis. Father and Mother Norman were for Hoover; Edward and I favored Roosevelt. Hoover's failure to provide leadership had been inexplicable. To consider the fate of thirteen million unemployed, of Hoovervilles and bonus marchers, in the face of reactionary ineptitude, enraged us. How could one remain unmoved by breadlines, soup lines, beggars, widespread despair, and poverty? To hear that Hoover had great plans meant nothing to us. Why were they not carried out?

Since Hoover was sure to be defeated, I asked myself why I should vote for Roosevelt, even though I was for him. Certainly he would become President by an overwhelming majority. But would he make the necessary reforms? Norman Thomas, who as head of the Socialist Party had a certain standing and backing, had spoken out for drastic changes in our society. Roosevelt had been in favor of more conventional reforms. Perhaps a large enough vote cast for Thomas would force Roosevelt to take the radical steps for which the nation was crying out: to redistribute wealth, raise wages, find a constructive way of avoiding unemployment. Thomas's dreams became more and more plausible to me, although I fully realized he couldn't win the election and I wasn't certain I wanted him to, despite my admiration. I cast a protest vote for him, as I had the first time I could vote, in 1928. Again, although not a Socialist, I thought it the only sane thing to do.

Mercifully, Franklin Roosevelt is elected. In dramatic contrast to Hoover, he moves swiftly; in rapid succession imaginative emergency measures are enacted. A new social consciousness is awakened throughout the nation. Eager, public-spirited individuals crowd to Washington to help draft and fight for innovative legislation. A disaster has been needed to make us act as we should have before. Roosevelt becomes a hero to the majority, and "a traitor to his class" and "that man in the White House" to a vocal minority. His insensitive enemies long for an illusory past, believing that rugged individualism alone can eliminate every problem. They must not be permitted to return to power.

The struggle for daily survival is a cruel one for most Americans. The reality and depth of the Depression touch the lives of everyone except a wealthy minority that, I fear, includes Mother Norman. She confides—with something akin to awe—that one of her friends has said "most admirably" that she doesn't mind in the least giving up her limousine and taking taxis!

6

Stieglitz receives word during the late spring of 1929 that he must vacate the Room. The Anderson Galleries, in which The Intimate Gallery is located, are to be torn down. O'Keeffe has gone to the Southwest. With the aid of Emil Zoler, Stieglitz's loyal assistant since the days of 291, I help him close the Room. A sad moment, especially so because Stieglitz declares he doesn't want another place.

I find it unthinkable that the Room should cease to exist, not only for the sake of the artists shown, but because of the unique role Stieglitz plays in the world of art. He should function in even larger quarters where he can receive the public and properly exhibit his photographs. (They haven't been shown at the Room.) He also needs a darkroom in New York, which he doesn't now have.

In the autumn O'Keeffe (back from New Mexico), the Strands, Rosenfeld, Herbert J. Seligmann (a writer close to Stieglitz), and I argue with all the force at our command that Stieglitz must create a new gallery. He is reluctant, but finally decides that to leave the "Seven Americans" without a congenial center in which to exhibit during this troubled time would be unfair. As always, he dislikes not seeing through any task he has begun. He is distressed, too, by rumors that a Museum of Modern Art is about to open with a loan exhibition of Cézanne, Van Gogh, Seurat, and Gauguin—in his opinion,

French "Old Masters." Everything he hears about the proposed venture makes him feel more than ever the need to gain support for his "own children." He is appalled by the idea that an expensive showcase is to be set up—that most of the money will be spent for staff and upkeep, rather than for the livelihood of American artists.

Someone asks him how he can be so sure that artists who are guaranteed a living will continue to work; he is nonplussed. "Work is life for the artist. He can no more stop working than breathing."

O'Keeffe, the Strands, and I devise a plan to raise a three-year guarantee fund that will take care of rent and overhead for a new gallery. We proceed with a sense of urgency, writing letters and visiting everyone we can think of who might contribute. In spite of the crash, well before the end of the year An American Place is founded in an unpretentious office building at 509 Madison Avenue. Stieglitz chooses the title because of its simplicity. He has always disliked the term "gallery," feeling that his work can be carried out in any "place" in America.

From the very first he sees just how he wants to use the new space, dividing it into a large exhibition room and a smaller one. A still smaller area serves as his "office." No doors close off one area from another. In the office are a used, unfinished wooden worktable, two unfinished wooden chairs, and the old, dilapidated armchair from The Intimate Gallery. Along the office walls are low, built-in, unfinished wooden bookshelves. On them Stieglitz stands pictures, sculptures, books. Next to the office is a vault in which, for the first time, he can stack paintings and boxes of his photographs. There are no chairs in either of the two main galleries.

Beyond the large room is a darkroom in which Stieglitz has no elaborate gadgets of any kind, only the usual red and yellow lights. He uses no automatic developing machine. Before printing, he places his negatives in simple wooden proofing frames and exposes them in daylight, so he can examine their potential print quality.

The Place is created in the briefest possible time; it is the first New York gallery with a total absence of decor. No false steps are taken, no decorators or architects are consulted. "I'd like the new rooms to be bare," Stieglitz writes to me. "Very bare. No attempt to arrange—to make 'look.' " The unadorned walls and floors are painted in subtly differing shades of gray and white. He feels that the Place is at its best when in a state of severe austerity—empty—its walls, ceilings, floors freshly painted, its shades clean. He claims, "Only innocence could have created the Place."

From the moment it opens, An American Place—beautiful and lively—creates a stir. Far more people visit than ever came to the smaller Room, even though we are in the midst of the crash.

The view from the Place, on the seventeenth floor, is not spectacular, but skyscrapers and other nearby buildings represent a constant challenge to Stieglitz. There are moments when relationships between the old and the new, the ornate and clean-cut—between darkness and light—are striking. He photographs the distinctions like one possessed.

"If what is happening in here," he says, "can stand up against what is out there, this Place has a right to exist. But if what is out there can stand up against what is in here, this Place does not need to exist."

Charlie Chaplin appeared one day. He looked out the window, grimaced, and said, "How hideous." The two men talked a bit, then Stieglitz showed Chaplin some of his photographs taken from the same windows, said nothing. Chaplin's face lit up. For a moment he, too, was silent, then exclaimed with wonder, "But these are marvelous!"

A Marin exhibition formally opened the Place in December—before the announced January 1930 date. As always Stieglitz refused to do more than send out a few announcements to the press and to interested individuals. I suggested that I put files of correspondence and other papers in order. Stieglitz: "You are an integral part of the Place. You must write, read, look at, do, whatever interests you." In old cardboard file boxes, the first treasures I came upon were Marin's letters to Stieglitz. The sentences flowed for me with the same magic I found in his pictures. I was reminded of the phrase about poet-painters whose pictures were "silent poetry," their writings "spoken paintings."

Marin's down-to-earth wonder before nature and its laws, his respect for his materials and for the demands of whatever medium he uses, delighted me.

I don't paint rocks, trees, houses, and all things seen, I paint an inner vision. Rubbish. If you have an intense love and feeling towards these things, you'll try your damdest to put on paper or canvas, that thing. You can transpose, you can play with and on your material, but when you are finished that's got to have the roots of that thing in it and no other thing. That's the trouble with all the lesser men. And an inner vision of your own has got to be transposed onto your medium, a picture of that vision. Otherwise, there's no use, no excuse, for, basically, you're not different from any other living thing, other than an intensity, other than direction of vision.

I feel the letters must be published. Stieglitz responds with enthusiasm and is tempted to issue them at once under the imprint of the Place, then hesitates. He knows no one at this point who can design a book properly and deal with printers. I suggest that a friend, Robert Josephy, who works for some of New York's best publishers, might take care of both problems. Stieglitz meets and likes him. He asks Herbert Seligmann to edit the letters, then publishes them at the Place, taking the financial burden upon himself. He watches over choice of type, paper, and binding with close attention, but never interferes with Seligmann or Josephy.

I love to talk and walk with Marin, to go to exhibitions and concerts with him. As we wander about the city, he puts together or takes apart what becomes a living painting to me, according to his pleasure. He regards the recently constructed Empire State Building with rapt attention: "Do you know why you feel dissatisfied with its rounded top? Because nature won't allow such a form at a great height. If you look at high mountains, or at great tall trees, you don't find rounded forms there. Let's say you're building a painting. If your structure isn't strong enough to hold up what you want it to, or if it's too strong, you'll feel restless when you look at it. You can address an envelope way over in the corner if you like, but you'll soon feel it out of balance. It's the same with your building, your picture."

We walk on. Marin's long, slender fingers gesticulate with a peculiar grace that deflects my attention from what we pass. "If you're painting a picture, you have to see your objects in their movement. You seek for the backbones of these swaying forms. You must hold to their backbones with all you're worth. All good writing, music, painting obey the same principle. As the back-bones bend, the whole structure bends. I would conceive the picture—writing—music—as structures related, bending, swaying on their backbones."

At the Metropolitan Museum Marin stops before El Greco's *Toledo*, a great Tintoretto, a modest Boudin. He loves them. His eyes squint. "If the structure you build inside your picture is strong enough to carry itself, it doesn't so much matter what happens at the edges. But if you have something so violent going on at the edges that it destroys the feeling of solidity in your inside structure, something is wrong. Your picture must be complete in its frame. You should never feel its strength going off from it. Your picture has to stop at its four edges through the magnetic force of the weights and balances operating from inside, controlling it from its axis."

Marin dislikes what he calls the professionalism that kills art. He plays the piano—Bach in particular—with enormous enthusiasm. He exclaims: "It makes me furious to see all those *pianissimos* and *adagios* written out on a sheet of music. I get so furious that when I see a *pianissimo* written down, hell!—I just can't help it—I simply come down with a bang!"

We go to a symphony concert. The orchestra tunes up. Marin turns to me, smiles happily. "That's nice." He beams until the conductor enters, raises his baton. The orchestra comes to attention and starts to play. He whispers, "Now, let's go home."

Marin writes to Stieglitz: "Art is produced by the wedding of man and material. . . . When man loves material and will not under any circumstances . . . destroy its own inherent beauty, then and then only can that wonderful thing we call art be created." In an article about himself, he says: "Seems to me the true artist must perforce go from time to time to the elemental big forms —Sky, Sea, Mountain, Plain—and those things pertaining thereto, to sort of re-true himself up, to recharge the battery. For these big forms have everything. But to express these, you have to love these, to be a part of these in sympathy. One doesn't get very far without this love."

While in New York, Sherwood Anderson visited the Place often. We were introduced and I told him about an experience I had had at Smith. I discovered his writing at the Hampshire Bookshop in Northampton and admired it enormously: the warmth and simplicity of his style, the compassion he felt for his characters.

Shortly after I read *The Triumph of the Egg*, our English professor gave the class an assignment to compose a theme in the manner of a living author we admired. I chose the style of Anderson, which liberated my own writing. I received an A minus, but also an angry note: "Please see me in my office after class." An infuriated teacher greeted me. "How could you choose such a second-rate author to imitate? I am shocked!" I, too, was outraged. How dare anyone insult a writer of such quality and distinction?

Anderson laughed heartily and thanked me for my early admiration, but his face—tired and lined—alarmed me. He had aged considerably in the few years since Stieglitz portrayed him in a more romantic phase of his life. Although he was careful to seem relaxed and in no sense troubled, I felt him to be greatly perturbed.

On his return a few days later, he again laughed a good deal, but even when he was talking with Stieglitz, his gaiety seemed forced; behind an aura of bravado, which he wore like a mask, I glimpsed a weary man. I tried to photograph him but knew the prints would not be good. They weren't. I had failed to penetrate the haunting face.

Yet my special feeling for Anderson and his work remained; nothing shook it, despite the merciless satires of his style that appeared. His new books had much less power for me than the early ones, which was saddening. But in my heart he remained a heroic figure.

Soon after the Place opened, the poet Hart Crane appeared—excited, tense, keyed up—carrying a sheaf of typewritten pages: his major poem, *The Bridge*. In the cardboard files, I had found, among his letters to Stieglitz, a statement, "I feel you as entering very strongly into *The Bridge*."

Crane had come to read his manuscript aloud to Stieglitz, who introduced us and asked me to stay and listen. The younger man's voice had an exalted ring as he was caught up in reading, but his face had a gray, unhealthy cast to it. As he raised his eyes occasionally, I noted how fervently he sought a warm reaction from Stieglitz, who, clearly moved, responded with enthusiasm.

Not knowing Crane, I had little sense of contact with him; it was impossible to judge so complex a work at first hearing. Yet the scope and sweep of the poem were magnificent and I told him so, sincerely. There was, nonetheless, something I couldn't formulate, that I found disturbing—forced. I tried to express this to Stieglitz later, explaining that the use of "thee," "thou," and "thy" put me off.

Once it was published, I read the poem and was scarcely aware of the "thees" and "thous." But the sections I had felt inflated still bothered me, suggesting an overpoetic attempt to emulate Whitman. I had not sensed this in Crane's earlier *White Buildings*. Yet I remembered and learned from what Stieglitz had said: "If I am blind to someone's work, it is just then that I know I must question myself the most."

An American Place, like The Intimate Gallery before it, becomes an important factor in my life. Marin and Strand, a young writer named Gerald Sykes, Waldo Frank, Paul Rosenfeld, and Dorothy Brett form a kind of family that nourishes, stimulates, and delights. Together with Stieglitz, they release me to be my real self.

Being an integral part of day-by-day occurrences at the Place provides a natural environment in which I can breathe freely and mature. The family circle expands.

Robert Josephy introduces me to Catherine Bauer. Both work for Harcourt, Brace. Catherine is brilliant, witty, alive to every nuance of good sociological thinking. Her main interests are modern architecture and public housing. She is strongly influenced by Lewis Mumford, whom I have met at the Place and the New School. I cherish him both as a person and as a writer.

After the Place opens and Catherine observes its satisfying simplicity, she says to Stieglitz: "I hear you know more colors of white than any other living man." Stieglitz: "Knowing the difference between whites is the only way of knowing white."

The friends I respond to most—including Catherine—are those at the beginning of their careers whose alive, penetrating approach to life attracts me. We share likes and dislikes, regale one another with our more bizarre experiences, and display a fierce loyalty toward those we most admire. We read avidly; discuss Joyce and Proust, Mann, Dostoevsky, Chekhov; debate the writings of Eliot, Pound, Anderson, Dreiser, Hart Crane, and William Carlos Williams. Our talk and my notebooks abound most of all with thoughts about Joyce and Proust.

Shaw's and O'Neill's stars, like that of Lawrence, wane for the moment. In the arts, Picasso and Matisse strike us as the greatest contemporary masters. We become aware of Braque a bit later. Marin is our first choice among American painters; Stieglitz, then Strand, are the favored photographers.

I see a good deal of Gerald Sykes. Because of his pitiless piercing to the core of a situation, he is dubbed one of the "New Barbarians." Although we prefer Russian films, Gerald and I go to see *Anna Christie* because of curiosity about Greta Garbo, and the *Blue Angel* because of Marlene Dietrich.

Gerald is a close friend of the composer Aaron Copland, whom Edward and I have met frequently at the homes of friends, at the New School, the League of Composers, and Copland-Sessions concerts. His music is impressive, individual, dissonant, American; his rhythms rapid, influenced by jazz, and again surprisingly noble, sustained, pastoral. With enormous generosity, he provides opportunities for promising young composers to receive a hearing.

Harold Clurman, whom Paul Strand takes me to meet in 1929, tells me with emotion that he and his colleagues at the Theatre Guild, Cheryl Crawford and Lee Strasberg, are in despair about the state of the American theater. Having experimented with independent productions, the three are ready to give up their secure jobs to found a new theater; several promising actors have agreed to join them.

Clurman, young and intense, has keen brown eyes that look straight at you, but as though you weren't there. His mouth is sensual, his hands expressive. Talking excitedly, he explains his position: "In America today the theater has no sense of direction, reflects no philosophy of life, has no central aim. No governing principle guides it."

He continues at top speed: "Actors must believe in the plays in which they perform, if their lives are to have meaning. But neither they nor directors in this country have the opportunity to develop to their fullest capacity. Nor do playwrights. Craft is important, of course, but content is paramount. A play must reflect not only the concerns of those who create and produce it, but of the actors and audience. Making money can't be our primary goal and we are not interested in a star system. What Lee, Cheryl, and I hope to establish is a theater larger than ourselves, to which we are all committed."

Clurman's eyes flash, his passionate approach endears him to me. His logic seems unassailable. But I see inevitable problems ahead, not only financial ones. Even though the Wall Street disaster has occurred, and panic and retrenchment prevail on all sides, still the world proceeds. Because we raised money so swiftly to establish An American Place in spite of the Depression, I believe—naïvely, perhaps—that anything one attempts with intense devotion can be accomplished. Harold fills me with faith that the theater of which he dreams will come into being.

He invites Edward and me to talks he is having with young theater people and other creative figures who may be part of or interested in the new project. Almost all who hear him respond warmly. Funds are raised—I do what I can to gain help—and Clurman, together with Strasberg and Crawford, succeed in founding the Group Theatre. Its members are talented and eager, ready to make whatever sacrifices are required. Salaries are small, the venture is cooperative, and no assurance can be given that first-rate plays or financial backing will be steadily available.

Father Norman is unexpectedly responsive when I seek support for the Group, which touches me. He most kindly gives five hundred dollars, just as, a year before—thanks to him—Edward and I could pledge five hundred dollars a year for three years to the American Place Rent Fund. Under his stern mask, Aaron has proved most generous with me.

Opening night of *The House of Connelly* by Paul Green: members of the Group perform under the spell of Strasberg's inspired direction. The play, which deals with the conflict between the decadent Old South and the more vigorous New, comes painfully alive. Lee's talent and intelligence, as well as the ability of the Group's actors, are responsible for the power and magic that pervade every moment of the performance.

The curtain falls; the audience is caught up in a spontaneous and tumultuous display of emotion. I weep and clap, like everyone else. The play is hailed, the Group is firmly established.

Shortly after *The House of Connelly*, the Group presents a play about the Depression by Claire and Paul Sifton: *1931*. The critics are hostile to its realistic portrayal of the country's economic and social dilemmas. I write a letter to the press in protest against its ostrich-like refusal to admit we are in grave trouble, but am rebuffed by the printed response that Rolls-Royces continue to drive up to theaters as they always have.

The Group asks me to be on its Executive Committee, which—sensibly —never meets. The new company's approach to our collective problems and dilemmas makes other theater seem suddenly tame and remote. A literature of social protest is rapidly developing; a new spirit permeates the arts. The Group's influence on the American theater is incalculable.

To my surprise, Clurman writes to Stieglitz about our first meeting; Stieglitz shows me the letter.

> I met Mrs. Norman the other day. We sat and talked in my office at the [Theatre] Guild. My impression of her derived more from her face than anything she said. In a description of her one would have to point out the intelligence and luminous shine of her eyes, but I think what I saw was not her eyes so much as a sort of remote presence as of something abstract to which one could *talk* freely. One is easy with her because she *receives* so effortlessly that one feels no check on one's own personality. It was like talking to a lake or rather like talking to a mirror in which one didn't see oneself but someone else! I can readily understand why such a girl might at first (superficial) sight be *overlooked*. She presents no problem, no burden of personality to be dealt with. One can be with her and at the same time alone with oneself. It is as if she did not come to you but was brought before you by some superior force. Her presence does not represent her will but the agency of some selfless mover. The impression I have of her face and demeanor is stronger than anything she may have said. (She makes one remember what one has oneself said and makes one careful to say the truth). This is a first impression but I feel the thing that her presence means is more important now than any intellectual attribute she may have, that what she *is* is more valuable even than anything she thinks. I hope to see more of her and get to know her better.

At a party given by the *American Caravan* publication, I became aware of a young woman about my age, Mary Hughes. She had come to the gathering with Aaron Copland, I with Gerald Sykes. She and Aaron, who introduced us, were warm friends; both knew Paul Strand. Gerald was close to Strand and Stieglitz, as each of us was by now to Clurman.

For some unaccountable reason, the actress Mae West appeared. Who among such intellectual editors as Lewis Mumford, Paul Rosenfeld, Van Wyck Brooks, and Alfred Kreymborg could have invited her? The next day Stieglitz, who was also present, asked me in all seriousness whether I knew that Rebecca West was at the party and did I meet her? I said no. He told me that, unfortunately, he didn't either. He hadn't the slightest idea who Mae West was.

From the moment I met Mary Hughes, no matter what I did or where I went, there she was: at the Women's City Club, on a train to or from Philadelphia, at Group Theatre talks or a contemporary music concert. We were shy at first and barely spoke. Although temperamentally we seemed so different, our interests dovetailed to an astonishing degree. Gradually we became close friends and I talked to her about matters I felt free to discuss with almost no one else. I trusted her completely—her quick but sound intelligence, her intuition.

She soon married the distinguished modern architect William Lescaze, whom I had met briefly in Philadelphia, where he, in partnership with George Howe, designed one of the city's—in fact the country's—most beautiful buildings for the Philadelphia Savings Fund Society. Mary was my only friend who automatically crossed over from one category to another, emerging as an integral part of my life at many levels.

Moving to Woods Hole each June, I experience a pang about leaving friends and work in New York, even though only for the summer months. But the family is closer in the summer, our life together more relaxed, more joyous. Flare-ups seem more poignantly out of key. Edward and I are so fortunate; how can we ever spoil a single moment?

All has been going along relatively smoothly until, in despair, I must write a letter:

Edward, dear, dear Edward. What makes you suddenly turn on me? Today you confessed it. You feel I am secure, sure; you tell me you are not. How can this be? How can you be jealous of a self-confidence you feel I have, but of which I am unaware?

When I married you I was so shy. I still am. Perhaps not as painfully as I was then. I felt you a tower of strength. You seemed certain about everything. I feel we have given each other new assurance—each in a different way—through our love for one another. What still makes me feel humble is my sense that others have accomplished so much in the world, while I have done nothing of value. I have achieved nothing. I am full only of dreams. Of what, then, can you be jealous?

Yesterday, on our trip to Martha's Vineyard, I took along my Bible, because I have never been able to read enough of it. You looked at me with blazing eyes. "How can you bring that to read on the boat?" you asked in a fury. Of what were you afraid? That someone might see me reading so "serious" a book, and scoff?

I had looked forward to having a quiet day with you. We would read, talk, be silent, look, wander. I anticipated the glory of our seclusion, the privacy of being alone together on a boat and on the island, which we both love. I loved the idea of being without telephones or other interruptions. And you were ashamed. No, you were not ashamed. You were scared. Frightened. Of what? Of whom? Of social acquaintances? Afraid of their contempt? Contempt of what? You are in conflict, I know. Because after each scene, you apologize; you say you wonder how I can put up with you.

If you are jealous of my security in not caring what people might think seeing me with the Bible in public, that is ludicrous. *The Bible.* The sacred book that everyone is supposed to treasure.

Oh, Edward. What has happened? How can I reach you? I love you. I love you very much. You know that. Oh, darling.

I cannot finish the letter. Nor can I give it to Edward. If I could, I wouldn't have needed to write it. I sit and weep. And put the letter away.

———————

Stieglitz photographs me often in New York. He never asks me to pose for him, to smile or relax. Before he takes up his camera he has seen something that moves him. When he is about to photograph, he says only, "Remain perfectly still." His excitement is contagious. I try not to blink my eyes. I discipline myself to remain motionless, to breathe so unobtrusively it will not disturb. I learn to hold my breath longer than seems possible.

Stieglitz uses no artificial light. He requires great depth of focus in order to attain the fullest possible modeling when he prints. Exposures are rarely short. I do not freeze, because I already am at rest, natural, being what I am. I hide nothing—my inner conflicts, my searching, my ecstasy. I know no one else who photographs the way Stieglitz does. "Each time I photograph," he says, "it is as though for the first time. Each time I photograph I make love."

I live through the eye, am held spellbound by beauty—faces, flowers, places, shells, New England spires, the feeling of white. At camp, at school, when traveling, I have used a Brownie camera, then a more advanced Kodak. In spite of my enthusiasm, my pictures are always disappointing.

Strand's and Stieglitz's prints have opened my eyes to the power of photography in the hands of the artist. They tempt me to use a better camera, even though I am without illusion I can make comparable pictures.

Stieglitz suggests I borrow his 4″ × 5″ Graflex. Without knowing how to control it, I make a few portraits of him. He generously develops and prints them for me. Again, failure—I haven't focused properly.

Although just looking into the Graflex has made me even more eager to photograph well, I find the 4″ × 5″ heavy and awkward. Because of the Depression, I hesitate to ask Edward for permission to buy a good camera. Stieglitz apparently reads my mind. "You should have a 3¼″ × 4¼″ Graflex. I'll buy one for you. Pay me back whenever you can. I'll show you how to get started and how to develop and print." Stieglitz speaks with such caring and simplicity that to accept his offer is as natural as to breathe. Yet I am startled, since he has told me he never teaches.

After the camera arrives, he says to shut down my lens as far as possible and take the longest exposures I can. He smiles and cautions me: "Don't be afraid. Just go ahead—photograph, photograph, photograph. That's the only way you'll learn."

At first I want to take pictures of everything I see, but soon refrain because I, too, find I can photograph only with love. I had thought I would take satirical pictures, mocking the absurd. But no.

Looking through the reflex mirror in my beautiful Graflex opens up a new world for me, even though each day I am confronted by fresh problems. When eyes are in focus, the background is not. Choices having to do with what to emphasize, what to sacrifice, must be made in split seconds, but with exactitude. I become increasingly challenged and entranced.

I photograph, photograph, photograph. I learn as much from Stieglitz's making portraits of me as I do from my own mistakes. Portraying him becomes more and more difficult. While I remain beautifully still for him, he makes comical faces, sticks out his tongue, at times smiles broadly—anything to make me laugh—before he settles down into being whichever self takes over. I should like to photograph Edward more often but he finds it difficult to relax. Nancy and Andrew never move or pose; they behave like angels.

Influenced by Stieglitz at first, I nonetheless refuse to photograph anything I think he would. Soon I work with independence. Watching him develop and print trains my eyes. I note he uses a special toning process that helps him achieve an extraordinarily rich print quality, not attainable with ordinary materials. I never ask him which chemicals he uses. He has earned the right to his discoveries without being questioned about them, because of his genius and lifetime of experiment and practice. I follow only the advice he offers. The rest is up to me.

Stieglitz is eager for me to be with him at Lake George and see where he lives, photographs, and prints in the summer. Since I cannot leave Edward and the children, he comes to Woods Hole. Together we go to Boston. His photographs are at the Museum, but he has never seen them there. They are beautifully cared for, and he is pleased. We stay overnight and then return to Woods Hole.

To call Stieglitz "Alfred" is still difficult, in spite of our deepened relationship. He photographs me in our little garden and moves close to focus on my face. Raising his head from the camera, he looks at me intently: "I love you." He never has said this with exactly the same intonation or intensity. I look up, startled. He repeats the words even more fervently. It is as hard to accept them, to the extent he wants me to, as to utter "Alfred." Why, when I know this man so intimately, can I still not entirely believe?

As so often, I feel he is reading my mind. He whispers tenderly, "Call me Alfred." But I cannot say the name. "Say Alfred," he whispers even more softly. "Say it," he coaxes.

Finally I whisper back, "Alfred." My eyes open wide, in wonder, almost in disbelief. I see my look later in the photograph he takes at this extraordinary moment. He speaks of the day always as the "Day of Transfiguration," and writes the words or the initials "D.O.T." on the back of all the portraits made at the time.

From Lake George, after he leaves:

> *You heard the Voice—you saw the Light—The Hour—The Hour—*
> *—I sitting beside you*
> *—You sitting up straight—*
> *suddenly transfigured—*
> *God's light in your Face—*
> *Transfigured—*
> *Whoever saw such Beauty*
> *as I beheld—*

The world of flowers takes on new dimensions for me. Stieglitz tells me I have courage to photograph them. He says he does not feel himself good enough to photograph or pick them. I never consider flowers in this way. I simply love them.

I peer into my camera, obsessed by the trembling edge and texture of white in a petal—sharp, cleansed, with a tinge of unearthly yellow, green. The veins of gray-white are so delicate they must surely vanish. A moon flower. Petunia. Cosmos. Water lily. Round. White. The feeling of white. Flowers that will not stay immobile in the wind. And then the wind is quiet for a split second, before it blows again. It has a whirl, then rests. Bless it. I thought it just blew. I discover its timing. No one has told me about this. During the wind's rest I click. Everything is magically still. Have I caught what I see? The absence of color in the prints bothers me for a while, then doesn't.

The petal behind, beside is blurred, thin, almost transparent. The one I concentrate on becomes sharp. I shut down my lens, hold my breath. Click. Again and again. Each moment the light changes. Worlds are born, live, pass. Have I caught anything or not? I am never certain, but I am transformed. Whom can I tell? Stieglitz.

A voice cuts the air. I remain mesmerized, cannot look up. You don't make a sound when a calf is being born. The spell breaks; I look up. Edward is going to our car to attend to an errand. I rush to him. I want to share the vision I have had with him, to tell him, include him. I throw my arms around his neck. I press my mouth against his hard and kiss it. Oh, please, dear one, hear me, hear me—but I don't say the words. "Dearest," I whisper. Edward looks away. It unnerves him when I take up my camera, take up my pencil; when I pick up a shell, a flower, or even look at one with fixed attention. He feels I have gone away from him. Is jealous. It isn't true; I want him nearer me. Why doesn't he come to me, as I want to go to him at a moment like this? He has been doing his own work; I haven't resented it. We both need a certain privacy, then we should share. He is hurt. "Oh, darling," I whisper, "I love you so." He smiles, gets into the car; the door closes. I am unnerved by his being unnerved. It will build up, then blow up. And then Edward will be abject.

In our room I throw myself on the bed, suddenly tired. I am afraid I shall cry. I dislike crying. Self-indulgence.

Nancy and Andrew have just finished their naps. They are delicate, beautiful. I love them so, I embrace them, I bring them flowers. "Look," I say, and hold up the flowers. The magic is there but it is another splendor, not the same as when framed, intensified in the camera.

I have chores to do but walk to the beach with the children. The feverishness from which I have been suffering, and that had disappeared, comes back. A strong wind blows mercilessly. Shall I stay with the children or be alone, back in my room, resting, quiet? My throat aches; I don't want to be ill.

I explain I must return to the house. I rush indoors and write:

Damp sea sand
Bringing rocks to rest
In folds
When tide is low
Like an arranged bouquet
Of scattered wild-flowers
In a vase
Ordering a countryside
Bringing quiet form and style
To turbulence.

I call the lines "Transient Order."

I felt bewildered on being first aroused by Stieglitz. Nothing else had brought me alive in the same way. The miraculous frenzy of awakening, of being fulfilled, must be hidden. The order, the equilibrium of each of us—of society—must be maintained.

Does our love really interfere with the rest of our lives? With the lives of those closest to us? Or does it contribute? We never think of breaking up our marriages. We are nourished by and nourish them. Each of us loves the core of the rest of our lives. I want to hurt or tear apart nothing. Nor does Stieglitz. One day he says to me, surprisingly almost on the verge of tears: "Never get divorced." I reply, "Of course not." (He was himself divorced in the early twenties to marry O'Keeffe.)

To stop loving—what would it help? And how do you stop? The rules haunt me. I have a sacred feeling about them, as I do about Edward—about Stieglitz. About the children and the flowers I have photographed. The sky overhead. Our little white fence. The lines I have written.

Oh, world—stop. Just a moment, as the wind stops. Just one split moment. But of course not.

———

From Lake George Stieglitz writes:

Oh Dorothy Child— What is it you give to me?— What has happened
to bring me the complete acceptance of everything you are—have been
—will be—all without the loss of an iota of continuous wonder—the
continuous sense of ever greater beauty— A oneness incredible yet
absolutely beyond all question.

Yes you love me. And I love you. And I know it is no crime. Not
before God. Not before right thinking Men and Women.

ILY
beyond all measure
It's beyond belief
My feeling about You.
I'm very quiet
At Peace—
Goodnight

I was working on a print of you . . . Dorothy it's certainly a beautiful picture of you. Really one of the finest things I ever did. But there
should have been hundreds more.

Dorothy God I DO— Wherever I look I realize how I DO. Nothing else seems to be a reality. Even the Mountains, the Lake, the Sky,
Rain—Lightning—Trees—Leaves—the Soil—all seem an illusion compared to the reality. I DO—all seem equivalents for that reality—I DO.

We are alike— So alike— We both do. And it's wonderful to hear
you say "I finally know completely." And all of you tells me you do.
As I do.

A floodgate opens wide and I am swept along by a strong double tide. I am
both liberated and trapped. Just as I was swept by Edward into the great
world. Freed and caught.

I was a small child, unknowing. I am a larger child. The tides—myself
at war with myself—close in, open out. Life called to me, and now has called
again. Is this permitted? There is no answer. I shall spend the rest of my life
paying the price for life.

Stieglitz continues to photograph me. Harold Clurman writes of the portraits that I look as though I were searching for truth, struggling "to steer clear in the midst of a dear pain. . . . She is almost on the point of seeing It, the secret, the thing that must be found. . . . If she gives the question a little more thought, she'll have the answer—oh surely she shall."

No one in our generation has appeared who can compete with Edward in my eyes. I continue to love his honesty, intelligence, integrity, but we grow differently. I have known this, hate to admit it. I have my faults; he has his blowups, which steadily grow more dangerous. And where are our dreams, where are they? I have tried to hold on to them; Edward has, too. If only they could come back in full and be realized. Yet sadly I know better.

Secretly, I have begun to realize that Edward is psychologically disturbed, but refuse to put it into words. Everything is allowed to drift. I cannot bring myself to take any action that might upset him. *We are married*, and there are the children.

Summer 1932. Woods Hole. Fever—low, but persistent—will not go away. My throat—my Achilles' throat—aches. Emily Wheeler insists I go to her doctor in Boston, who orders an operation. My body is heavy, hot. I am un-nerved by the thought of anesthesia: it leaves me unable to breathe properly for weeks. I have been writing, writing, but not what I meant to write. The lines that pour out are personal—born of conflict, love. Sometimes passages come out whole. I make the fewest possible changes, not wanting to tamper with the flow, immediacy, rhythm.

After the operation Edward is about to return to Woods Hole to be with the children; he flares up at me, seemingly about nothing, then writes a heart-breaking letter that leaves me speechless and torn.

Darling Angel,
I can't tell you how disgusted and disheartened I feel with myself after this morning's outburst—especially at this time when you so much

need the opposite kind of treatment. Sweetest, I really just adore you to the utmost possible limit. I couldn't live without you at all, and I wouldn't want to go on if I couldn't be with you. I must be almost a psychopathic case, with my ungovernable temper—that I despise more than you or anyone else could. I do so want to keep our lives on a smooth harmonious plane, but no matter how much I try, I seem unable to restrain myself. Dearest, I don't know what to say about me. I am very discouraged. I wish you were built so that you could control me, and keep me from letting loose on you. But I suppose that's an idle wish, because I know very well that you will not undertake to hold me down. I know that you hate personal conflict, and your natural impulse is to avoid it. But just when you do that is when you have the openings through which my aroused passions rush out and create what I think must be worse scenes than if you were to meet me coming and resist me in a way that would be effective. I'm sure, though, that you just can't do this, and I'm all the more discouraged.

Kitten, I'm the most terrible person, and I do wish something could be done about it—for your sake, for the kids, and for me. I know now that I can't rely on myself. I'm so spoiled that my anger comes up before I know it, and pops off at once unless I am met by stern force. And you, sweet kitten, haven't that in you, and you can't arouse it in yourself. But, love, it just can't be that we can't work the matter out—unless, of course, you should decide that it's not worth trying, because I'm so far gone. Angel, angel, I love you so—I just want to live close to you and love you. And only my temper prevents me. Oh, darling, I can't bear these thoughts. What are we going to do? I'd give anything I could to make up for the misery I've caused you.

Kitten, about Dr. L. He said there was no question that you were ill, yet he was sure there was nothing wrong with you organically—except the adenoids, which caused the local trouble, but were not serious enough to cause the general debilitated condition. He said he had no sufficient evidence to think of a neurotic condition, and yet all signs pointed to it. That's why he wants to question me at length. I was much upset by all this, and have been crying a lot, and that is why I said some of what I did this morning. Darling, I can't escape the thought, which I no doubt have no right to have, that your life for a long time has been too internal, too introspective—and it is my fear that your associates, Stieglitz especially, innocently encourage this. Baby, please don't be too troubled by these thoughts of mine. I'll try to get Dr. L. to talk me out of them. But my mind is whirling around in circles, thinking about us, and I am at a loss. Forget all this, sweetest. No matter how bad it all is—it must work out in the end, dear, because the underlying thing between us is right—honesty and love.

Our dear little children are too sweet. Andrew is just an angel and Nancy too. I haven't shown her your "cat and dog" letter yet, as she is still asleep. This is just after lunch.

I will phone you tonight.

I love you.

Ed

The doctor never talked to me about his meeting with Edward, nor did Edward refer to it again. They had no further conferences. The doctor simply smiled when I left and said to take care of my throat. I felt he understood.

I sent my writings to Stieglitz, who responded with warmth and to my surprise wanted to publish them. I had a sinking feeling they were too young, perhaps of no value. Stieglitz showed the passages to visitors at Lake George, including Paul Rosenfeld. Paul sent me an unexpected letter: "I have an impression of a new spirit using the form of didactic poetry to a new end; an impression of a deal of knowledge and a deal of innocence; but above all . . . I have the sense of a new order coming into life, in you as much as anyone." He wrote that the poems gave him a "new desire and joy for writing and daring more intensely and purely than I have hitherto been able to do." To have the first positive responses to my spontaneous, intense young lines come from Stieglitz and Rosenfeld was overwhelming.

I called the volume that Stieglitz published at An American Place *Dualities*. He asked Josephy, who had designed the 1931 Seligmann edition of Marin's *Letters*, to produce it. I chose for the binding a Dutch paper—black—and a rich white vellum. Up to the moment when the book went to press, I was uncertain about how to refer to the outpourings. In an Afterword I wrote of having had no intention of calling the segments poetry, of not having attempted to make them into anything they were not, in their own inevitable way. The form was implicit in what I had to say. In my experience love, art, and religion were born of a single impulse.

Dorothy Brett had been working on her book on D. H. Lawrence, while I had been writing my poems. I sent them to her, eager to know whether they would mean anything to her. Her reaction amazed me.

Taos, Nov. 1, 1932.

Dodo dear,

I have waited to write you—wanting to keep the poems quietly in me for a while. They are beautiful. What do I seek. I think the same Religious Extasy that to me is the Cause—perfectly crystalized into an utterance that is incorruptable—that is your poetry to me. Life so completely realized—so deeply experienced—strangely belonging to Life rather than to you. It seems to me that the intense personal extasy becomes at its highest point—Impersonal—thus belonging as much to the receiver as to the giver. I feel they are a part of my unuttered self. As well as my painting, which is myself. Would that I had the clearness of your vision, the purity of your art. Can I keep them for a while longer. I want to know them well. They are drawn into my painting—"The Immaculate Conception," Dodo, nothing less than that—of the Vision—and the Utterance.

Yours,
Brett

Nov. 22, 1932
TAOS

Dodo dear,

I wrote you about your poems—our letters have crossed—our thoughts have crossed. I have said to you what you have said to me. In your poems you said all I would say if I had the gift of speech. There is that that we know—that Katherine [Mansfield] knew—that Lawrence sought—You and I hold it.

There is a great shining Morning Star that rises out of the silver twigs of the Cottonwood Tree—in the cold sleet coloured dawn before the warm rays of the sun reach over the low hills. I sing to it.

Yrs,

BRETT

The first three-year guarantee fund for An American Place had been spent. I worried that the growing severity of the Depression might cause the gallery to close. After much persuading, Stieglitz allowed me to raise a new fund, but only if I did it alone. Thus I sent out on my own not only pleas to possible contributors, but notices to the press as well, to create as much public interest as possible. Edward Alden Jewell of the *New York Times* was especially helpful. In his column he wrote: "These are difficult days for art galleries and museums. . . . As for Mr. Stieglitz's An American Place, an SOS brought such cordial response, shepherded by Mrs. Dorothy Norman (whose campaign is still on), that there now seems little doubt of this gallery's being able to make the grade. If worse comes to worst, says Alfred Stieglitz, 'I'll take half a room,' and should worse climb to the ultimate and catastrophical worst, there is always the friendly street corner (again glancing back a cool few thousand years one remembers Socrates)." The response was swift and generous. The Place was saved.

Years later, our son, Andrew, would recall in writing his reactions when I left him—a small boy—for an hour or two alone with Stieglitz at the Place. I include his words, since they reaffirm for me the atmosphere Jewell mentioned.

Stieglitz's hair was white, thin, longer than that of most men I had seen. He wore a black suit, a black tie, a black cape—the only cape I had seen on a man. He was quiet but not silent. He would, perhaps, accompany me around the two or three rooms of the gallery, ready to answer my questions and to respond to my responses or non-responses to the paintings or photographs. Then we would go to his room just off the main room of the gallery, where he would lie down on his couch, under a large Marin oil of grey and white gulls standing on grey-brown rocks amid grey-green water. On a ledge, near the chair I took facing him,

112

stood a nude female torso in alabaster by Gaston Lachaise. The room was spare but not bare, full of things but far from cluttered. The grey floor, white walls, simple furniture, and the black-garbed, white-haired, quiet old man combined to express an austerity that satisfied no need of mine. But it was this man's chosen and created austerity. Why did he choose to spend his days in such surroundings? Could the complex, seething water in the Marin mean the same things to him as to me, the dual sensuousness of the alabaster and the sexual in the Lachaise?

We talked about baseball, horse racing, early automobiles, why somebody would paint a picture that did not look as exactly as possible like a bird or a mountain or anything at all. On the latter he told me virtually nothing. "Does it mean anything to you?" he would ask. "Well, I see this," I might say. "I like the way the water seems to move in that picture with the gulls, and I sort of like the colors in that big picture in the small room." "All right," he would say.

Many years passed before I understood that Stieglitz had taught me, or helped me prepare to learn, that whatever fills you with delight or wonder or love or awe is wonderful; that it is the encounter, the transaction, the event that counts. A person, a bird, a flower or sea shell, a ball game or a horse race—even an automobile—may produce a wonderful response, and when it happens it is good in a way that needs no explaining, no confirmation or justification beyond itself. What produces such a response in you may not in me, and what produces it in me at one moment may not at another. A work of art may produce it, and when that happens it is wonderful in a special way, because the other person—the artist—has given you a gift of it, which is an act of love and an added source of joy and wonder. When it does not happen, you are a fool if you get angry or start to argue—with the work of art, or the artist, or the person who seems to find something there that you cannot see or respond to. To demand an explanation is to miss the whole point.

And there is another kind of joy and wonder that art can produce: the enhancement of one's ability to respond to other stimuli—sight, sound, motion; relationships, patterns, sequences; contrasts, complementarities, analogies, transformations. Are not our special favorite artists those who expand our vision by adding some of theirs, so that we see or hear more and in new ways and have more marvelous encounters in our daily lives?

All this seems self-evident, and I often feel that everybody knows it. And yet it cannot be so, or there would be fewer pretentious and joyless works claiming to be art, fewer books and college courses that omit and ignore the joy and the wonder of art and literature—that assert and belabor the importance of everything except the joy of response. It cannot be so self-evident, and so universally understood, or there would be fewer people marching through museums in lock-step obedience to guides and arrows and taped lectures, fewer museum officials declaring that the mission of their institutions is mass education rather than making possible those private, personal, always surprising, individual encounters that are all art is really "about." Where people shuffle past paintings in solemn trances, with immobile faces, art is absent. Where hordes troop through a show of Saul Steinberg and not three in a hundred laugh or smile, something has gone as wrong and sad as between Victorian novelists and sex.

The analogy between art and sex is not trivial. It is not really an analogy but something between analogy and identity. Though Stieglitz, I now know, made this point often, sometimes so explicitly as to offend people who were ill at ease with their own sexuality, he never said a word on the subject to me, an eight or ten or twelve-year-old boy who clearly had no articulate awareness of adult, loving sexuality. And yet the Lachaise torso that was the third participant in all our conversations said it all. Without being aware of it or understanding it, I think that I knew it then.

Stieglitz would be seventy on January 1, 1934. Paul Rosenfeld and Waldo Frank asked me to join Lewis Mumford and the educator Harold Rugg in editing a collective volume in honor of the occasion. We all agreed that a book about a man who had so ardently devoted himself to the living artist should appear during his lifetime.

Mumford and I talk to Richard Walsh at the John Day Company about our project; he accepts it and gives us a firm contract. He likes the list of twenty-five contributors, including, in addition to the editors, Sherwood

Anderson, Harold Clurman, Dorothy Brett, Demuth, Dove, Marin, Hartley, Victoria Ocampo from Buenos Aires (editor of the avant-garde magazine *SUR*), Gertrude Stein, the young American writer Jean Toomer, and William Carlos Williams. The illustrations will include works by the major artists Stieglitz has exhibited and his own photographs.

Waldo and I spend the summer months on Cape Cod; Mumford, Rosenfeld, and Rugg are far away, so they leave the editing to us. It's my first job of the kind. So much younger than the others, and inexperienced, I fear I won't function as ably as I'd like to, yet to my relief the task goes smoothly. Waldo is serious, generous, quick, and flexible. He has the only kind of concentration I understand—total. We agree perfectly and work together so well, I'm amazed. I must have been born to edit, it comes so naturally, although when the first manuscript arrives, I have no idea what is expected of me. I am surprised to learn how almost automatically, if alterations are required, the needed changes dictate themselves. I find, again to my relief, that almost no writer, no matter how accomplished, always spots his own occasional repetitions, omissions, misspellings, or imperfect structure.

When we were ready to give the almost finished book, called *America and Alfred Stieglitz*, to the publisher, we found him frightened by the number of pages and reproductions, about which we had told him in advance. He reneged on our contract for a volume that he now termed too expensive an undertaking. We refused to be discouraged and completed it as though we had a publisher.

By chance, in September I heard that Carl Van Doren, chief editor of the Literary Guild, was looking for a Christmas art book. In a rush I took our manuscripts and illustrations to him. As he turned the pages, he was delighted. I could scarcely believe it when, the following day, he accepted the book and speedily sent it to the printer. Because Doubleday, Doran was associated with the Guild, *America and Alfred Stieglitz* had broad distribution. Thirty thousand copies alone comprised the Guild edition—in the midst of the Depression! A joyous irony, in view of the first publisher's timidity.

Our little house at Woods Hole has become too cramped and we buy a larger one on nearby Penzance Point. The property lies between Buzzards Bay and

Woods Hole Harbor; the constant movement of yachts and small boats seen from the house is enchanting.

We become close friends of Winslow Carlton, son of the head of Western Union, a heroic younger man who agrees with the James Warbasses and Edward about the promise of Consumers' Cooperation. Like Edward, he believes his family has sufficient money and so devotes himself to founding one of the country's first group health insurance organizations, and to promoting public housing. He and his wife, Margaret, who has been active in Washington with the New Deal, are ardent Democrats. Friendship with Mary Draper and the endearing young Gerard Swopes also greatly enriches our lives.

In a natural way, we become part of the summer community. Edward organizes a modest yacht club and is chosen its first commodore. I am elected president of the Children's Science School—an excellent small institution almost every child in Woods Hole attends. Edward and the children enter weekend sailing races. Our tennis court is used often by scientists from the nearby Marine Biological Laboratory and some of our neighbors. The country club, which I have no desire to join, doesn't admit Jews—the ironic result of Justice Louis Brandeis having requested membership one summer. Yet I'm invited to play tennis there, even to participate in the club's tournaments. As they grow older, Nancy and Andrew are asked to its dances. As is my custom, instead of saying no, I hope saying yes will break down barriers. During our first summer on Penzance Point, we learn that one mother disapproves of her son going about with a Jewish child, but soon he and Andrew are happily playing together. Later the family invites all of us to the young man's wedding.

Theodore Dreiser came to Woods Hole to talk to the great scientists at the laboratory, in order to confirm his intuition that they were the equivalent of the priesthood of the past. We met him at a scientists' picnic, where he told me he had explained his theory to a Nobel Prize winner who had no interest whatever in religion. The man had even resented being likened to a priest. The same experience had been repeated with every scientist Dreiser interviewed. He was heartbroken, but was pleased at my telling him that Coomaraswamy also felt modern science had taken the place of the Church.

Dreiser came to our house and I photographed him. I was aware of the sensitive face hidden behind a somewhat gruff mask. He was one of the few writers who looked exactly the way I expected. The compassion of his writing was mirrored in his expressive features. From our conversations, I could understand what impelled him to portray trapped human beings with such close identity: his own entrapment. Our friendship continued in New York.

Dreiser had been one of the first to interview Stieglitz at the turn of the century. Some critics had found a resemblance between Dreiser's descriptions of city scenes in his early novels and Stieglitz's photographs. It occurred to me that perhaps the two men might enjoy meeting again.

At An American Place each was genuinely glad to be with the other; their faces lit up as they spoke. Yet too much time had gone by for them to be able to pick up the threads of their brief relationship of long ago; they had little to say, despite their mutual admiration. Dreiser preferred looking at Stieglitz's photographs to viewing the paintings on the walls.

7

The international picture becomes increasingly bleak. 1931: Japanese overrun Manchuria. 1933: Hitler comes to power in Germany. 1935: Fascist Italy invades Ethiopia. 1936: German troops reoccupy the demilitarized Rhineland zone, in violation of the Locarno Pact.

Americans in general feel remote from Europe and Asia. There is fear of becoming involved in war. The country is steeped in depression. Yet to be so blind to atrocities and aggressions daily staring us in the face is inconceivable. Hitler's persecution of Jews alone is barbarous and ruthless beyond belief. Threats to peace and human freedom everywhere mount relentlessly, without any effective opposition. We are "unprepared," to be sure, but appeasement, ignoring reality, and inaction simply add to the dangers already confronting us.

Ingrid Warburg, a member of a rich, powerful, and highly cultivated German-based family of world fame, comes to New York. Energetic, distinguished, with a sophisticated, liberal political attitude, she works diligently to alert Americans to the evils of Hitler and the need to help those Europeans most endangered. She is one of the first persons I know who is directly involved both in assisting German Jews—especially children— and in cooperating with the anti-Nazi underground movement.

Drawn to each other, we work together feverishly and become fast friends. Very much alike in many ways, we have been unable to feel religiously

Jewish, yet never have denied our heritage. We rebel consistently against confining dogma of any kind: Catholic, Communist, whatever. We value the freedom to make up our own minds and to protect that sacred right for others.

Ingrid brings Paul Hagen to see me. He is a leader of one segment of the labor-oriented German underground, has a sensitive, intelligent face and an impassioned but reserved manner. He inspires respect and confidence in the sensible and well-laid plans he describes. He cannot divulge his program in detail, but his general aims are clear. He and his carefully chosen coworkers hope that a movement may arise to overthrow Hitler. One can doubt such a possibility but one must help its advocates. At the meetings I arrange for Hagen and his associates, their intense dedication and willingness to take risks, to move about in clandestine fashion, to build their movement and save the lives of others, impress me deeply. First I try to raise funds for refugees, subsequently for the underground.

From the opposite extreme of Hitler's opponents, Ingrid introduced me to a handsome young German aristocrat, Adam von Trott zu Solz. He was highly secretive about his work. Perhaps because of his outstanding good looks and perfect manners, several people I knew tended to mistrust him, warning that he might be a spy, which seemed impossible. I believed in him. Later, when von Trott returned to Germany, he became involved in a bomb plot to kill Hitler. The conspiracy failed and Hitler's life was spared, whereas the beautiful, idealistic Adam and his associates were executed.

Even before anti-Nazi Germans came to the United States seeking help, I had worked with groups trying to gain support for leading Italian anti-Fascists. Throughout the thirties I became involved with a number of active and highly cultivated Italian writers. Our major task was to arouse public opinion against Fascism and to get whatever help we could for those who, persecuted by Mussolini, remained trapped in Italy or tried to escape.

I am introduced to the anti-Fascist Italian author G. A. Borgese at a dinner party given by Rita Morgenthau, head of the Neighborhood Playhouse School. He has a magnetic quality that holds my attention. Borgese's eyes blaze. His sensuous mouth pulls down at one corner as he speaks. The words that pour forth could be about anything and they would interest me, because of their clarity, passion, humanity. We meet often.

Gaetano Salvemini—eminent historian, educator, and fighter for democracy—urges me to bring together a group of Italians and Americans interested in Italy's plight. He and a few colleagues hope to issue and circulate a bulletin to give the latest news about Mussolini's activities in greater detail than is available in American journals—an enterprise for which they lack funds.

Among the anti-Fascists who crowd into our living room are Max Ascoli, Paolo Milano, Niccolo Tucci, Borgese, Randolfo Pacciardi, Nicola Chiaromonte, as well as such American coworkers as Frances Keene, Marya Mannes, Adrienne Foulke. As I stand at the doorway to greet the guests, every Italian in turn surveys the room. Each whispers to me, "Oh, please don't put me near X. You know, at the beginning he was a Fascist." Or: "Please don't seat me near Y. In the past, he was an ardent Communist." As the room fills, I whisper to an American friend, "There isn't an honest man in the house."

We smile wryly; I wonder if any movement can exist without internal tensions. Of course all greet one another with lavish Italian warmth; all, in fact, trust one another and work together harmoniously in these most difficult days.

In 1933 the New School for Social Research founded a University in Exile for leading intellectuals from Nazi- and Fascist-dominated countries. It was Alvin Johnson's inspired idea to create this badly needed center for threatened, uprooted, talented intellectuals and professors from abroad, to help them again write, teach, and exchange ideas freely. The school at once became their spiritual home. Not all universities in the United States had been equally hospitable.

Edward, who was on the board of directors of the new University, and I attended a dinner honoring Albert Einstein. His beautiful and extraordinary head made it impossible for me to look at anyone else. Einstein was introduced with great éclat, and reference was made to how much he had suffered in Germany. As he rose to speak, the audience burst into thunderous applause. He smiled shyly like an embarrassed youth and said slowly, gently, "I—did—not—suffer." The audience responded even more enthusiastically to his unvarnished, understated, mild reproof.

———————

Edward's fervor for a free Palestine has been passionate and sincere ever since his college days. In view of the rise of Hitler, any attempt to alleviate the plight of the Jews calls for sympathy and rapid, decisive action.

At heart, Edward is a planner. The American Palestine Fund for Cultural Institutions is one of his brain children. Its aim: to make available the best of music, theater, and the other arts for Palestine. Soon it becomes a functioning reality. Yet acting as head of it in New York makes Edward anxious and nervous. He has also been intent on working out a scheme that would give Palestine's Arabs a place in which to settle once they had divested themselves of their land. Handsomely paid by Jews for their holdings, the Arabs, in Edward's view, could best be resettled in Iraq, a country desirous of attracting immigrants with agricultural experience. If sufficient funds were made available to finance resettlement of Arabs by the Iraqis—the funds to be secretly made available by Jews—the problem would be solved. Edward was hopeful that the Iraqis would take the initiative, rather than accept the idea from outsiders.

In 1938, he explored the matter thoroughly and entered into negotiations with highly placed, fully informed individuals in Britain and America. A study by an expert on Iraqi affairs was commissioned, with the stern injunction not to put down on paper any specific plan. Edward attempted to go ahead with his idea well into 1939, but the war put a stop to the project. If only the plan could have been carried out sooner, quietly, as first intended, it might have worked. To see all his sincere and thoughtful efforts frustrated was a constant heartache for both of us.

At the time of my marriage I naïvely believed that all social injustice could be eradicated by a single, concerted, inspired action; that freedom could be obtained once and for all; that wars between nations could be eliminated forever by way of one preconceived doctrine—pacifism. Through my work with the A.C.L.U., I quickly learned the absurdity of believing any isolated act in any field—no matter how noble or seemingly decisive—can bring about perpetual order. I have become increasingly aware that every event must be decided on its own merits; that "Eternal Vigilance"—the watchword of the A.C.L.U.—is a prime necessity. Now, in the thirties, I realize, ever more fully, the dangers of generalizing; that each situation threatening peace or freedom must be evaluated on its own terms.

The Spanish Civil War determines my new point of view. Earlier I couldn't have imagined taking sides with any combatant in any war, but now my heart is with the Loyalists. I am deeply upset that the United States, in adopting a position of neutrality, is giving them no help, while on the other hand—inadvertently or otherwise—assisting the Fascists and their allies.

At the home of friends I meet a young American who is going to Spain to fight on the side of the Loyalists. For the first time, I warmly sympathize with someone volunteering to kill and possibly be killed in a war. This reversal of a deep belief brings about an agony of thought; I must gain more clarity about many other convictions I have held.

Those whose attitude toward war has most affected me are Roger Baldwin and the pacifists of the remarkable periodical the *Seven Arts*, published in 1917—mainly Waldo Frank and Van Wyck Brooks. Their position—like that of Randolph Bourne, whom I am too young to have known, but who has become a hero to me—was staunchly antiwar. This has made them anathema to both the general public and the sponsor of the magazine, which folded after just one year.

On the whole, the editors of the *Nation* and *New Republic* also opposed military action throughout the thirties. After Lewis Mumford wrote his famous books *Men Must Act* and *Call to Arms*, he was practically ostracized by his coworkers and many other associates. A wave of criticism blasted him for his so-called uncivilized ideas. Yet before long his critics were agreeing with him; Mumford's "heresy" was forgiven and forgotten.

Quite on my own, I decided no choice was left. We had actively to oppose totalitarianism. We had taken insufficient preventive action: war was clearly and tragically inevitable.

During the daytime I attend meetings about the predicament of the poor and threats to civil liberties. At An American Place I encounter artists and writers, each of whom has undergone any number of hardships in order to work in accordance with his conscience. The Depression has presented nearly insurmountable difficulties for almost everyone. Yet I'm amazed to find so few artists aroused by censorship, persecution, and cruelty elsewhere in the world. In the evenings I see more and more exiles from dictatorial regimes, and am haunted by the question of how I would behave under similar circumstances.

My morning mail includes little magazines—both from Europe and the United States—filled with writing by young authors, mostly unestablished. Much is of interest but few express an awareness of contemporary issues. Only too often they blindly imitate the language of Joyce or Lawrence, thinking themselves daring because they use four-letter words, mainly in a vulgar manner. I also become impatient with complaints about censorship from those who take little action against it.

The urgency to oppose repression in all forms obsesses me. My inner conflict—interest in the arts and in social action—begins to resolve itself; I want to share this resolution with others. I dream of issuing a periodical quite different from any now printed, based on no confining dogma, in which the various strands of my recent experiences can be correlated. I have more faith than ever before that the creative artists of our time can have a startling influence, that their freedom and all life-enhancing freedom must be protected.

In 1936 the editors of the *American Caravan* had invited me to be a co-editor. Mumford, Rosenfeld, and I worked together well on *America and Alfred Stieglitz*. Their invitation gave me both a new sense of confidence and a shudder of surprise. I greatly admired the *Caravan*, but as I contemplated its past numbers, I realized it was not a purely literary magazine with which I wished to be affiliated.

During long talks with Mary Lescaze, we write out prospectuses for my newly proposed project, which she agrees to coedit. Something I think of as "An American Quarterly" begins to take shape in my mind. The title is simple and makes no claim. We send out perhaps a hundred letters to authors whose work attracts us and to young writers who are only names, but who seem promising.

Lewis Mumford responds:

I know very well what you are driving at, for the publication that you have outlined has always been in my own mind as an alternative to the sort of thing that we did in the *American Caravan*. Two years ago I discussed the project vaguely with Waldo [Frank]; and perhaps I would have gone ahead with it, instead of sinking back, as it were, into the more obvious form of the *Caravan*, if I had been sure that the necessary amount of "related writing" were available: or rather, perhaps, if I had sufficient time and patience to get at the writing that probably is actually or potentially in existence, but which would still be hard to assemble. There is need for such a publication: I have no doubt of that. . . .

Your notion about actually bringing a group of people face [to face] is important: it is for lack of this contact, as it is for lack of someone to hold them together, that so many fine ideas get dissipated and so many initiatives are lost. Stieglitz of course has always known this; and when we did our good work on the *Caravan* we spent a great deal of time establishing personal relations with people: but this is a place where you, as a woman, have an enormous advantage, if you have the courage and persistence to use your special powers and opportunities. You might influence the feeling and thought of a whole generation, if you would devote yourself to bringing into a social-intellectual relationship the creative spirits around you: people who are shy, diffident, lonely, suspicious, incapable of joining with each other unless some polarizing center comes into existence, capable of drawing them out of the narrower orbit of their egos. You have done this on occasion in the past, first with the Theatre Group, then with the Stieglitz book: but now it needs a longer, more patient, more persistent attack: something that perhaps had to await the gathering of the necessary forces in your own life.

I tell Stieglitz about my desire to publish a magazine and of the conversations I have had with Mary. At this time the writer Edward Dahlberg visits An American Place rather often. He has recently left the Communist Party and seems friendless and depressed. Stieglitz feels he has a certain brilliance and, because of the man's intelligence and unhappiness, urges me to give him a place on the periodical I am contemplating. Stieglitz has never asked me to do anything. I am amazed by his suggestion; my previous encounters with Dahlberg and my intuition tell me that he and I cannot possibly work together in harmony.

In deference to Stieglitz, I confer with him; his face is contorted and sad. His life, partly spent in an orphan asylum, has been lonely and impoverished. I feel compassionate toward him and want to be patient, but his repeated arrogance repels and estranges. For a while he calms down; perhaps we can cooperate, but I continue to doubt it.

Dahlberg's heart is certainly in the publication; he, too, makes various requests for material. I have no clear hope the articles we have asked for will arrive, yet we go ahead as though certain we shall receive them.

One day, while talking to Mary, I am perplexed. "How shall I pay for it all?" I know with certainty the magazine cannot possibly support itself. Even now I don't know how much money Edward has; I have none of my own and I don't want to ask for funds. But then, unexpectedly, I'm told the ten thousand dollars I was offered by the Normans as a wedding gift is to be put in a special account—after all these years. I'll be able to spend it as I wish, without asking permission from anyone. The rent fund for An American Place is sufficiently guaranteed, so this is not a worry at the moment, nor are my parents' finances. I decide to use the gift for the magazine.

Edward is less than enthusiastic—in fact quite skeptical—about the project, but I'm so certain it is right in spirit that I go ahead. A good but reasonable printer gives me an estimate for producing one thousand copies of a six-by-nine journal of perhaps two hundred pages, and one or two reproductions of top quality. The publication is to be printed on inexpensive but good laid paper and will have cardboard binding, not cloth. Perhaps a few copies for library use can be hardbound. What should be the selling price? Certainly not fifty cents. Four times a year? Impossible. The seasons pass so quickly; so many students are away in the summer. Because I envision the magazine especially for them, the price must be low; it will certainly not have a popular audience. And we're still in the Depression, although we hope near the end of it: it is 1937.

I tell Mary I think the publication should come out only twice a year; that's all I can afford. In his splendid hand Stieglitz is diligently putting down titles as they are suggested. "An American Quarterly" is dropped; no other name appeals to me. "Why not call it simply 'Twice A Year'?" I ask. Everyone to whom I mention this finds it absurd except Mary and Stieglitz, who writes it out at once so beautifully that I want to see it on the cover. And so the publication is named *Twice A Year*.

I ask the editors of several little magazines what they pay their authors.

Some can afford nothing. Others pay a cent a word for prose, and by the page for poetry. Each translator is considered separately in terms of his fame or lack of it.

Costs begin to mount in my mind: packing, circularization, postage, secretarial work, publicity. My head swims. How can I ever support the enterprise of my dreams? At least something should come back by way of subscriptions. But I fear it will be far too little.

I ask Frances Steloff at the Gotham Book Mart if she will be the leading agent for *Twice A Year*. She is delighted with the idea and is cordial and encouraging. I inquire what discount bookstores will want, what she will want. The dollar a copy I hope to charge dwindles before my eyes. Exactly how much will I lose? The amount I have set aside must pay for at least two issues, if I call the journal *Twice A Year*. I cannot accept subscriptions and then not deliver the promised numbers.

Dahlberg is so absolute in his antiwar attitude, he rebels against presenting any other views, whereas publishing opposite opinions helps clarify my own beliefs. My conversations with him sharpen my perceptions about pacifism and war, but this does not in any way change my mind or bring us closer together.

We discuss plans to print Thoreau, whom I see as both a defender of John Brown and an advocate of peaceful civil disobedience. I am perfectly satisfied with this seeming inconsistency, but Dahlberg eyes me with hostility for suggesting that Thoreau would defend violence.

At first, in an effort to be sympathetic, I praise Dahlberg's writing, though in reality I find it too florid and bitter: it makes me uncomfortable, I cannot identify with it. My own writing, I'm certain, is far too simple for him.

Dahlberg disapproves above all of my insistence upon printing Roger Baldwin's statement about being a conscientious objector. He fumes, taking me to task for approving anything so unliterary. Baldwin's straightforward and courageous credo strikes me as a most important document of our time; I am firm about the the necessity of including it.

Unless we agree totally, Dahlberg becomes insulting, derogatory, and inflexible. I don't know how to deal with him. Arguments about almost every subject create an atmosphere of unbearable tension. Meanwhile Mary and I work in beautiful harmony. When I talk about the publication with her, there is nothing but light. When I have any contact with Dahlberg, everything is a deep, morose black. Finally I tell him we can go no further; to work together is impossible.

This is a sad moment. Dahlberg is deeply upset and I know he is hurt. He is an established writer; I am not. The one piece he has brought to the magazine is a marvelous essay by Charles Olson on King Lear and Moby Dick— Olson's first writing to be published. I admired it enormously at once; meeting Olson, I also like him. As a result of his article's appearance, he receives much praise, a Guggenheim Fellowship, and his career is launched.

At first, Stieglitz feels sorry for Dahlberg and pleads with me, as does Olson, to permit him to continue as an editor. Certainly Dahlberg wants to, in spite of an ambivalent attitude, but our temperaments are too much at variance; his behavior is too hostile. Before the first issue appears, our split is final.

Ignazio Silone's novel *Fontamara* is the first work of art from Fascist Italy that attracts our attention. I know Silone has had to escape to Switzerland, but he seems to have transcended the trauma of exile and created a contemporary classic.

I am eager to learn more about the man. Why can't he be brought to America? Does he need financial help? What is he thinking and feeling? I want to see more of his work. Mary and I query him by letter, then publish his reply:

Reading Room of the Museum Society of Zurich
For the last seven years I have lived in Switzerland as a political refugee, under the special police surveillance of aliens. A residence permit of a political refugee in this country is always accompanied by a restriction: the political refugee can only practice a profession permitted him by the police and he must completely refrain from searching for other sources of income from any other work. . . . Having been authorized by the Swiss police to work as a writer (during the first year with the express restriction that I must not publish in Switzerland but only in other countries, because of the subversive content of my writings), I had to forego other occupations. When I could prove to the police that my earnings as a writer were absolutely insufficient for me to live on, I re-

ceived authorization to give lessons in business correspondence, in Italian, in a school in Zurich. I must confess that I was an abominable professor and that the business letters that I taught to my students (I had only young girls from 18 to 23 years of age) were absolutely fantastic. . . .

I strive not to become a professional writer and I rigorously absent myself from every congress, assembly, group or clique of writers. I want to try to stay faithful to the first impulse that led me to write and to safeguard my work from the debasement that professionalism always carries with it; I want to be careful to save myself from "Literature." . . .

I was born into a peasant family in comfortable circumstances. My orientation toward progressive ideas and toward the poor developed as a contradiction of the dominant psychology of my background.

The society of Southern Italy, where I was born, is torn to pieces by profound contradictions; it is the region which gives to Italy her most original philosophers and artists and in which ignorance is most extensive; it is the region of mystics and of sensualists; of anarchists and of policemen; of peasants without land and of the great landowners. It is one of the most inhuman sections of the earth (comparable in several points to Spain) and its contradictions are so old that they seem natural. My refusal to consider misery, ignorance, injustice as natural facts was the origin of my non-conformism.

Books did not play a great role in my intellectual formation. It was influenced strongly by certain events in which I took part, or which I witnessed, and by certain people. None of these was a university professor. When I was an adolescent I sometimes took a book with me when I went for long walks all alone in the mountains; then I thought about many things but I almost never opened the book, often putting it on the ground, on the grass, for me to sit upon. Later, I tried to find books which could feed my hunger for things of the mind. . . .

After twenty years I have taken up again to re-read the Greek and Latin classics that I studied at school and now I find in them a pleasure that then I did not even suspect. On the other hand, certain romantic masterpieces that I had to read secretly because they were forbidden in the college now seem to me unreadable.

I admire André Gide, Aldous Huxley, John Dos Passos, Faulkner, Thomas Mann, Gaetano Salvemini.

That is to say, I admire them for the little that I know of their life, above all as men. The influence of intellectuals on public life has increased enormously since the war. I believe that, in recent times, even the great public has learned to orient itself toward more serious and lasting values.

I have no personal theory of art. But I admire very much the theories of those who have them and I find that they are all correct even when they contradict each other. I should not be reproached as being negligent for not having an art theory. Had I known as early as my youth that I would end by becoming a writer, then, of course, I also would have equipped myself with a theory, but I became a writer by mischance. Now literary creation has become, for me, my way of living.

I have continued to write down what Stieglitz says because I find him so magnificent and independent an artist; he has battled for freedom of expression throughout his life. We publish some of his words and writings in the first issue. I have not seen them printed elsewhere.

I pore over civil liberties briefs that are stirring and important to me. Harriet Pilpel, a young and brilliant civil liberties lawyer, tells me a story that seems particularly apt. She lunched with a college classmate who says she is an author; she has published two or three short poems. The classmate asks Harriet about herself. Harriet has just prepared various first-rate briefs, but feels much too self-conscious to call herself a "writer." I am baffled by the lack of respect shown such work as opposed to the high praise often given to minor "literary" expression. The publishing of a coherent magazine, including just such material as Harriet's, seems ever more necessary.

I hear that the author and editor M. D. Herter Norton has been translating Rilke's wartime letters. I beg her to finish them in time for our first number. Even the smallest section I read strikes me as extraordinary:

Those two powerful old men going around—Tolstoi and Cézanne—uttering warnings and threats, like prophets of an ancient covenant that is soon to be broken—and they did not want to live to see that break. Whatever comes, the worst of it is that a certain innocence of life in which after all we grew up will never exist for any of us again.

We also manage to include three parables by Kafka in the first issue.

James Laughlin, editor of *New Directions*, had refused to print a story we accept—*Birth*—by Anaïs Nin. I love its directness, lack of inhibition, and fearlessness. Laughlin tells me I have courage to print it, but I have no sense of being courageous. He dedicates an early issue of his magazine to what I am still calling "An American Quarterly" at the time we meet—a most generous act on his part.

While plans for *Twice A Year* have been materializing, my friend Miriam Holden introduces me to Mary Beard. She and her husband, Charles, are eminent historians. Mrs. Beard, wanting to make sure women's accomplishments are recorded properly, is founding a World Center for Women's Archives. "Without memory," she claims, "there is no history. Without history, there is no civilization."

Mary Beard is large, motherly, kindly, intelligent; I am drawn to her at once. She invites me to be on the Archives board; I ask her to write an article for *Twice A Year*. Perhaps we can devote an issue to the idea of the Archives, to the extraordinary but unremembered achievements of women. Unfortunately, Mrs. Beard's concentration on the Archives and on writing with her husband prevents her from contributing to *Twice A Year*. We correspond, however, and her letters are provocative:

As for statements by the C.Os. [conscientious objectors]. It may be impossible for many of them to make them. I know one . . . who has been hounded from pillar to post by the Legion every time his friends get a job for him and he can only live on caution. But if you do have men who can make declarations now, that would be immensely interesting.

On the matter of the last war, Charles' position was not that of a pacifist. He resigned from Columbia because the President fired three professors without a hearing, who were pacifists, and he thought that no way for a university to behave. He thought *that* war had to be. . . .

Nor have I ever been a professional organization pacifist. But I do hold that we should not and cannot police the world, that we should not engage in an imperialist war in the Far East, and that we can stay out of war if we want to. The World War seemed to me unequivocally horrible and I believed that all the nations concerned, except the U.S. perhaps, were guilty in bringing it on. . . .

We both have the disposition to place wars in history and look at them from that angle. We both think this continent and this republic should be defended. How to defend it has been one issue at the naval hearings. Proponents of the battleship declare that defense is best far over the seas. That to us spells imperialism. And whether the battleship itself is any good at all as defense is a prime issue too. Technicians say it isn't.

Twice A Year: A Semi-Annual Journal of Literature, the Arts and Civil Liberties takes final form. Beautiful proofs of two Stieglitz photographs are made by a famous Austrian printer Max Jaffe. To my relief—Stieglitz is critical of most attempts to reproduce his work—he approves of them.

Mary Lescaze and I are young, unknown. How is it possible that so many distinguished people trust us by sending contributions for our first issue? How do people have the faith to write articles we commission? I have almost nothing with which to pay authors. Yet something in our impassioned call finds response.

My original shyness with Mary has disappeared. I believe in her integrity and we trust each other. We can agree or disagree, but a beautiful spirit always underlies our relationship. Neither of us seeks power.

Stieglitz takes no part in editing or making decisions, but his willingness to allow *Twice A Year* to use An American Place as headquarters is enormously helpful and encouraging. Also my opportunity to talk to him and clarify my ideas is invaluable. He generously permits Andrew Droth, who works at the Place, to pack copies of *Twice A Year* and mail them. This is of major assistance. I pay for the services of Andrew, for postage, and all other expenses incurred at the Place. Yet these outlays are minuscule, compared to what I should have to spend if I had an "office" elsewhere. Working at the Place is nourishing and natural. How has all this wonder come into being?

I look at Number I with disbelief. Although I have discussed it a thousand times, designed it, read proof over and over again, it is a complete surprise to me. There is a supreme logic to the contents I would have been hard-pressed to define clearly as they evolved. The issue feels to me like a clear embodiment of love.

Mother Norman is in bed, ill, when the first number is distributed. I visit her and rather hesitate to take *Twice A Year* as a gift, for fear she will dislike it. She looks at it carefully, turns the pages slowly, with respect, raises her eyes to mine, and says, "Why, Dot, I'm so proud of you."

In spite of all our previous differences about values, hearing these words spoken so simply by this frail woman—Edward's mother—brings tears to my eyes and to hers. We embrace with sincerity and love.

Twice A Year attracts both old and young. The publication broadens the base of An American Place, even though the journal is quite separate. I have meetings there with many of the authors who write for us. Younger men and women who see Stieglitz for the first time are deeply affected by him; the give and take that occurs is healthy, heartening. Insiders at the Place automatically expect *Twice A Year* to reflect only its preoccupations; but as they discover the breadth of the journal's interests, they respond with unexpected approval.

I discovered several approaches to mailing the publication. A special postage rate existed for books; another for periodicals that came out at regular intervals—at least four times a year; another for parcel post. I was advised by the post office to mail the first issue as a periodical. Andrew Droth wrapped the copies most beautifully, took them to the post office, and stamped them precisely according to instructions. The cost of mailing seemed larger than the amount received by way of subscriptions. Giving the copies away might have been less expensive.

The day after the first issue was sent out, every package was returned.

Reacting like a bewildered child, I rushed to the main post office, taking a copy with me. Ushered up to the highest official in the huge building on Thirty-third Street, I asked what had happened. The official looked at me as though it were I who was mad, not the Federal Government. He said calmly, "You are not a periodical." I asked, with as much restraint as I could muster, "Then what am I?" He replied, "I don't know." "Then why did you send all the issues back?" "Because you are parcel post."

"I asked for full information before I mailed *Twice A Year*, at great expense. I was told how much postage to put on each copy as a periodical. Now every one of them has come back, which means I shall have to pay postage all over again. What is the point?" The man looked at me coldly. "You will have to either publish books, or see that your publication comes out more often than twice a year, in order to be rated as a periodical." The tears that could easily have come to my eyes stopped halfway.

I told Stieglitz my tragic story. He looked at me without expression. "My dear Dorothy, didn't you know this would happen?" "No, I didn't." "You are reliving my life. Nothing I ever did turned out differently. Nothing that you do will ever turn out differently."

"But I've made commitments. I've received money for subscriptions. The issue is oversold. This is a catastrophe! I'll not only pay some fantastic sum to mail the copies out again, but I have to print a second edition." Stieglitz embraced me but, for once, failed to comfort me.

The expense of the second edition was enormous: the price of paper, the price of printing, the price of everything had gone up. Again I asked the post office how to avoid disaster. Another official replied, "If you call your publication a book instead of a periodical, your problem is solved. Then it can go out at the book rate." As a result, *Twice A Year* was called "A Book of Literature, the Arts and Civil Liberties." Now it was the critics who were confused—a further dilemma. They told me they didn't know how to review it.

Succeeding issues were mailed at the book rate, but other costs increased to such a degree that the resolution of the postal problem helped but little.

Mother Norman died in 1938, which brought great sadness to Edward and me. Unexpectedly, she left me a legacy of twenty thousand dollars. I had thought I couldn't go ahead with *Twice A Year*, but now I could. I knew she would approve.

Stieglitz was as excited as I was about each issue as it appeared. He admired the cover design and the contents. Even though *Twice A Year* was quite separate from the Place, Stieglitz had given me the courage to publish it; I dedicated it to him.

Among the writers in Paris we have invited to contribute is Henry Miller. I have read a few of his pieces in little magazines and send him a copy of *Twice A Year*. He replies promptly on November 23, 1938:

> Dear Dorothy Norman:
>   If your review had done nothing more than to publish Thoreau's speech at Concord, it would have been worth the trouble. I can't think of anything more fitting to the actual situation today than this speech which, to my mind, is far superior to anything Lincoln ever wrote or said. And how well Thoreau stands up beside our contemporaries! How much more alive, honest, really rebellious and just than the latter-day revolutionaries. That is the American spirit which is lost.
>   P.S. Make every issue a John Brown number! Until we all become alive again!!

My early correspondence with Anaïs Nin, with whom Henry Miller had suggested I get in touch, is invariably warm. When Edward goes to Europe before the war breaks out, I ask him to look her up. I worry that, in the worsening situation, she may need help. The first time she comes to see me at the Place, after her arrival in New York, there is something of the nun about the way she looks. Her gray coat with its simple rounded collar, her almost poke-bonnet gray hat, suggest a professional Puritan. But her small mouth is carefully painted; her exaggeratedly innocent mascaraed eyes stare at me ecstatically.

At first I don't realize our positions are similar in many ways. I have taken it for granted she is poverty-stricken and in distress, but her husband is a banker and by no means poor. He and Edward have much in common. They love their wives, as we love them. They don't understand our dedication to the contemporary creative scene in the arts, though they are tolerant of it, often even proud of what we're doing. Anaïs's husband makes delicate drawings and cooperates with her on her publications, but beneath the surface they are drifting apart in an unacknowledged manner, much as Edward and I are. How I wish Edward understood. We could do so much together, so tenderly.

The first issue of *Twice A Year* appeared in the autumn of 1938, immediately following the Munich Pact; the second comes out in a time of further crisis—1939, when Germany invaded Czechoslovakia and was preparing an attack on Poland.

With the greatest of difficulty I pursue my desire to print Randolph Bourne's unpublished letters. I follow every possible lead and at last discover they are in Princeton with Bourne's sister, Mrs. Fenninger; I write her and ask whether *Twice A Year* could possibly publish the correspondence. I receive no reply; in despair, I telephone, much embarrassed to take up the time of a stranger. I explain I have written, had no answer, and am being extremely brash in telephoning, because I am so serious in my hope of including the letters in *Twice A Year*. Is there no way this might be possible? The sound of friendly laughter, then: "I have a theory. I know if a person wants something badly enough, he'll pursue a first unsuccessful attempt. The fact that you've phoned and didn't just give up makes me feel I can trust you. When will you come to Princeton? I'll get out all the letters; you may go through them and print what you like."

I feel as though heaven had descended. When asked how I have gotten hold of the rare and as yet unpublished letters, I can only blush and say I was lucky.

I write to an old friend, Max Lerner, an admirer of Bourne, requesting that he write about him for *Twice A Year*. Lerner's reply:

Your note brought me back to Bourne with a jolt. I had been so busy watching the egg-shell of Europe being crushed by this mystical gangster-conqueror that I had forgotten Bourne warned us once against too passionate a concern for Europe. . . . My thought on Europe has shifted. I want to help *if* and *while* there is still time. But that has not shifted my allegiance to Bourne. There are things in him that are even more valid

135

if we go to war than if we don't . . . that our first concern is the American promise. We must grimly recognize [it] first, and guard against being crushed by the very power we must use. And we must, once survival is assured, try not so much to recapture the old America but build a new one, as far beyond the old democratic image as Hitler is beyond the old dictatorship image.

The architecture section of Number II, which Mary does much to help create, covers the spectrum of the great and revolutionary spirit emerging in that discipline. George Bernard Shaw and the distinguished pioneer Louis Sullivan give overviews—timeless and magnificent. From a younger generation we select articles by Mary's husband, William Lescaze, and by Walter Gropius, as well as Mumford's eloquent criticism. We ask Frank Lloyd Wright to contribute but he refuses, complaining that the issue contains too many representatives of the "foreign" International School, of which he disapproves.

A map of outstanding modern buildings by living architects in America shows students what is to be seen and where. It presents not an abstract picture of theories but a specific arrow pointing to the most adventurous structures in America. With Randolph Bourne, we think that a civilization is to be judged in large measure by its architecture.

Working on the issue intensifies my impatience with the building in which Edward and I live. Our Park Avenue apartment fills me with dismay. The façade, like that of its neighbors, is designed to look imposing. The entrance hall is gloomy and pretentious. A uniformed doorman and elevator man make us feel uncomfortable. Our rooms are badly proportioned. The ugly and forbidding windows belong to an institution, not a home. False moldings attached to badly painted walls, sconces with pointed electric light bulbs imitating candles strike us as absurd.

Lescaze recently has remodeled a brownstone for his family with great distinction. I dream of his re-creating an old-fashioned, narrow house into a simple contemporary one for us. Edward shares my horror about the building we live in and agrees we should move.

I tell our requirements to a representative of a large real estate firm. We seek a house that has not been made over, no wider than twenty feet, with no tall buildings in front or back. The rear of the house should face south. It cannot be near an elevated or bus line, since we both sleep badly; we prefer to be neither above Seventy-ninth Street nor below Sixty-eighth on the East Side. The list of suitable properties boils down to five. The one we choose is exactly what we had in mind: a Victorian brownstone, nineteen feet from wall to wall inside, with a high front stoop. It is in bad shape, inexpensive, and crying out to be renovated.

Many months go by before plans are completed. War breaks out in Europe and building supplies are limited. I envisage a whitewashed brick exterior, but am voted down because of New York's well-known atmosphere. The most practical solution: walls of glass brick surrounded by light-gray glazed bricks. The front of the building is moved as far forward as permissible; the rear is slanted to allow the greatest amount of daylight to enter. Interior space is reorganized imaginatively; the spare, clean lines throughout the house are as satisfying as I had hoped.

We move in in 1941. The starkness of the interior seems a bit forbidding at first, but soon our furniture, books, art, shells, and plants transform it. "124" is voted one of the city's two best new buildings of the period: photographs of it are exhibited at the Museum of Modern Art. Architecture students frequently stand in front, studying and sketching the building; many ask to be shown through. Living in such a house is a delight; sharing it with friends and visitors, an added joy.

Late summer, 1939. The radio is new to us in the country and we are snobbish about it. It makes raucous noises and tells nothing we want to know. The sound of its vulgar advertisements is a blemish on our quiet New England house and landscape. But suddenly it becomes an integral part of our lives; each evening we are glued to the instrument—our guests, Edward, and I. Dr. David Gurewitsch—born in Russia, then an exile in Germany, Palestine, London, and now New York—is painfully aware to his fingertips of every event occurring in Europe. His wife, Nemone Balfour—British, an aristocrat, unaccustomed to our passionate involvement in the horrors we hear—sits with us, silent, regal, handsome. Edward is so emotionally upset, as am I, that we can speak of little else but the announcements coming over the now miraculous airwaves.

Perhaps because we're in the country and, except for the radio, news reaches us with less immediacy than in New York, it is difficult to assimilate the staggering blast of the Nazi-Soviet Pact on August 24. Every value or lack of it strikes us with a sickening thud.

In the city, most party-liners for whom Stalin can do no wrong are now confronted with an embarrassing situation. As I circulate at meetings and parties, aware of the red faces of those who cannot look me straight in the eye or give a logical reason for their sudden change of heart, I feel despair about the Far Left—about a number of so-called intellectuals who had once seemed brilliant, humanistic, sincere. Now, nothing they can say means anything to me.

Only one week after the pact was signed, the unbelievable turned into reality. September 1: Germany invaded Poland. September 3: Britain and France declared war on Germany. September 17: Soviet troops entered eastern Poland. September 27: Warsaw surrendered. September 28: Poland was partitioned by Germany and Russia. November 30: the U.S.S.R. invaded Finland. (In a horrifying chorus, pro-Communists insisted the reverse had occurred.) Although America was secretly terrified of becoming embroiled, everyone knew we would be sooner or later. Meanwhile, Hitler's devastating success in Poland was the most catastrophic event of all.

Twice A Year continues to attract to it precisely the type of material we want. G. A. Borgese develops the theme of the perennial exile in an essay that we publish in Number III–IV.

Many things have happened in the past which, in our forgetfulness of history, seem new to us. There have been other exiles in other times, other fugitives who learned new languages and abandoned their mother tongues, other fertile hybrids, other coalescences of cultures. There have been other ages in which men became aware better than we have so far of the creative meaning of exile. Hebrew poetry and prophecy reached their apex in and through the trial of exile. Dante, the father of what is lasting in my native country and will far outlive all barbarization and darkness, the exile *par excellence*, could never have written his poem and reached his own stature, had destiny been lenient to him, and it is only incidental if, instead of conquering a foreign language, he built his own, almost equally new. Practically all the Middle Ages knew how fixed fidelity to one's past and place hamper the creative spirit, how good and generous exile is. . . . It was the very sapient Bernard of Chartres who stated that no one can become a scholar unless he leaves his own country and becomes an exile. It was Hugh of St. Victor in the same twelfth century who . . . added: ". . . He has a delicate soul who still loves his native country, but he is stronger, to whom all the earth is a country, and he is perfect to whom all the world is exile." . . . The words of the mystical medieval doctor remain supreme in their main significance; there is no unity if there has been no separation, there is no real stability unless there has been *exile*.

Thus exile appears as permanence in metamorphosis; a gift, not a doom, to those who have wanted the privilege of a reconstructed life in the plenitude of this country, a land of new covenants, United Uniting States. The best answer to the question with which we started, "How can Culture survive in Exile?" is another question. For I wonder: "How could a European culture survive today except in exile?"

Gaetano Salvemini sends a brilliant article, "Mussolini's Foreign Policy," which is also printed in Number III–IV. I see a good deal of Salvemini's extraordinary young friend Frances Keene, who speaks perfect Italian and knows many exiles. She gives me a copy of a virtually unknown and crucial piece of writing, "The Journal of a Militiaman," by Carlo Rosselli, coeditor of an anti-Fascist weekly in Italy in 1926. Arrested for organizing the escape from Italy of a Socialist leader and sentenced to a year's imprisonment, he escaped to Paris, founded a secret society named Justice and Liberty, and edited its weekly until 1927. He volunteered to fight in the Spanish Civil War and, with his brother Nello, was murdered in France by Fascists. The Rosselli journal alone makes Number III–IV worth publishing.

I meet Ernst Toller, whose *Man and the Masses* already has made a deep impression on me. We print passages from his "Swallow Book," written in prison. Toller is one of the most beautiful men I have ever seen, but he is obviously troubled. When the 1914 war broke out, he served fifteen months at the front before being seriously wounded. During his convalescence he became actively interested in socialism and played an important part in the Munich revolution, for which he was sentenced to five years' imprisonment on charges of high treason. During that time he started to write the "Swallow Book." His hair turned gray—he was barely thirty—but he tells me, "My heart was not tired."

In 1933, when Hitler came to power, Toller was traveling abroad and thus escaped being thrown into a concentration camp and most likely executed. Attempting to rally anti-Nazi feeling, he came to the United States in 1936 and helped raise fifty million dollars to supply the Spanish people with food and medicine. The defeat of the Loyalists added to his already growing depression.

Toller is a patient of a renowned diabetes specialist, who warns him that if he doesn't take insulin regularly, he may die. Whenever the specialist is called out of town, he arranges for Toller to be under the care of a psychiatrist. (The rumor is that Toller consults secretly with more than one psychiatrist; some claim three.)

One afternoon Toller tells me our conversations are good for him; they have given him a new sense of life. Although he hasn't been writing, he promises, "I will do a short story for you." His eyes light up. His subtly modeled features become elated and transformed. I share his surge of emotion and am hopeful that an unusual story will be written.

A few days later I hear of his suicide. Sorrowfully, I visualize the situation: he failed to keep his psychiatric appointments as directed and didn't take insulin. "Oh, God," is all I can say to myself, "oh, God, if only I could have helped. What a ghastly loss!"

Ingrid Warburg not only works for the anti-Nazi underground and for beleaguered German Jews, but also becomes involved with aiding Italian anti-

Fascists. Our paths cross more and more often. She takes me to meet her friend Veniero Spinelli, an ardent anti-Fascist.

Ingrid and Veniero fall in love and decide to marry. To obtain a license, Veniero, an émigré, must have papers: a passport, proof of his place of birth, the date of his arrival in the United States. Veniero gives me the following account of the dialogue at the Marriage License Bureau:

Clerk: "Kindly hand me your passport."

V.S.: "I have no passport."

Clerk: "You have no passport? How did you get into this country?"

V.S.: "I'm an anti-Fascist and was jailed in Italy for my position. They took my passport away. I escaped, made my way to the Swiss border, and crossed to France. Then I went to Spain and flew with the Loyalist forces against Franco."

Clerk: "Without a passport?"

V.S.: "Of course. We did that in those days."

Clerk: "On what date did you arrive in Spain?"

V.S.: "I don't know."

Clerk: "Then what did you do?"

V.S.: "After the Loyalist defeat I went back to France and got a job. When the Germans invaded France, I joined the Foreign Legion. Next, I fled in Arab clothes and hopped a steamer to America as a stowaway."

Clerk: "Again without a passport?"

V.S.: "Of course. And I got into New York City."

Clerk: "How did you do that?"

V.S. (smiling): "I swam in."

The clerk, who can think of no more questions, issues a license, and the Spinellis are married.

To my surprise, Coomaraswamy has agreed to write for *Twice A Year*. From one of his letters:

I might be able to contribute something to your magazine—scarcely, however, an article on symbols, since the subject is so vast (I have before me the prospectus of a French book on Christian symbolism, the *first of three* projected volumes—1100 pages and 1075 illustrations!). One could hardly do more than deal with one thing at a time, e.g., cross, wheel, lotus-rose, seven rays of the sun!

We have been reading two large books on Philo, who has extraordinary parallels to Indian and other traditions. I feel that everyone who wants to understand the essentials in Christianity must follow through from Plato to Philo, the Hermetica, John and Paul, Plotinus, Dionysius, Origen, Eckhart: the continuity is extraordinary.

Coomaraswamy's enthusiasm for the works of Meister Eckhart and René Guenon had intensified his involvement in Catholic thought, although he was always a Hindu first.

From another of our dialogues: I asked how it was possible to justify the Pope's blessing Franco and Mussolini.

A.K.C.: "The Pope, in such instances, speaks *ex cathedra*."

D.N.: "But isn't it possible that those Catholics who are most humane—therefore most valuable to the Church—would prefer the Pope not to bless mass murderers?"

A.K.C.: "Franco and Mussolini are members of the flock; the Pope is their shepherd. It is his function to bless, not to judge. All departure from tradition is destructive."

D.N.: "Then why is anyone ever excommunicated?"

A.K.C.: "For reasons of importance to the Church."

Pause.

D.N.: "Why, if all traditions are one, does the Catholic Church claim it alone is the Way?"

A.K.C.: "That is its one flaw."

D.N.: "If it has one, isn't it possible it has others?"

A.K.C. (shaking his head): "You make a great mistake in rebelling against tradition."

D.N.: "I don't rebel against tradition. But I do object strenuously to institutionalization that distorts tradition."

From another Coomaraswamy letter of November 1938:

Many thanks for Once a Year [sic]. It is really what the English would call a "good effort." It looks well too. I'm glad to see the war question emphasized, but feel that what *most* needs emphasis is that "they (most people) desire peace, but not the things that make for peace." There is a price to be paid for peace. Only the man who is himself at peace is really a paci-fist ("peace-maker").

To my surprise, I learned that Coomaraswamy's middle initial stood for "Kentish." His mother was English. He had spent much of his life in England and America, not in Ceylon, where he was born. No wonder he was steeped in the religious tradition of the West as well as the philosophies of Hinduism.

In its issue of December 25, 1939, *Time* solved the problem of how to review *Twice A Year*. The book column contained a section entitled "Twice to Once" that began: "First published in autumn 1938, *Twice A Year* has established itself as a distinguished periodical, more original in essence if less 'experimental' in a literary way than the *New Directions* annual." The column concluded:

> *Twice A Year*'s . . .latest issue [Number III–IV] includes a prophetic piece written by Heine in 1834 ("There will be played a drama in Germany compared to which the French revolution will seem but an innocent idyll"); a Civil Liberties review of the year 1939 commending 23 actions, condemning 25; a 38-page analysis of Mussolini's foreign policy by Gaetano Salvemini ranking as the calmest, hence deadliest deflation of post-war diplomacy yet in print.
>
> By tone, price ($2), format and program, *Twice A Year* seems limited to an upper-crust liberal audience, and its quota of contemporary creative work is a bit less "free" than its documentary content. Yet in everything it prints it conveys a sense of the seriousness of writing which few U.S. journals attempt to match and which is pretty well indicated by Editor Norman's touchstone for documentary contributions: "Someone who talks about the thing must be someone who would do the thing."

Father Norman died in 1936. Edward responded to the loss with overwhelming sorrow, then steadily his entire demeanor changed. He gave sudden, curt orders, much in the manner of his father. He became dictatorial, stern, forbidding—harsh with the children and with me. I grew terrified. All the character traits against which Edward had first rebelled he now adopted.

I posed a hypothetical question to a psychiatrist whom I met at a friend's: "I know someone who, after his father died, became his father in every action. He now displays the very characteristics he most disliked in his father. Is this a common occurrence?" The psychiatrist: "Yes. It happens often."

The issues on which Father Norman and I had at first taken opposing sides but had finally agreed upon are now often the ones that divide Edward and myself most cruelly. With greater resources after Aaron's death, Edward is in even deeper conflict about how we should live. We have a small sailboat; he speaks of buying a large yacht. He wants me to dress in a more splendid, conventional manner. No one can know how long the Depression will last, but this seems not to worry him. Yet when I need a new tennis racquet, I'm told it's not a necessity but a wasteful expense.

Edward remains liberal in politics, but in other important respects he becomes far more conservative. Although still as serious about his work as ever, he craves more time for relaxation than before. This confuses me, because his father was anything but frivolous. I see the new development as an assertion of independence, but in some ways as retrogression.

The more involved I am in my work, the more I arouse a kind of jealousy difficult for me to understand. Outbursts over trivial matters are more frequent and the usual dejections that follow seem more deep-seated. I try as always to be comforting, but the quick shifts from anger to self-recrimination grow more difficult to handle. If I speak up against a "tantrum"—which Edward has always begged me to do—this upsets him to a staggering degree. Ironically, as the world situation becomes more worrisome, it brings us closer together. Yet my nerves are jangled and I live in constant fear of sudden violence—fear that I try my best to hide.

Edward grows abnormally strict with the children; this distresses me and I am often more permissive with them than I mean to be, in order to compensate for the rages. I love the children; Edward does, too. Our contradictory behavior sets up conflicts within both Nancy and Andrew.

I admit I am a complicated person and must strike others as difficult. I simply cannot be at Edward's side every moment, as he periodically says he wants me to be; he needs as much freedom as I do. We depend upon each other, but he has sudden surges of wanting me to stop all my serious activities. His desire is illusory, but to know this helps nothing.

After Mother Norman's death in 1938, Edward has become his mother as well. The luxury-loving, feminine side of him develops. He wants me to wear large, floppy hats and elaborate, expensive Bergdorf Goodman dresses.

When I first fell in love, Edward appeared to be a tower of strength and wisdom, yet he was also a vulnerable boy. I looked up to him in one way and wanted to protect and help him in another. I am forever committed to this dual role.

Our actions clash so intensely, we are unable to function as whole human beings at the very moments when this is most required. I can no longer share my insights with Edward; it would hurt him too much. I am full of humility and love, yet have an overriding will to survive. I am playing no game and have no desire to win. I am trying to sustain my equilibrium and to function as well as I can. To give in to demands about which Edward himself is ashamed in his more lucid moments would spell disaster for both of us. How can I help? How?

I must write and photograph surreptitiously. My darkroom is at first a bathroom; later, the damp basement of our larger house. I never feel free to work in sight of the family—neither in New York nor in Woods Hole. All is done in secret. Papers are pushed out of sight if anyone appears.

At Stieglitz's galleries I work at will; Stieglitz liberates my entire being. I send and show him manuscripts and photographs even before they are perfected. He seldom offers suggestions but is always encouraging, leaving me free, exalted. Showing him even the incomplete helps clarify my aims; his not offering criticism, but being loving and trusting, makes me solve problems myself.

8

In April 1940 Germany invaded Norway and Denmark; in May, the Low
Countries and France. Italy entered the war, France collapsed. The Nazi
bombing of Britain began.

Nothing, nothing can compare with the horror of the actuality of war.
Nothing the country offers to Europe—Lend-Lease, a fantasy of our sense of
involvement—makes up for our failure to act earlier in more important ways.
England is still unprepared, but at least it has discarded Chamberlain and
his Munich Pact in favor of the determined and aware Churchill. The French,
British, and United States governments are hostile to the one man who
understands the reality of France's situation: Charles de Gaulle.

Because England gives asylum to De Gaulle after he flees Vichy France,
great hopes are stirred that a new alignment may result. Instead, Churchill
and Roosevelt continue their opposition to him. But De Gaulle's Free French
movement gains momentum; many of his backers join the Resistance. A
number of adherents—threatened by Pétain's compliance with the Nazis—
flock to New York. At once I become involved with their efforts to gain
support for De Gaulle.

Edward, ardently pro–Free French, is apt to lose his temper with anyone
who is not. At a small dinner, he asks Mrs. Roosevelt how Churchill and the
President possibly can be anti–De Gaulle; I tremble. Mrs. Roosevelt states

only what is already evident, that her husband and Churchill are not pro–De Gaulle. I quickly take up De Gaulle's defense in the hope it will fend off Edward's fury. We make no impression whatever on our beloved Mrs. Roosevelt.

Henri Bernstein, the French playwright and a firm defender of De Gaulle—witty, elegant, effective, with a lashing tongue and a profound knowledge of the political situation—left France on June 17, 1940, when Pétain assumed control. He described his departure; we include his account in *Twice A Year*.

This writer was crossing from Bordeaux to England on a little coaling vessel called the *Madura*, a tiny ship with a capacity of one or two hundred passengers, but carrying 2,000, herded like cattle. The trip took three days and four nights. My companions were Frenchmen who, like myself, would have been persecuted in France because of their staunch anti-Nazi attitude.

On the evening of the 18th a group of us, anxious for the B.B.C. news, were crowded around a small radio when suddenly we heard these words, uttered in French, by a superb voice:

"I, General de Gaulle, speaking from London, ask those French officers and soldiers now on British soil or capable of reaching it, I ask those French engineers and workmen now on British soil or capable of reaching it, to communicate with me immediately.

"I ask all Frenchmen who desire to remain free to hear me and to follow me. France has lost a battle; she has not lost the war. A makeshift government may have capitulated, giving way to panic, forgetting honor, delivering its country into slavery. Yet nothing is lost because this war is a world war. There are immense forces in the universe as yet unleashed.

"These forces will crush the enemy. When they do, France must be present at the victory. This is my only goal. This is why I ask my compatriots wherever they may be to unite with me in action, in sacrifice and in hope.

"The flame of French resistance burns strong as ever."

These lines will be recited by our schoolboys as long as there is a French language.

I first met Bernstein at a weekly luncheon given at the Ritz by Mauricio Hochschild, a "tin king" from Bolivia. Until the outbreak of war, each lady at the luncheons had received an orchid, pinned to her napkin. After hostilities broke out a gardenia was substituted, with apologies.

The next time I saw Bernstein, he scolded me for not having invited him to our home. To my amazement, this man who I assumed knew and was known by everyone, declared, "Didn't you realize I'm lonely?" We quickly discovered our mutual interest in De Gaulle and worked together ardently.

He made many speeches in favor of the General, often asking me to help him with their final editing. He had a keen sense of style but, in spite of his fluent English, he wasn't certain about every turn of phrase.

Somehow he had been able to salvage his beloved paintings. On the walls of his suite at the Waldorf hung exquisite French masterpieces, including a fine portrait of him as a child by Manet and a unique collection of Constantin Guys. He told me the work of all great contemporary French painters was overvalued.

André Geraud—who signs his writing "Pertinax"—is a most distinguished French journalist; his articles are outstanding and of great historical importance. We, too, work together for the Free French and become fast friends. He confesses that if his assignments in Paris hadn't included going to the Quai d'Orsay each day to read the official documents there, he would gladly have paid for the privilege of doing so.

An American Place remains of vital importance to me. I find the various antitotalitarian organizations that proliferate in New York, local social work committees, and the Civil Liberties Union face greater responsibilities than ever. My schedule—including publication of *Twice A Year*—curiously never feels heavy. There is no strain if one is youthful and concerned. I am convinced that, although primarily intent upon the family, I must go on devoting time and energy to those in constant danger and need.

Twice A Year's contents continue the trend established in the first issues. Although the publication has aimed chiefly at printing current material ignored by most other journals, we sense that much from the past can throw added light on events today. To our self-critical eyes, Number V–VI represents *Twice A Year* at its most varied, human, and stimulating.

Henry Miller, among the first expatriate authors to whom we wrote while planning *Twice A Year*, had sent many manuscripts and we corresponded voluminously. His *Tropic of Cancer* and *Tropic of Capricorn* both had been forbidden entry into the United States because of their alleged obscenity. Anaïs Nin, one of his greatest admirers, often spoke of him to me, just as he had written of her with admiration. Until 1940 he insisted on staying in Europe, but then—from Greece—I received an SOS cable announcing his desire to return to the United States and asking for funds; I sent a check at once. Soon after his arrival, he came to see me.

I was taken aback; from his writing I had expected a sensual-looking, rather ferocious man. Instead, standing before me was a modest and proper figure, resembling a serious, conventional preacher. Our greetings were genuinely warm and I was happy he had escaped from war-torn Europe. After an hour or so he apologetically explained he had promised to attend a gathering but would return as soon as possible. He reappeared and looked at me, wide-eyed. "A most disagreeable incident occurred. Imagine: a woman used four-letter words when speaking to me. It was appalling!" Later I took him to An American Place and introduced him to Stieglitz.

From a Miller letter to me, written soon after his return to America:

I am surprised and pleased thus far to see how much real sympathy and understanding the few people who count have shown me. This is in itself the greatest sustenance. When I wrote [my] books I knew full well what I was up against. In a way, I have succeeded far beyond all expectation. The real obstacle lies deep and the process of overcoming the difficulties which stand in the way of recognition is a slow one, I believe.

Perhaps the most valuable service people can render me is simply to keep on telling the public that my work is of value—not necessarily ramming it down their throats. I believe that we come to everything we desire or need in time—precisely when we are ready for it, not before. My time may lie further in the future than most writers. It may be my fate. I see the law, public opinion, taste, etc. as a reflection of the true inner condition of a people. I don't believe in bucking my head against a stone wall. Less and less do I care about altering things. I am working on myself more and more. Not that I am trying to adjust myself to conditions which are bad—or even good—but that more and more I feel like accepting full responsibility for my actions. I believe that nothing I have done has been in vain, nor will it be overlooked. Really, as I see it now, the primary thing is that I should be able to continue to work. There will always be some place in the world to have my books published. And those who want to read me will always find the way to get my work. For the present it looks as if I may be taken care of financially—it is not definite yet, but it looks promising. And even if it fails, I shall not perish. I am destined to go on, I know it.

My role is simple and large—it is *to love*. And I think, in expressing myself, that is what I am doing. I am learning to accept everything—and that is the way to love. Hatred cripples and paralyzes. And playing a role is restrictive too. I am working towards greater liberation always, and in doing so I find I become more indulgent, more tolerant, more forgiving. My emotional reactions are spontaneous and erratic, as they should be. I don't flare up emotionally on principle. If I seem irritated at times it is a passing thing. Deep down I am confident and tranquil—and fairly joyous. The question of censorship is more a nuisance than a grief. The law is not my enemy—it is the stupidity and narrow-mindedness of people. I hold the people responsible for the laws which harass them or make life easier for them.

I am going through a very trying period and it is doing me good. It is a supreme test for me—and I relish it, however painful. I have caused a lot of suffering to others in my efforts to liberate myself. Now

I *am* liberated I want to give, to help, to bring peace and joy to others. Whatever happens later, in the way of fame, success, money, means very little to me. If I can keep my head above water and do what I feel necessary that is all I ask. So you see, I am really quite well off—rich, you might say. Remember that!

After a meeting of writers and editors in New York, Miller wrote me:

What I saw the other night was the artist versus the critics. It wasn't at all muddled or confused to me. On the contrary, extraordinarily clear— lucid. But anybody would get off the track in an atmosphere of that sort. What happened there I've seen happen everywhere—it's inevitable. And the upshot is nil. I suppose the only thing is for you to keep the whip hand over us all. I mean it. After all, a magazine must represent what the editor believes in. If you try to be impartial you make a mess of it. The ones you like will gravitate towards you—and the others away from you. Everything is personal. We shouldn't try too hard to be fair— only be what we are, maybe. . . .

This New York crowd, this gang of intellectuals, leaves me utterly cold. I have no use for them. [They're] barren and sterile and ugly. Words, Words. Nobody gives a damn about the man, about what he's *trying* to say. And for me all that matters is the man. I don't live with theories. The country is hollowed out with theories. . . .

By the way, I can't talk on the telephone. I seldom use one. I don't like the instrument. I must watch the person speaking else I lose interest.

After an apology for not having had time to come to An American Place, Miller wrote:

I feel worse not having run in to see Stieglitz. I hope he will forgive me. If it's any consolation, tell him I've definitely decided to open the book on America by paying my long-deferred tribute to him—and Marin. I find that the only worthwhile people in this country whom I meet are either seventy or over . . . or else youngsters from 15 to 22!!! But the old ones interest me more. They are *younger*, so to speak.

I am given the manuscript of a play, brilliantly conceived, with drawings for stage sets, color plates, and a score, written, illustrated, and composed by the talented young mime Angna Enters. The play, *Love Possessed Juana*, takes place in the Inquisition Spain of Ferdinand and Isabella; it concerns the struggle of their daughter, the Infanta Juana, for love and justice as opposed to the tyranny and hypocrisy of that dark age in Spain.

I first saw Angna Enters's recitals in the twenties, shortly after moving to New York; I had been impressed by her special genius as a mime, but also by her painting and writing. *Twice A Year* has included material from her journals, and several of her essays.

Since no one in New York will produce her play, I decide to publish it as a book under the imprint of what I call Twice A Year Press. Preceding the text is a quotation from Leonardo da Vinci: "It is better to resist at the beginning than at the end." The dedication reads: ". . . To the heroic people of Republican Spain who, defenceless, oppressed, and starving, fought and will fight again for the liberation of the human spirit."

A chain reaction begins. A special section on Franz Kafka for *Twice A Year* becomes too extensive. I decide to publish it as another Twice A Year Press volume, *A Franz Kafka Miscellany*. During the same period John Beecher, a descendant of Lyman and Henry Ward Beecher and of Harriet Beecher Stowe, walks into An American Place to see me with *Two Talks to the American People* under his arm. He has named the double manuscript *And I Will Be Heard*. The title is taken from a statement by the abolitionist William Lloyd Garrison: "I am in earnest—I will not equivocate—I will not excuse—I will not retreat a single inch—and I will be heard." The *Talks* are not great poetry but their integrity merits publication. They are issued as another Twice A Year Press volume, as is a long poem by Beecher, *Here I Stand*.

William Carlos Williams writes a generous letter:

The two copies of Twice A Year have arrived and are being read by the whole family. I read my own piece first, of course, looked at the pictures which are outstanding, glanced at the Anaïs Nin, a writer whom I have enjoyed, and then turned to the John Beecher pamphlet.

The publication of such works is very necessary. No matter what may be their effect as works of art, and they have a place there too, their voicing of the public mind is their great virtue. This is a man who speaks for the conscience of the people. It is a special sort of writing whose basic honesty, lack of pretence and posturing is American at the foundations. I think he will be heard. Let him keep on pounding it out, he comes of a distinguished family and is carrying on a family tradition that is the backbone of our beliefs. I'm all for him. I'm glad you gave him your assistance to allow him to be heard.

From the side of poetic structure his style is rather lean—which is, of course, as he intends it. What could a poet learn from his form? I am wondering. At least the man speaks our language. He uses colloquial turns of phrase for a sort of effect he wants to achieve. Well, observation, information and wit are the essence of such a style. Its force comes from the acuity of the vision and the sharpness of statement, the freshness of the phrasing, the paragraphing for dramatic effect in the best sense, the firmness of the sentences. I say all this because I presume this is a young man. I hope his powerful convictions and belief in the power of the spoken and written word will not disdain what the art of writing may teach. Let him labor with the words a while and he will gain even more force than he has now. I wish him luck.

Number VII is something of an adventure for us. During conversations with Beecher he shows me poems by his six-year-old daughter, who has been ill. It happens that I have been writing down what our own children, Nancy and Andrew, tell me each evening. I call their spontaneous outpourings "Dark Century in Never World." The curiously wild beauty of the child's imagination enchants me. We print a sequence of writing by the young.

The rest of the issue is as usual eclectic, broad in sweep and, in view of its wartime background, timely.

A group of articulate liberals—educators and writers—often gather in the evenings and invite me to join them. Our main topic of discussion, against the background of the dire events in Europe, is how to awaken Americans to take more effective action against Nazism. For this purpose the Union for Democratic Action is formed. The eminent Reinhold Niebuhr of Union Theological Seminary is elected chairman. From his past position, I expected him to be antiwar. Now he, like the rest of us, has decided the United States must fight the Nazis. I am asked to be a member of the board of directors. James Loeb, young, active, liberal, is chosen to run the U.D.A. Other ardent and vocal non-Communist intellectuals who play decisive roles in its activities include Louis Fischer, Robert Bendiner, George Counts, Mark Starr, and John L. Childs.

Finally American public opinion is aroused by Germany's occupation of Denmark and invasion of Norway, by its invasion of the Low Countries and France, and by Dunkirk; Roosevelt's third term is assured. But the U.D.A. program consists not only of support for the Allies; it also seeks to make certain that no American reactionaries will succeed in curtailing the rights of labor in the name of the war effort; civil liberties might be endangered in the name of patriotism. Thus our slogan: a two-front fight for democracy.

At an early U.D.A. board meeting I was introduced to Louis Fischer, who sat next to me. His articles, which I had read with admiration, were invariably brilliant, succinctly phrased, simple, and wise. Carefully documented, they revealed a disciplined sympathy for revolution-weary Europe. Fischer himself looked somber and withdrawn. Glancing at him, I noted his drooping eyes, suggestive of a mysterious person. He fascinated me. I kept looking forward to his analysis of the problems we discussed as the meeting progressed.

During a recess we discovered that each of us was born in Philadelphia. In a roughly humorous way, he attacked me. Sharply: "Where did you live when you were growing up?" "2317 North Broad Street." He regarded me with an at once serious yet faintly amused stare. L.F. (again sharply): "That was two doors from the synagogue I walked to every week—miles from South Philadelphia, where I lived. You were right there, right where I was walking, and you never threw me a nickel. Didn't you know how far I had to walk?" He was teasing, but I felt his deep awareness of his boyhood poverty. "I didn't know you were there," I said lightly, to hide my compassion, and my surprise at the turn our conversation had taken. As he repeated his accusation relentlessly, I felt like a naughty child.

Circumstances throw us together often. A friendship develops; Fischer becomes an important figure in my life, even though I find him not at all mysterious. But I delight in his intelligence and wild humor.

We lunch, walk in the park, discuss politics—everything. He loves to come to our house. Friends say it makes him secure to feel at home there. He wants to meet everybody; I sense an eagerness he tries to disguise behind his drooping eyes. He is obsessively inquisitive and will do anything to satisfy his curiosity; I am precisely the same. Our desire to find out is at the root of our passion for writing. We go to great lengths to explore the fields that interest us and then want to tell about them, to share them. Louis begs me to have gatherings, dinners; he even tells me whom to invite.

He speaks often about being poor as a child; of his concern for wiping out poverty everywhere, in view of the world's plenty. "We had no electricity at home, nor running water. Until I was seventeen, I never lived in a heated house. Our rooms were mere cubicles. We were forced to move constantly— the rent was always too high."

I visualize Louis, a serious child, doing his lessons by the light of kerosene lamps, while I was ignorant of hardship in my privileged neighborhood. His early interest in Russia becomes totally understandable. "One night I stood on a hill; there were no lights as far as the eye could see. At which point I decided to work for the development of that great sleeping country. Buildings, homes—everything devoid of light—moved me. I had to become involved."

He tells me how, while still at school, he planned to be a teacher in order to earn his living. "I bought a canoe and went out in it so I could get some fresh air. I paddled along the Schuylkill River and I might have run into you one of those days."

The way in which Fischer educated himself, constantly in search of knowledge; his quick success as a writer for the best liberal journals; and his subsequent ability to travel abroad and report, while still quite young, impress and inspire. During his first trip to Europe, in 1918, Zeppelins were hovering over London, the Allies were not yet victorious, and lines of women in black stood along the sidewalks. "It was all very beautiful but sad. I didn't understand much of what I saw."

The U.D.A. board meets regularly, has public dinners, and issues statements to gain support for its program. It is formally established in the spring of 1941.

Meanwhile, American Communists and their sympathizers are almost unanimously against the war effort. Their foremost interest is Russia. But then on June 22, 1941, like a thunderbolt, Germany invades Russia. The "imperialist war"—to Communist sympathizers—suddenly changes into something quite different. The vocabulary of the Communist Party alters overnight, but most alarming is the German Army's penetration deep into Russia. Italy and Britain struggle back and forth in North Africa, then in December comes—for Americans—the greatest blow of all: Pearl Harbor.

The entire rhythm of life changes; the nation seems united as never before. Everyone becomes involved in the war effort, sons are drafted, husbands and fathers go off to serve. Everywhere fear of death, awareness of death. Edward, who is overage, enlists. He is fit and feels he has a duty to perform. He joins the Navy, is sent to Columbia University to be trained for Military Government of Occupied Territory. I support and admire him, and hide my fear for his safety. We try to keep the children from being too unsettled by events, but I doubt if anyone of any intelligence is ever quite the same again.

At home everyone copes not only with the emotional strain of war but also with such seemingly insignificant matters as gas and food rationing; we participate in air-raid drills and we dim lights during "brown-outs." I attend a Red Cross class around the corner. During the summer grating contrasts hold my attention: commando boats and idle sailboats; soldiers drilling and tennis games; uniforms and smart, soft summer clothes; troop trains and pleasure trains; army trucks and speeding roadsters; Russian war films and Rita Hayworth; khaki tents and flamboyant gardens; hardship elsewhere and our overfull bakeshops; radio war news and vulgar commercials.

I help at a U.S.O. center near Woods Hole, to make life a little more pleasant for the military. To my amazement the soldiers, who come from Texas and doubtless have never known a Jew, are fiercely anti-Semitic. The noisy atmosphere in the rooms and the constant movement make it impossible to argue any point. Hostile remarks are hurled at the air, about no one in particular, but their repetitive ugliness gives a clear indication of how widespread prejudice is throughout the nation. Discrimination against Negroes in the armed services is one of the most shocking flaws in American democracy.

Summer after summer there are race riots, symbols of our largest minority's dissatisfaction with its lot. To my relief, the leaders of the organizations in which I am involved in New York join forces, the most courageous and concerned pooling their efforts to see if we cannot work out an overall plan to transform the destructive forces so regularly let loose.

A cluster of incidents involving Negroes comes to mind. An Urban League meeting held for the first time at our apartment in the 1920s, when I had to instruct the doorman to show the members to the front elevator. The many times I have traveled by train out of the tunnel from Grand Central Terminal through the shocking area of Harlem close to Park Avenue: the unloved properties, ugly streets, deafening roar of elevated cars crashing close to bedroom windows; no greenery except an occasional half-alive plant on a window sill; no beauty—only sorrow and pollution.

Going alone to meetings, or to speak in Harlem, half-frightened, ashamed of my fear. A group of young Negroes coming to see me about a theater and sitting on the sofa, looking at me blankly, asking, "Why do they hate us so? Why?" The many reports I have seen prepared, and have prepared myself; the work with well-meaning groups to change inhuman conditions. Yet the blight on our collective conscience has not gone away.

The newly formed City-Wide Citizens' Committee for Harlem becomes one of the most influential clearinghouses in New York for combating racial discrimination at a local level. I am asked to join its board of directors. Our first step is to subdivide into working committees, each of which handles a separate issue: education and recreation, housing, health and hospitals, employment, crime and delinquency.

One of the most difficult situations to correct is the attitude of the press toward the Negro; there are few black reporters. In almost all cases, if a Negro is said to have committed a murder, the account states—with or without proof—that a colored person is involved. No paper declares a "white" man has killed someone. Almost all stories are slanted against Negroes. Accounts of positive accomplishments are rarely given.

Little is known about the number of Negroes employed in stores, hospitals, schools; about how many more are qualified to fill skilled positions that are never offered. We make lists of Negro nurses working in hospitals and health centers; only nineteen Negro doctors serve in city institutions. There are virtually no Negro bank officials, department store executives, school administrators. In sports, major league baseball teams are loath to use Negroes; we campaign ardently for Jackie Robinson.

If a hearing of a court case is held at which a Negro is inadequately represented, we see that the best possible lawyer is called in. We attempt to persuade schools to give up outmoded textbooks that portray the Negro in the most ignominious fashion.

We fight against all infringements of civil rights. Negroes cannot stay at "white" hotels, attend downtown theaters, or eat in "white" restaurants. A seemingly small matter, but one that is resented: the word "negro," spelled with a small "n," is demeaning, while "nigger" is barely out of use even in the North. We encourage the press to refer to the colored peoples of America as Negroes with a capital "N." The amount of energy spent on this battle is incredible.

As we achieve positive results, I consider it vital that we announce them to the general public in order to gain increased recognition and support for the committee's work. I have learned that a news story must be followed up at once by another on the same subject or it makes little impression; I have noted, too, that four related ideas presented to the press in one day will be covered in only a single article. Why not create a carefully planned series of meetings to be known as "City-Wide Harlem Week"? On Monday, stress housing; on Tuesday, hospitals; on Wednesday, delinquency; and so on. In this way we can get seven times more publicity than if we send out only one report detailing too many subjects.

As a member of the press subcommittee, I ask prominent editors and publishers to change their writers' careless vocabulary, the unsympathetic approach of their articles, and their generally superior attitude toward the Negro. The response is surprisingly warm and encouraging, whenever I appear in person to argue in behalf of our beliefs. I think we should cultivate heads of newspapers and magazines more intensely—ask them to our meetings and present them with our facts as frequently as possible.

I offer my suggestions in some detail. The committee's reaction is immediate; it appoints me chairman of what we call "City-Wide Harlem Week." As I leave the room, I realize I have never before sent out sensational and complex releases that will catch the attention of all newspapers and surely be printed. I telephone a noted public relations expert, a friend whom I see often in connection with "good works." He generously invites me to his office.

I explain my problem, trembling, feeling like an utter amateur. The P.R. expert: "Dorothy, my dear, let me give you a piece of advice. In my job—let's say I'm asked to promote religion. The last thing I would do is to launch a huge campaign about it; nobody would listen. My first task would be to find some big soap company that would start an enormous promotion of its product. Make the whole country conscious of it. The next project would be to announce that 'Cleanliness is next to Godliness.' I would try to remind the entire country that soap is related to cleanliness; that unless you're clean, you can't be next to God. So to arouse your audience to City-Wide Harlem Week, follow the same formula—something akin to 'Soap, cleanliness, Godliness.'" I laugh but am forced to ask, "What on earth am I to do?" He pushes a buzzer. A secretary enters with a pad and sits next to me.

P.R. friend: "Dorothy, please dictate to Miss Smith what you want to accomplish." I shyly turn to her and describe the work of the committee and my proposals for the special week. Mr. P.R. repeats my ideas back to me, developing some of them most intelligently and sympathetically. Miss Smith writes busily as we speak, then leaves.

Our conversation continues; I go on spouting ideas. Five minutes later, a knock at the door; the secretary reenters. She has typed out on official stationery what we have said. I've given only the outline of the various subjects and points I wish to stress, but she has developed them briefly and eloquently.

Mr. P.R.: "How do you like it?" D.N.: "I'm flabbergasted. It's excellent. You mean, if this goes out to the press, it's guaranteed to make editors pay attention? You know I want to do this every day for a week—not just this once."

Mr. P.R.: "Now you know how to do it."

———

Thus begins my education in "public relations" for good causes. The requirements are clear: headings must be strong, proposals convincing, text short, decisive, to the point. I can never express my thanks sufficiently for the assistance I have received.

The press prints our daily releases. We arrange meetings to which civic leaders and reporters are invited. Each subject to be covered is singled out for special articles. Our program represents a clear blueprint for the many reforms we favor. The strategy works; many of our suggestions are acted upon by city departments.

John Beecher telephones me just as I'm calling newspaper editors. He tells me frantically that the national Fair Employment Practices Committee, for which he works, is to be curtailed, unless enough money can be appropriated within the next few days. He pleads with me to put pressure on as many newspapers as I can, so they will inform the public.

It is Thursday afternoon; I realize that any nonsensational news story given to a paper so late in the week has little chance of being featured during the weekend. I haven't phoned the *New York Post* or *PM* to plead my case for better coverage of events involving Negroes, because I felt they were doing an adequate job. Now, however, I decide to call Dorothy Schiff Backer —owner and publisher of the *Post*, whom I know and admire—just because I didn't approach her recently. We have worked together on committees at the Women's City Club; I sense she'll be sympathetic about the F.E.P.C. To my relief, she promises to give publicity to its plight, then says she has heard I'm doing a good job in the antidiscrimination field. Will I come for lunch and talk about it? This chance occurrence again changes the focus of my life.

I lunch with Dorothy; Ted Thackrey, the *Post*'s new editor; and Ed Flynn, the city editor. They ask me many questions. I explain the background of City-Wide Harlem Week and my attempts to change the attitude of the press. "It may interest you that I didn't come to see you during my campaign because I thought you were doing an admirable job. But now that I'm here, I could go on forever describing how matters could be improved." Thackrey asks direct questions which I answer with enthusiasm. The intensity of his and Dorothy's interest amazes and pleases me.

I haven't been home more than half an hour when the phone rings.

Ted Thackrey: "How would you like to write for us?" I'm nonplussed. "But I've had no newspaper experience." Thackrey: "But you write. You edit a publication. And you know your subject thoroughly. I'm sure you can do a good job. When can you come down to see me? How about nine-thirty tomorrow morning? Bring a list of articles you think would be of interest and we'll see how to proceed."

Astonishing! To be paid for what I do for love, and at the same time reach a large public, seems miraculous. I can use the money I earn for my parents, *Twice A Year*, An American Place, and writers and artists in need.

Immediately I make lists on long sheets of white paper. They start with Roman numeral I and have subheadings A, B, C ,D, etc. The roman numerals stand for the categories I wish to cover; the letters, for specific articles. By the time I reach Z, I say to myself, Thackrey will think me mad. I could list articles for a year at least, without having a new thought.

At 9:30 sharp, I show my penciled notes to Thackrey. He smiles. "This is wonderful. When can you start?" "Any time. I can easily fit writing articles for you into my daily schedule. I'm concerned with their subject matter all day anyway and constantly follow them." Thackrey: "Good."

I tell Edward of the exciting offer; he looks at me sternly and says, "You'll make a fool of yourself."

I reply lamely, "I know I've never done newspaper work, but I can try. If I fail, all right. I'm willing to take the chance."

Edward's fears are incomprehensible to me. Why should I make a fool of myself? If I do a poor job, I'll just stop. I'm tremendously stimulated by the idea of writing for the *Post*; I agree with its policies. The articles I have suggested would cover positive accomplishments, not just negative practices. No other member of the staff or any other newspaper is treating the particular aspects I hope to emphasize. I accept Thackrey's offer.

I'm not certain how to compose an article for a newspaper, but the *Post* editors are extraordinarily kind and helpful. They say to give my notes for the first article to a rewrite man, who will assist me. I have no idea what this means, but tell the facts to the sympathetic person assigned to me; he types them. I amend any errors, also passages I would express differently, and hand back the corrected pages. He retypes them and shows me the final draft. I approve it; he tells me it is excellent. He asks what by-line I have chosen. I don't know what he means but learn it signifies simply the signature I want to use.

The following morning an editor calls to congratulate me. He says my piece is on page three, a most desirable location.

My second article is also praised, which reassures me. The next few pieces are written in the same way: I obtain a story, take it to the office, tell it to the rewrite man; he types it, I correct it; he retypes it and it is finished. After a few days he says, "Now you're on your own." So this is what a rewrite man does. Bless him!

A few months later the managing editor, Paul Tierney, calls me to his office. "How would you like to do a column?" "A column? What's the difference between the feature articles I've been doing—no one ever tells me what to write—and a column?" Tierney: "You don't have to quote someone else as the authority for your story." I burst out laughing. "You mean I can save all that time finding someone well known to be the source of a story I have thoroughly researched anyway?" He smiles and asks, "What shall we call the column?" "I haven't the faintest idea." After a number of tries, he suggests, "A World to Live In," which I find excellent.

My first column rather frightens me: I must now take full responsibility for what I write. But after I gain confidence, it's a relief to be on my own. The scope of my subject matter greatly expands.

Ignazio Silone writes a touching note in French. He encloses a pressed green leaf:

Dear Dorothy Norman,

In recent days I have often thought of you; I have often had need to think of you; the very fact that you exist does me good. Oh, how tired I sometimes feel! In recent weeks the greater part of my day has been spent in useless efforts in behalf of my friends, more frequently, in behalf of people whom I have never met, in France, Lisbon or even here in internment camps in Switzerland; if only they were of some help. There is nothing in the world I hate more than government offices, than asking personal favors of indifferent strangers; as I leave the office I always feel like a whipped dog. Such is my life of the moment. If only it were of some help. Now then you will understand, Dear Dorothy Norman, American I have never met, why I so often think of you; but I imagine that you are a healthy, gay, optimistic young woman; perhaps even a beautiful one; in short, a happy person; oh, what a pity, Dorothy Norman, that you do not have need of me to visit the offices for you! Since I so often think of you I should at least write to you, but that, dear friend, is in fact my greatest problem: I was born in a little village, and in our village friends do not write to one another, friends talk. It is not difficult to see friends, you have only to sit on your doorstep and wait for them to pass by your house. In our village we write only to enemies and to government offices, which are enemies too; you can therefore understand my reluctance, my remissness, the fact that I write to you so infrequently. I have not been taught how to write to friends, that is the reason. What a pity, Dorothy Norman, that you live so far away, and that I cannot ask you to wait for me at your doorway, so that we might take a little walk together. And besides to write you in a tongue that is not my own and which, not being your own as well, adds to my difficulties in writing. What is more, I do not make friends easily. If this letter should seem too personal, Dorothy Norman, lay it to the account of a mind overwrought by daily life.

Yours

I. Silone

British-born Ivy Low Litvinov comes to New York to escape the official life of Washington. While still quite young, she fell in love with Maxim Litvinov, now Russia's Ambassador to the United States. Her early lack of interest in politics scarcely prepared her for the reality of Soviet Communism. Whenever Russia wishes to be friendly to the West, it makes use of Litvinov. Otherwise he is intermittently put on the shelf.

Louis Fischer is going away and asks me to be especially kind to Mrs. Litvinov during her stay in New York, to see that she meets interesting people—she is starved for them. Joseph Freeman, ex-editor of *New Masses*, has been to Russia and knows the Litvinovs well. Joe, a warm, sincere man, a poet at heart, was an early admirer of Communist ideals but one of the first American sympathizers to speak out against Communist actions. He couldn't countenance, among other atrocities, the purges or the transporting of Russian Trotskyites to Siberia.

Joe kindly invites me to his apartment to meet Mrs. Litvinov. She is large, in no way prepossessing, but unexpectedly humorous. Something decidedly aloof, impersonal, and British about her puts me off at first. I cannot find her; I stare, trying to make contact; she looks back at me icily.

She tells of being asked how she feels about American Communists; her reply: "Alas, I have never met one." She then abruptly asks if I am interested in Basic English, a passion of hers. It isn't one of mine, but I say, "Yes, it interests me"—a lame reply that seems only to widen the gulf between us. I feel I am letting Joe and Louis down.

I cannot remember ever having been so desolate at a first meeting with anyone I admire. I have read her writing and respect it greatly, as I do both her political position and that of her husband. Why is everything going so wrong? I suppose I'm trying too hard to be pleasant rather than relaxed. I can think of nothing to say, but before leaving, I make one final effort: perhaps Mrs. Litvinov would enjoy seeing An American Place and Alfred Stieglitz? We make an appointment.

She and Stieglitz like each other at once; the atmosphere is warm and the ice between her and myself is broken. She writes to me almost immediately on her return to Washington:

I somehow don't think it is necessary for people to give signs. But then I am a person who is so involuntarily expressive most of the time, and you are exactly the opposite. I don't know you, of course, but I feel that everybody should be him or herself to the n-th degree, for that is what will in the end most deeply suit them and every one else. I don't think we must try. I think if you "trusted" me at once, which is the most wonderful thing, then that should have been quite all-sufficient for us to be very happy before. But I think you spoilt (almost) everything, by wanting to "do" something about it too soon. I should have "got" you much quicker if you hadn't started handing yourself out. (And you know you can't do it!) Now, by seeing you with Stieglitz, and him with you, and somehow the way you went to the typewriter, I am recovering from the bludgeoning, and on my slow way to finding out something about you.

In the train on the way home I saw your column for the first time, about adopting, or perhaps just succouring, negro children as well as white. I thought there were some simple straight things in it. Things look blacker now for the negro than for many years, it seems to me, and the obstacles in the way of doing anything seem something ferocious. But we should believe more in *writing*, if we are writers, I think. I mean we (and I mean *me*) should believe that if there is something we want to say, the way is just in writing better. I get so easily discouraged and thinking things impossible. But writing is still the great weapon, partly especially now when there is so very little real writing, and partly it is in danger of being crowded out of the armory because there is such a lot of mediocre writing. But I must believe a great deal more than I have yet been able to.

I love Alfred Stieglitz.

When I give Ivy copies of *Twice A Year*, I'm surprised that she is enthusiastic about them, except for Number VII, which includes children's work. She writes:

I'm very glad you read [my] "M. Mystery" [*Moscow Mystery*] which I think quite a pleasing little book and I did take quite a lot of trouble writing the preface (which by the way I had to force myself to do, so do I hate writing anything in the form of an apologia). Of course this is quite an old book, and written in a special convention. My next will, I hope, have more of myself in it. . . .

So help me if I will read poetry that doesn't rhyme, yours or anyone else's. Nor, ever again, will I be lured into writing letters about t. good, t. beautiful, t. true, & may t. lord do so unto me and more also if ever again I take t. word "creative" into my mouth. I suppose I hate t. wicked, vulgar commercial age, but when I read cultured "affirmations"

I seem to long for the atmosphere of a drug-store counter. Glad to have TWICE A YEAR. . . .

The Walden School adolescent stuff is nauseating like all adolescents when encouraged to express their beastly little selves and be creative, goddam them. But the little child's poem about death is marvellous.

Well, my grouch is over. I hope you will be better. This ought to make you.

A few weeks later, another note:

Just to say that I shall be in N.Y. over the weekend and shall not dare to try to see any of my few friends, bec. I shall have a strange and jealous creature with me who is irritated at the idea of anything exotic in my life—which for him are all contacts that do not relate directly to him. But I will just call you up for a "sign."

Surely there can be no "crime" in giving signs involuntarily, nor will I plead guilty to the crime of not "quite" understanding. That's involuntary too. Dear Dorothy, the word "crime" occurs in your letter twice, also "guilty." You say: "Don't feel oppressed" (don't worry, I never do!). Of course (I think it is of course) most of us are guilt-haunted, but I suppose health consists in knowing what a sick feeling this is and therefore, somehow, compounding with it. It is the sick reformer and the sane artist in us trying to keep a balance. The artist loves what is, i.e. life. The reformer, poor tyke, wants to "mould it closer to his heart's desire." His poor miserable heart! And so we get the farce of "progressive" schools, the schoolmarm's dream of making everyone nice and timid and suburban like herself. ". . . As if we all need the rest of the world to be like ourselves" is too marvelous a piece of unconscious analysis! I am all the time uneasily skipping over aeons of time if I see a marvellous film like "Emperor Jones," when all these frightening wild people will be nice and "developed" and I can dare to think about them. Also vaguely dismissing all the things I don't like, like radio-commercials, and technicolor and war and good works, by imagining just a hop, skip and a jump into the idyllic future entirely shaped by my views. As I get older, however, some of the things I wanted to "abolish" have somehow gone into solution, and I am reconciled to their presence, in fact I have allowed them into my own bloodstream, like comic-strips and street-cars and other people playing billiards and city waste-lots and heaps of other things that used to worry me. Some years ago I drove my loved ones nearly crazy by talking about "manifestations of life." As *everything* comes under that heading, then everything is lovable. I went about quite ecstatic for weeks (to the fury of my daughter, who wanted to know "so-what").

Ivy comes to our house and regales me with an account of her mother's most ardent wish during her youth: that she marry a dentist and have him extract all her teeth, thereby saving her much trouble for life and enormous expense.

She is interested in English literature rather than Russian, with a special feeling for Jane Austen. She pleads with me to read the books of Harriet Martineau—a feminist—and is delighted by my success in finding copies of her volumes. We laugh a great deal and I am suddenly happy with her.

Andrew comes home from school while Ivy is having tea with me. I introduce them and they find an immediate bond. How this happens I cannot explain, but before I know it, they discuss her giving him piano lessons. Their time together is serious, glorious, hilarious.

Arthur Upham Pope's book on Maxim Litvinov has been sent to me to review. Curiously, Ivy has not seen a copy, nor did she read the text in manuscript. I hand the volume to her; she turns the pages and roars with laughter, takes out a pencil and scrawls on page after page.

The book's dedication reads:

> *To the memory of*
> William Wendt
> Richard Montague
> Herman Lathrop Tucker

to which Ivy adds:

> Abraham Lincoln
> Karl Marx
> and the Ziegfeld Follies

Pope writes, "After taking that name, Litvinov never really changed it. When later he became an English subject, he was naturalized as Litvinov." Ivy underlines "English subject"; her comment: "He never became one."

Pope: "His friends knew him to be gentle and amiable, and mamas with daughters to marry off looked on him with a friendly eye as a most eligible bachelor." Ivy: "Rubbish. He didn't know any people like that."

Pope: "Through Leeper, Litvinov got to know Ivy Low, a girl whom he had met in 1914 at a house party. . . ." Ivy: "Untrue."

Pope's paragraph: "When Ivy was thirteen she went to live with one of her uncles and promptly announced that she also was going to be a journalist. . . . Only two years later she began publishing. . . ."

Ivy's marginal note: "At age 15!"

Henry Miller's promised "Stieglitz and Marin"—in a special section in *Twice A Year* on Stieglitz—asks the simple question:

> What answer is there to make to a man who says, "I believe. I love. I cherish." . . . Stieglitz and Marin . . . are constantly fecundating each other, nourishing each other, inspiring each other. There is no more glorious wedlock known to man than this marriage of kindred spirits. Everything they touch becomes ennobled. There is no taint anywhere. We reach with them the realm of pure spirit.

Soon after Number X–XI appeared, I ran into a scientist at Woods Hole who had won a Nobel Prize but, being Jewish, had had to flee Nazi Germany. He was now working at the Marine Biological Laboratory. We greeted each other warmly; he had told me only recently how much he admired Waldo Frank when they met at our home in New York. Now he pulled me aside and whispered nervously, "How I wish Jews would stay out of politics when they go to foreign countries. It is bound to lead to greater difficulty for Jews everywhere." He added, critically, "I do wish Mr. Frank had not spoken up in Argentina against Perón and gotten into trouble. This will reflect badly on Jews everywhere." I was so shocked I could only reply, "Suppose no one from abroad had spoken up for you? Your problem was and is our problem. The fate of anti-Peronists is our fate. I really cannot share your opinion." I sadly walked away.

9

Since the thirties, I have followed news about India's struggle for independence with mounting sympathy. The repeated imprisonments of Gandhi, Nehru, and thousands of colleagues for their nonviolent civil disobedience campaign against colonial rule seemed cruel and ironic, in view of Britain's traditional commitment to civil liberties at home.

By 1941 Louis Fischer was following the Indian situation closely. He introduced me to J. J. Singh, a tall Mephistophelian-looking Indian businessman who had just formed the India League of America, hoping to make people more aware of the Indian situation. He asked me to be on the League's board—Louis and Roger Baldwin were already members. I joined it with enthusiasm. Pearl Buck's husband, the publisher Richard Walsh, was president; both were extremely active on the board. We held regular meetings and printed instructive reports for the public, press, and radio.

Throughout the forties, whenever private emissaries from India came to New York to plead their country's cause, someone was certain to telephone from the India League. Because Edward and I had a house in town and Pearl Buck lived in the country, I was chosen to receive one spokesman after another. I did this with a sense of commitment.

Louis Fischer, who went to India in 1942 and wrote *A Week with Gandhi*, asks me to lunch with Nehru's nieces, Chandralehka and Nayantara

Pandit, on their arrival in New York. They are on their way to Wellesley College—Lehka as a recipient of a Mei-ling Soong scholarship. Courageous, like the rest of the family, she has been jailed for activities in behalf of independence, as has her uncle, Jawaharlal Nehru, her parents, Vijaya Lakshmi and Ranjit Pandit, and other relatives.

Fischer also introduces me to Mai-mai Sze, an extremely handsome young Chinese woman who is brilliant, witty, and talented. Her East-West column in the *Post* has attracted my attention. Not only eloquent, it expresses an original and enlightened view. (Later she writes to me: "I used to try and think of new terms for East and West. They are so out of date and meaningless. What is East of what, and West of what, on a globe? Europe is no longer the center of the world.") Mai-mai has appeared on the stage, is a fine painter, and seems able to do anything and do it well. As recipient of the first Mei-ling Soong scholarship, she has been asked to befriend the Pandit sisters upon their arrival in New York and invites me to tea with them.

The dignity with which the young Pandits conduct themselves is impressive and touching. They are without bitterness. I admire their spirit and interview them for the *Post*. The "girls," as we call them, stay at our house during vacation periods. Edward and I, Nancy and Andrew, take them into our family as though they have always been part of it.

Nehru's sister, Mrs. Pandit—nicknamed Nan—is the first Indian leader permitted to come to the United States directly from India since the beginning of the war. Her husband, Ranjit, released from prison because of deteriorating health, dies a short time later. Mrs. Pandit makes a lecture tour, speaking effectively throughout the United States in behalf of India's freedom. As an observer, she attends the San Francisco Conference, at which the United Nations is created. We become friends and she, too, often stays with us. I write about her to help the "cause" and have various gatherings in her honor.

By 1944 proponents of a hard-line settlement for postwar Germany appear to be in the ascendency. Louis Fischer, in particular, convinces me that such a policy is blatantly shortsighted. Eager to issue a longer piece on the subject than can be included in *Twice A Year*, I commission a political affairs writer and lecturer on postwar problems, Hiram Motherwell, to express the opposing view in a pamphlet, to be entitled simply *Germany*. Through the good offices of a friend, Edward Bernays, a leading public relations expert, we arrange to have Western Reserve University in Cleveland print and distribute copies to students, university libraries, and interested citizens as part of a series to be called *Toward a Democratic Foreign Policy*.

During the course of many conversations, Mai-mai Sze admirably clarifies for me salient aspects of China's history and its current situation. I invite her to prepare a second pamphlet, *China*. When I ask her to send me a detailed biography for the publication, she replies: "I have no biography. . . . I can't say I was born in Tientsin and have spent the past 30 years running away gypsies and all. Won't my name and that I'm Chinese serve the purpose? If not, then you as my editor should make up a nice life for me, please."

As I see more of Mai-mai, I discover that her father, a high-ranking diplomat, served as Minister to the Court of St. James's and Ambassador to the United States. She was educated in England, as well as at Wellesley. Since 1931 she has lived in France, England, the United States, and made several return trips to China.

Mai-mai has crisscrossed this country many times since 1937 on lecture tours, and has spent long periods in California. She tells me that before one speech she was introduced as "Miss May-I May-I See," and before another, as Mme. Chiang Kai-shek. Her keenly observant letters are a joy to receive.

[Boston. January 12, 1944]

I walked back from Washington St. up Bromfield—up one end of the Common and then down Beacon St.—something Nathaniel Arden [of Santayana's *The Last Puritan*] would never dream of doing. He always walked *up* Beacon St., remember? There was a London air in the greyness and over the Common and the alley ways. The old houses made me quite homesick for London, the only place I've ever felt homesick for. . . . I walked along very slowly looking at the houses and thinking about London and watching cloud shapes in the sky. So many pictures are born from cloud shapes, perhaps most of them, for isn't the sky one of the first things we ever notice and watch? A tall old gentleman who might have been related to the Ardens came up to me and said, "May I tell you how much I admire the Chinese?" and held forth for ten minutes or so on his trips to China and his admiration for my countrymen. Then he said, "What on earth are you doing in Boston?" I had been wondering that myself and his putting it at me made me decide the encounter was not a pick-up but one of those chance meetings which are perfect of its kind—never repeated but never forgotten. It's the human touch people talk about so much and are usually afraid to do anything about. He walked with me back to the hotel. We talked of Beacon St., of course, of the codfish noblesse, of tradition, of Puritans, of London, scooters and squirrels in the parks of London and we talked long at the door of the hotel of heritage and the things one owes to ancestry and the bondage of those "things"—it could have gone on forever. . . . But we said goodbye at last and he said, "Would you tell me your name? I should like to send you a book tomorrow." The book just came—Santayana's *Last Puritan*! The pattern carries on, it seems, no matter where one goes. The card with it just said: "It was a great pleasure to talk with you. You made me think of a man who once spent some years in exile here whose book I am sending you." No name—no identification. No one to whom I can say thank you and that I enjoyed the walk and talk too.

[Connecticut. January 19, 1944]

I might just as well be in Timbuctoo or on another planet as here in Connecticut. It was awful getting up in the dark this morning and crawling to the station and crawling here in 3 long hours. I can't describe how I hated starting out again. It's the whole business of touring and speaking. When one talks of "all men are brothers" and humanity with a big H, one must take a deep breath. Nevertheless, God Bless America. This is a typical New England town. It is proud of its public buildings, its citizens are what is called stalwart. There seem to be an awful lot of little girls around. The meeting was a Sunday Forum they have four times in the winter, open to all and held in the school auditorium. The mike bounces back on one, the younger married couples participate in local dramatics and giggle about it, the old people have the best faces. They have roots. There was a lively question period—lively in that there were plenty of questions and a good deal of laughter. No one knows anything about anyone else let alone each other's countries. And I do not know much either. Fundamentally every lecturer is a disappointed actor. The lecture platform is a poor second to the theatre for sheer exhibitionism. In the middle of speaking the thought flashed through my head God, I'm talking an awful lot—what a lot of words—do they mean anything? The people who come up afterwards and press your hand fervently do it because you're from the outside. It's sheer relief to see, hear, touch somebody from outside the small world of their town. When they say that what you said told them a lot, they only mean it's nice to have someone dish it out. And if it's personal compliments—well, China is a romantic place for so many people. The pretty picture—and they don't want to know about the hunger, pain, misery and suffering—only the pretty side.

[New York. July 17, 1944]

[In] the evening I went . . . to meet [publishers] Kurt Wolff and wife [Helen]; very nice they were, warm and full of enthusiasm. Very continental in taste and expression which is only natural. Do you know them? I think they have done a marvellous job in the three years they've been over here. Thought they would be interested in the Chinese painters' "Bible" and told them about it. It's a wonderful book, beautiful and full of wisdom and practical instructions for paint; never been done in English.

Heard an Indian say, "Shakespeare is the most profitable British export."

In 1940 I was not directly involved in city politics. Although La Guardia had been a refreshing mayor, by then he was "pinching pennies"; excellent programs had become diluted and uncared for. His opponent in the coming election possibly would be William O'Dwyer, whom I looked upon as a member of the Christian Front, favoring reactionary and destructive forces. People were tired of La Guardia. But after the *New York Times* came out against him, I went to the editor, Mr. Cyrus Sulzberger, in despair, pleading that, whatever La Guardia's faults, the *Times* not back O'Dwyer; I left with a dismal sense of having accomplished nothing. By 1944 matters locally had gone from bad to worse. La Guardia was no longer interested merely in New York but, rather, in international issues. Who would be our next mayor?

The American Labor Party had been formed because of disgust with Tammany politics, and the enthusiasm of its leader, Sidney Hillman, for Roosevelt. Hillman and his colleagues in the new party might or might not be fellow travelers, but the widespread rumor was that they were. In any event, they favored for mayor the man I had labeled with such disdain a member of the Christian Front: Bill O'Dwyer.

Louis Fischer, George Counts, John L. Childs, and David Dubinsky—the last an energetic labor leader and head of the International Ladies' Garment Workers' Union—disagreed with Hillman's political position. As a result, together with Alex Rose and others of like mind they founded the Liberal Party. All were Democrats and strong advocates of Roosevelt. I was asked to be one of the directors; Fischer urged me to accept.

Theoretically I was against a third party, believing that splits in major parties were bound to play into the hands of a minority. The Liberal leaders assured me they agreed, and that the present division was only temporary. As soon as they gained sufficient power, they would move back and take over the leadership of the Democratic Party. Persuaded they were sincere, I joined, became a director, and worked for the Liberals.

Heated arguments between left-wing friends broke out; to followers of Hillman, Dubinsky was virtually a reactionary—which was nothing compared to what people called Hillman. Attending Liberal Party meetings, I found the general program we devised satisfactory; as more and more idealists joined, I became hopeful something good might evolve.

After Roosevelt's nomination, Alex Rose pleads with me to make a radio broadcast for him. Never having spoken on the radio, I write out my fifteen-minute talk with some trepidation. Clearly, radio statements require rhetoric quite different from writing. I have no talent for oratory or for projecting myself dramatically, being accustomed only to speak seriously and address audiences in a straightforward manner.

As my speech progresses, I become more relaxed, but I'm convinced as always that I wasn't born to be a public speaker.

As a result of praise for the broadcast, Station WEVD invites me to give a weekly evening radio program. In spite of my dislike of the medium, I accept, since I can talk about anything I choose.

Requests for speeches and broadcasts on social issues increase. One evening I debate an important labor relations controversy with an arch-conservative member of an antilabor vigilante committee. As we argue, I point out he cannot have read the document in question with care, since his conclusions are illogical and unwarranted. The discussion becomes so intense, and I so outraged, that after the program ends I cannot shake hands, but turn on my heel and depart in a fury.

A week later there is another broadcast, again involving a labor dispute. The weather is humid and hot, my back aches. I step from the elevator and find only a heavily cushioned bench; what I require is a hard-backed, wooden seat. I writhe in agony, trying to perch on the bench's edge without sliding off.

To my horror, my vigilante foe steps from the next elevator, accompanied by his wife. Noting my discomfort, they approach me with great solicitude, ask if I am having back trouble, assure me they both have suffered from the same ailment, suggest I drink gallons of orange juice, and demonstrate a series of exercises—all in the most kindly manner. He and I are summoned into the studio.

I listen to the complex dispute to be arbitrated and can discern only one fair solution. To my amazement, my former adversary and I agree on every point. The program ends; he takes my arm and escorts me carefully to the elevator. He and his wife continue their flow of friendly advice, find me a taxi, help me in, and bid me a cordial good night.

The time arrives when the Liberal Party must choose a candidate for mayor. As a director, I am automatically a member of the nominating committee. Sitting like a dutiful child in the literally smoke-filled room of a tawdry midtown hotel and listening to endless debates on who has a chance of winning and who does not, I become disenchanted. Aren't the labor leaders attempting to nominate someone they can control, just like Tammany or any other political group? Their preferred candidates exhibit no talent, no charisma, nothing to recommend them; they are only fairly well known, lack dash, put forward no dynamic programs, maintain no contacts with large groups of citizens.

A strange thought occurs to my innocent mind. It is now said that O'Dwyer is hostile to the Christian Front, and intends to run his own primary in order to be beholden to neither the American Labor Party, Tammany, nor any other political bosses. Why not capture him and make him our candidate? He will surely win.

I present my suggestion. Polite rebuttal: "Bill O'Dwyer is in the hands of Tammany and Boss Flynn. Don't believe a word he says." "He's tied up with the Labor Party, too, because that's what he believes in." "You'll no more get O'Dwyer to become part of the Liberal Party than you'll fly to the moon."

I sit down, baffled. "How," I ask myself, "can O'Dwyer both be committed to the American Labor Party and be a tool of the bosses, yet run his own primary campaign?" On the other hand, most of the politicians favored at our Liberal Party meetings are themselves close to Tammany. Nothing makes sense.

Local newspaper reporters are eager to find out who the Liberal Party's choice will be. At ten o'clock one evening we hear a loud knock on the door. Alex Rose answers it, looks back, and says, "It's a *Times* man. He wants to know the name of our candidate." General consternation. Dubinsky replies, "Tell him we haven't decided. He mustn't print anything until we make our announcement." The meeting continues.

I leave the room at midnight and go downstairs to buy a copy of the "Early Bird" *Herald Tribune*, so as to check the day's events against my already written column. A headline in the *Times* proclaims our candidate to be one of the men for whom I have little enthusiasm, and for whom I believe few votes would be cast.

Debates continue about whom we should select; feeling against O'Dwyer grows daily more virulent; I become increasingly curious about the man and decide to interview him, both for the *Post* and with an eye to Liberal Party deliberations. He is in seclusion in California, planning his strategy. I put in a long-distance call, not expecting O'Dwyer himself to answer, which he does. I tell him my name, that I write for the *New York Post* and am a member of the Liberal Party. He says, "Put it there, Dorothy. What do you want to know? Just ask me and I'll tell you." Taken aback, I reply calmly, "I want to know everything about you. I want to know what you think about every political issue. From womb to tomb." He laughs. "Okay, shoot."

D.N.: "I have been trying to get the Liberal Party to make you its candidate. But I've had no success." O'D.: "You'll never have any success. They hate me more than they do Tammany. They're tools of Tammany and they know they can't control me." I smile to myself and continue with my queries: "I used to think you were in the hands of the Christian Front. Are you?" O'D.: "I sure am not. I am totally against the Christian Front." D.N.: "Can I quote you?" O'D.: "Sure thing. You can quote anything I say." D.N.: "Can I print it?" O'D.: "Of course you can print it. I've nothing to hide. What else do you want to know?"

I am forced to think fast about the most controversial questions. D.N.: "Are you for birth control?" O'D.: "Of course." D.N.: "Are you for wiping out discrimination in all city departments?" O'D.: "I'm from a minority myself. I'd be an idiot if I didn't believe in equal opportunity for everyone." D.N.: "Are you for all-day neighborhood schools—that is, for school activity after hours? La Guardia has been neglecting this." O'D.: "Of course I'm for it." D.N.: "Are you for reforming the health department and hospitals? They're in shameful condition." O'D.: "Naturally." D.N.: "When are you coming back to New York?" O'D.: "As soon as I make up my mind just how I'm going to run my primary. I refuse to knuckle under to Tammany or any of the other bosses. You just watch what's going to happen!"

O'Dwyer gives me a number to call in New York within a week. We make an appointment to talk things over. I have never seen the man and am rather astonished to find how different he looks from his pictures. His face is red, his eyes blue; he is well built but in no way handsome, as many people have described him. We shake hands and sit down; I am ill at ease. O'Dwyer's sense of humor is typically jolly and Irish, but has an edge that makes us both self-conscious.

I repeat that if he would come along with the Liberal Party, I'd work to make him its candidate; he would be obligated to no one and could carry out a truly liberal program. He looks at me askance. "That's a beautiful theory,

*My father, Louis Stecker.
Early 1920's. Photographer
unknown*

*My mother, Esther Stecker;
myself and my brothers,
Robert and Jack Stecker.
1908–09. Photographer
unknown*

*Andrew E. and Lottie
Norman (Edward's parents).
Early 1920's. Photographer
unknown*

Dorothy Norman, wedding picture. 1925. Photographer unknown

*Nancy Norman by Dorothy
Norman. 1931*

*Edward Norman, Woods Hole, by
Dorothy Norman. Early 1930's*

*Our second child, Andrew, by
Dorothy Norman. Early 1930's*

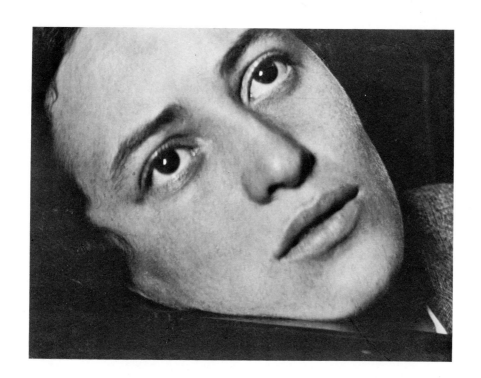

Dorothy Norman by Alfred
Stieglitz. 1930's

Dorothy Norman by Alfred
Stieglitz. 1936

Dorothy Norman by Alfred
Stieglitz. 1931

Hands—Dorothy Norman by
Alfred Stieglitz. 1932

L.G.
8/28/26

You ask me about Objectivity &
Subjectivity. I had years of such
discussions at "291." — Some of
the discussions led to "action" —
most of them were just academic
twaddle. I don't care whether
something living is "subjective" or
"objective" — All I ask is for
the livingness. The rest of it I'll
leave to the discussionists. —
They'll find everything but the
living of the moment — Object —
or what-you-will.

Greetings —

*Letter from Alfred Stieglitz to
Dorothy Norman. 1928*

*From New York Series by
Alfred Stieglitz. 1935*

Number One
Fall - Winter 1938

RAINER MARIA RILKE: Some War Time Letters
RANDOLPH BOURNE: The War and the Intellectuals;
    A Letter to Van Wyck Brooks
THEODORE DREISER: Randolph Bourne
HENRY DAVID THOREAU: from A Plea for John Brown
ALFRED STIEGLITZ: Writings and Conversations:
    by Dorothy Norman
ANDRE MALRAUX: from Man's Hope
IGNAZIO SILONE: Some Facts About My Life;
    A Chapter from The School for Dictators
E. E. CUMMINGS: What About It?
FRANZ KAFKA: Three Parables
ANAIS NIN: Birth
CHARLES OLSON: Lear and Moby Dick

ALFRED STIEGLITZ: PHOTOGRAPHS
    Reproductions by Max Jaffe

CIVIL LIBERTIES SECTION
ROGER BALDWIN: On Being A Conscientious Objector
    (1918-1938)
IRVING BRANT: The Struggle for Civil Liberties
T. V. SMITH: Repeal of the Espionage Laws; K. PATCHEN: Poem
RAY ABRAMS: Conscientious Objector; ANGNA ENTERS: A
    Letter

In addition to further material . . . .

A SEMI-ANNUAL JOURNAL OF LITERATURE,
THE ARTS AND CIVIL LIBERTIES — IN BOOK FORM

Twice A Year, *Fall–Winter 1938*

Twice A Year,
Tenth Anniversary Issue, 1948

A R T and A C T I O N

MALRAUX   CAMUS   SARTRE   DE BEAUVOIR   MAGNY

TOLSTOY   GANDHI   RICHARD WRIGHT   VALLENTIN

SPENDER   CARLO LEVI   MARIN   NOVALIS   SILONE

BRECHT   CUMMINGS   VIERTEL   ROGER BALDWIN   FREEMAN

LOUIS FISCHER   V. L. PANDIT   SACCO-VANZETTI   PERRY

KONVITZ   MARSHALL SPEECHES   GERMAN WAR TRIALS

WORLD CONSTITUTION   CIVIL LIBERTIES   RACE RELATIONS

POLITICAL DOCUMENTS   LEYDA   MAIER   JAARI   YOUNG

UN-AMERICAN ACTIVITIES COMMITTEE HEARINGS

YOUNG WRITERS: ANDERSON   YORCK   DOUGLAS
FRANKENBERG   SELVIN   HARPER   KUNIHOLM   POWELL
PUCCIANI   REPLANSKY   STIEFEL   ZYLBERBERG

PHOTOGRAPHS OF: MARIN   STIEGLITZ   LACHAISE
COOMARASWAMY

BY: PAUL STRAND   BRETT WESTON   DOROTHY NORMAN

10th ANNIVERSARY ISSUE

TWICE A YEAR

A BOOK OF LITERATURE, THE ARTS and CIVIL LIBERTIES

Editor and Publisher: DOROTHY NORMAN
Associate Editors: MARY LESCAZE, RICHARD WRIGHT
Assistant Editor: BROM WEBER

Mary Lescaze. 1940's. Photographer unknown. Collection of Dorothy Norman

Norman house, Penzance Point, Woods Hole, by Dorothy Norman. 1937

Moon Flower—Cape Cod by Dorothy Norman. 1930's

Woods Hole house, interior, by Dorothy Norman. 1930's

Equivalent by Alfred Stieglitz. 1933–34

BELOW: *Equivalent by Alfred Stieglitz. 1930's*

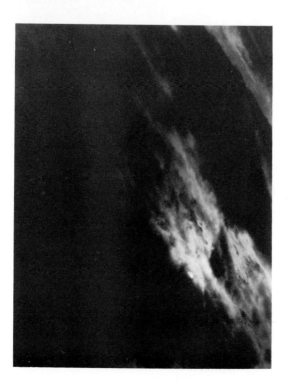

Walls—An American Place by Dorothy Norman. 1940's

*Alfred Stieglitz by Dorothy
Norman. 1940's*

*Alfred Stieglitz by Dorothy
Norman. 1940's*

East Hampton house. 1950's. Photographer unknown

East Hampton house, interior, by Eric Kroll. 1960

Church Steeple—Cape Cod—by Dorothy Norman. 1930's

Dorothy Norman with Jawaharlal Nehru. 1949. Photographer unknown

*Nehru with grandsons Sanjay and
Rajiv Gandhi, by Dorothy Norman.
New Delhi, India, 1950*

*Nehru (in Western suit), New York,
by Dorothy Norman. 1949*

*Nehru, India, by Dorothy Norman.
1950*

Indira Gandhi, New York, by Dorothy Norman. 1949

124 *East 70th Street, New York, Rear,*
by Gottscho Schleisner. 1947

124 *East 70th Street, New York,*
Interior, by Gottscho Schleisner. 1947

*Dorothy Norman with Jackson Pollock
and others at the Museum of Modern Art,
New York, 1950. Photographer unknown*

*Georgia O'Keeffe by Dorothy Norman.
Early 1930's*

John Marin, Cliffside, N.J., by Dorothy Norman. 1940's

Charles Demuth by Dorothy Norman. Early 1930's

Elli Cartier-Bresson, New York,
by Dorothy Norman. 1940's

Henri Cartier-Bresson, New
York, by Dorothy Norman.
1946

Dr. Stella Kramrisch with mandala, Philadelphia. Early 1980's. Photographer unknown

Amanda K. Coomaraswamy, Boston, by Dorothy Norman. 1947

Ignazio Silone, Rome, by Dorothy Norman. 1950

Theodore Dreiser, Woods Hole, by Dorothy Norman. 1930's

Lewis Mumford by Dorothy Norman. 1940's (RIGHT)

Gaetano Salvemini, Rome, by Dorothy Norman. 1950

*Natacha Rambova and Rudolph
Valentino by James Abbe. 1920's*

*St.-John Perse, Washington, by
Dorothy Norman. 1950's*

Richard Wright by Dorothy Norman.
1940's

Honorable Dorothy Brett by Edward
Weston. 1930's. Collection of
Dorothy Norman

Harold Clurman, New York, by
Dorothy Norman. 1930's

Edgard Varèse by Dorothy Norman.
Early 1930's

Sherwood Anderson by Alfred Stieglitz.
1923. Collection of Dorothy Norman

Mai-mai Sze by Dorothy Norman.
1940's

BELOW: *Mme. Gaston Lachaise*
by Dorothy Norman. 1940's

Louis Fischer by Dorothy Norman.
1940's

U Nu, Rangoon, by Dorothy
Norman. 1959

Ivy Litvinov, Soviet Union, by
Mary Lee Leatherbee. 1960's.
Collection of Dorothy Norman
(BELOW LEFT)

Paul Richard by Dorothy Norman.
Early 1950's

Dorothy Norman by Arnold Newman. 1970's
© *Arnold Newman*

my lovely lass." I laugh but answer seriously, "You don't realize that you could be one of the great mayors of New York, if you wanted to. We're at a point where many reforms are being neglected. La Guardia is squandering his largesse, so that the city is gasping for the leadership you could offer!" I smile as I speak, afraid that to be too obviously serious may shut O'Dwyer up or off.

He looks as though he's reading my mind. "Young lady, you don't understand this city. You don't understand a guy like myself. I didn't go to any of your Harvards. I'm not a member of your exclusive clubs. I went to night school. I got my education the hard way. I got to be a lawyer after a lot of hard work and I'm a nobody to your aristocrats. I never will be anybody to them. Don't kid yourself that I could be a great mayor—not in your sense."

I argue. "You're wrong about the way people judge others. The very fact you've achieved what you have is admirable. Why not just believe in yourself? You don't need Tammany, you say, or the Bronx and Brooklyn machines. You've already struck out on your own. Why not go on doing that? If you're going to be your own man, be a great one. This city needs to be made over, needs leadership. Why not head a splendid administration? It will help you, help the Irish, help the city. Why not?"

As I speak, I realize I am taking on the responsibility of standing up for this man against the better judgment of my peers, if only he will accept my suggestions. No matter that others disagree—I have decided to trust him. I have no power, but is it not possible that the faith of just one person in another may increase his strength of character and resolve?

We say goodbye. O'D.: "Telephone me whenever you want. Keep me informed." D.N.: "I can't give you confidential material from the Liberal Party. But I can tell you how I think you could be a wonderful mayor."

O'D.: "Make out a program and send it to me." He writes down his address and private phone number. "Tell me what needs to be done in every department. Call me up at eight-thirty in the morning every day." D.N.: "So I've lost? You won't be the candidate of the Liberal Party?" O'D.: "You go back to your party and tell them you've seen me and you want me to be its candidate. You'll discover their reactions. But call me! Promise. And tell me what to do." I promise.

As I leave, I'm trembling. I say to myself, "What an extraordinary moment—when I decided to take on Bill O'Dwyer!" This man has been hurt. He's not a great man, but he could do great things for the city. Knowing he might not makes me more eager to convince him.

The next meeting of the Liberal Party. The words spoken sound hollow. The solutions I have written out for the city's problems by now seem much clearer than do those of the party leaders. I feel heartsick. I joined the Liberals because I was assured that, once the battle with the American Labor Party was resolved, the membership would join ranks again with the Democratic Party and take over its leadership. Now I find no one has any intention of rejoining.

All my enthusiasm has disappeared. I become a Democrat once more. None of the candidates is perfect, but each day shows more clearly that O'Dwyer will win. Let him have his fling at running his own primary—he has no competition. Let the Liberal Party stick to its second-rate candidates. I will not spend one more moment listening to their vapid arguments or trying to believe in them. I tell the head of the party, George Counts, I intend to resign. Without argument, my withdrawal is accepted.

At the polls O'Dwyer is the overwhelming choice of the people. What irony! During the last election I was against him, but he has acted manfully, standing up against the Christian Front, against Boss Flynn, against Tammany. Is he really in tune with the American Labor Party? I doubt it, but he has their votes. Now he is mayor of New York City.

Every morning at half past eight I call O'Dwyer on his private line. Our talks—often hilarious—usually begin with his reading me a passage from Yeats. His voice changes; he becomes the actor, the reciter of great poetry. He loves Yeats. Strange that I want to laugh when he reads with such passion.

Then we get down to the concrete suggestions I make, one after another. I tell him what I think should be done about health and hospitals, about day-care centers, delinquency, and the rest. He listens, is responsive, asks for specific recommendations. He reads the memos I send him and acts on most of them. An example: one of my early proposals is that the city should appoint a Board of Hospitals to function in the same manner as the Board of Health; nonpolitical leaders can then act as watchdogs of the department and make suggestions of an independent nature to improve services. O'Dwyer creates such a board.

People think we are having a love affair, although I never see him alone. I speak to him on the phone in the morning, occasionally we're at the same meetings or dinners—that is all. I deny the rumor to a first-rate journalist-friend, who replies, "Of course you're having an affair. Everyone knows it." I'm furious.

People play up to me, hoping to meet O'Dwyer and gain favor with the city administration. I make no attempt whatsoever to influence the Mayor, except in our private talks about urgent city problems over the telephone.

O'Dwyer asks if I want some position in the city government. I assure him I don't; nothing is further from my thoughts. Various members of the Liberal Party approach me, even though I have resigned, to see if I might run for the City Council. Only when asked to accept a political appointment or to seek office do I realize how wrong either would be for me. I know how unable I am to compromise. O'Dwyer offers me the chairmanship of the City Planning Commission, but I say a firm No.

10

April 12, 1945. I walk up Lexington Avenue on my way home, where I have an appointment with the foreign correspondent Edgar Ansel Mowrer. A stranger stops me and says in a toneless voice, "Did you know? The President is dead." I look at him, disbelieving. "The President is dead." "Oh, no." I glance around. Everyone is crying. I am almost home. I walk on in a stupor. President Roosevelt. Gone.

Edgar arrives promptly, comes up to the living room; we put our arms around each other and sob. I turn on the radio; the news blares. We stand listening. He tries to comfort me. "Dorothy, don't be *too* upset. Margaret Truman is a wonderful person. She keeps her father right in line." I continue to cry. Margaret Truman, Harry Truman. Franklin Roosevelt, Eleanor Roosevelt. There is no equivalence I can sense.

Edgar—unusually intuitive, well versed in politics, and a most skillful journalist—repeats his words. We embrace again warmly but my tears will not stop, until at last we turn off the radio, sit down and try to talk—as we have on committees or as friends—about the future. What will happen now? Edgar stares unseeing into space; I stare at him.

The end of the war, so long almost unimaginable, turns suddenly into reality. The shock of the atomic bomb neutralizes the otherwise joyous news of peace.

Number XII–XIII of *Twice A Year*, printed at the war's end, is dedicated to Lewis Mumford's son, Geddes, killed in action. No matter how dehumanizing mass murder and atrocities are, the death of a single individual close to someone we love has an immediacy, an impact, a symbolic meaning out of all proportion.

The same issue includes major conference reports pouring forth from council chambers all over the world. The mounting hunger for a new world order finds eloquent expression; a note of hope pervades almost every document.

In the spring of 1944 Theodore Dreiser gave a party at which Richard Wright—whose books I admired—and I never stopped talking, as though we had known one another always. Wright expressed his enthusiasm for *Twice A Year* and suggested certain writers and topics he felt would be of interest to the publication. Our ideas coincided. We met again to discuss them, frequently. Wright's first appearance in *Twice A Year* was marked by an exchange of controversial letters between him and the Uruguayan painter and engraver Antonio Frasconi.

At the same time a young writer, Brom Weber, visits An American Place in the hope of obtaining permission to include Hart Crane's letters to Stieglitz in a book he is editing. Respecting his enthusiasm for Crane, I help secure Stieglitz's cooperation.

Our friendship develops; I respond to Weber's extreme sensitivity and generosity. He loves *Twice A Year*, wants to help it, and is willing to perform the most demanding chores. No one else has ever volunteered to read proof or check facts. To receive an offer of assistance from someone of Weber's intelligence and sensibility is a heartwarming experience.

After much discussion of Crane's writings, we agree to publish a selection of the poet's prose in Number XII–XIII. As a result of our mutual interests and harmonious relationship, I name Weber assistant editor.

———

In June 1946 I leave for Woods Hole heavy-hearted, saying goodbye to Stieglitz with tears I would rather not show. He looks frail and weak, and tells me, "I don't want to go to Lake George this year. I'd rather stay at the Place, on the job. I love the young people who come in."

Early one morning at Woods Hole, the telephone rings. The young photographer Henwar Rodakiewicz is calling from New York. "Stieglitz has had a stroke and is in the hospital. You must come down at once. Georgia is in the Southwest." I tell Edward that Stieglitz is dying. He is kind and understanding and does not object to my going back to New York immediately. I reach the city in a daze. The weather, toward the middle of July, suddenly has turned cold. I am wearing a woolen suit, yet shiver as I rush to the hospital.

Henwar and the sculptress Mary Callery, a warm friend of O'Keeffe, stand beside Stieglitz's bed. He is in a coma; I have a strange feeling he has already died. There is not the slightest movement in his body. Mary says, "Touch him." I can't do this in front of others. We remain motionless, speechless for hours. Stieglitz's condition does not change. We know he will not revive. How noble he looks, how at peace his face.

Henwar and Mary—both close to O'Keeffe—are exceedingly kind to me. Late in the day Mary takes us to her apartment. I break down, I weep. Mary and Henwar try to comfort me, but there is no comfort. Henwar spends the night at our house so I won't be alone. The next day O'Keeffe arrives; our paths do not cross at the hospital. I make no effort to go to Stieglitz's room again; some extrasensory perception tells me he is dead.

I walk up and down in front of the building in which An American Place is located, yet I cannot go in alone. I call the French photographer Henri Cartier-Bresson, whom I introduced to Stieglitz only two weeks before. Henri made a beautiful sequence of little photographs of him. They liked each other at once. I say, "Please, Henri, go to the Place with me. I'm afraid to go by myself." Sweetly, he consents. We walk in and it is like entering a world that never existed. The walls are bare. The Place is dead, too.

The dreary day before the funeral drags on. At home I try to write an obituary for the *Post*. My mind goes blank as I think of all I wish to say in a brief article. Another problem: this is one piece I must type myself—no matter how slowly. How can I? My machine is in Woods Hole. The telephone rings. Harold Clurman calls, sounds understanding, sympathetic, but cheery. He suggests I have dinner with him.

I am torn; dare I go out or will I make a show of myself, weeping? Harold offers me the use of a typewriter in a friend's apartment on Washington Square, near the restaurant to which we are going. I pull myself together and drive downtown.

My piece is painfully composed, typed. Harold and I cross the avenue to Longchamps, sit dejectedly at a small table outdoors. I look up. A familiar figure looms toward us—Mrs. Roosevelt, walking by with a companion. She sees us at the same moment, smiles, comes to me, and puts out her hand in her usual gracious manner. "What are you doing in New York on this miserable day?" Her high-pitched voice is warm, cordial. I can scarcely answer. My love for her and her friendliness make my tears flow even more profusely.

"I'm here because—a great friend, Alfred Stieglitz, has died. I've come down for his funeral." My words sound banal. Mrs. Roosevelt looks at me; I can tell the name means nothing to her. How could this be?

The irony of the situation brings forth a new flood of tears that I try unsuccessfully to hide. The paths of this great woman and that great man have never crossed! Looking at Mrs. Roosevelt with almost unbelieving eyes, I can only utter a perfunctory: "How nice to have seen you. I do hope you are well."

I return to Woods Hole as though walking into a changed world. The aftermath of Stieglitz's death is traumatic, excruciating. Edward is noble, kind; he and the children seem more precious to me than ever. Sympathetic messages pour in. Stieglitz's daily letters lie beside me, but I shall never receive another, nor feel his touch nor hear his voice. The lovely little flowers I pressed into envelopes for him will now have nowhere to go. The last note he wrote me, the day before he died, was in pencil in beautiful, tiny handwriting—tender, caressing.

I put down lines I can show to no one.

The petal lies
precisely where it falls
its final resting place

The pace retarded now
all rebirth curbed
(Oh did that loved one live
it were revived
were flown at once to his sweet lips
once more to give it life)

It was so tender then
   in briefer absences before
   to pluck the flower where it grew
   from sweet oblivion
   to shower it afar before those deep all-seeing eyes
   preserve its bloom
   miraculous reprieve of perfect tracery
   the faultless drawing by the heavens dropped
   and found as though by prearrangement
   to my need
   engraven image of my ecstasy
   to render it more possible
   to bear the interludes of parting
   through such delicately conceived and fragile messages
   of rejoining
   now turned to nothingness
   as though the petal were itself a triple thrust of death
   now stricken in a silent void

Thrice killed
Oh death: to slay in measure multiple
   In losing what I love am lost
   the petals lost
   just as before we were thrice alive
   (the reaching from within
   together then
   in fully joined song)
But now: not now my love not now

I bend I waver pluck a wondrous flower as before
I think to hold its beauty for a while the longer
but the magic fades before my eyes
(Its destination mirrored in my hand of old
increased the beauty
now denied)

I let the petals fall:
their presence even on the ground
become too harsh reminder of the needed ritual

Oh glory: lived for further bearing beauty
it to me to him
and so itself survived the longer then than now
Oh death to rob in measure multiple

Stieglitz died on July 13, 1946. During the week before I return to Woods Hole, Paul Rosenfeld and I speak to each other on the phone, tearfully and lovingly. One evening he calls: "But Dorothy, what a giant he was. It should comfort you." And then with unexpected ecstasy: "I believe he was the first man since Goethe who truly understood art."

On Saturday, Paul, too, is dead. I rush to New York for his funeral. The next Saturday, news comes from Paris that Gertrude Stein has died. Not long before, Dreiser, too, had gone. In so brief a span of time, four giants of our era have vanished.

I must honor Stieglitz and decide to issue a memorial portfolio that will include tributes and some of his photographs. I send out letters to which everyone replies with extraordinary spontaneity. Lewis Mumford writes from London:

You are right, dear Dorothy: Stieglitz's death can only unite, in a more durable bond, those of us who were originally united by the living man. I first saw about his death in the *London Times*; it seemed to me then to have some of the quiet resolution of his whole life, active and daunt-less up to the last moment, like Socrates in the description of the *Symposium*, parrying blows with the enemy as he slowly retreated. I had a talk with him the very morning before I left and bless the impulse that made me turn to him then in the midst of that harried day. Of course I shall want to write about him; and when I have had a little time to collect myself . . . I hope to turn out something worthy of the man.

I wish Stieglitz could know for all time how much he was loved, how he was appreciated for the wonders he wrought throughout his life.

It had been a spontaneous gesture on my part to photograph Henri Cartier-Bresson at the Place. After printing the pictures, I discovered that by accident the best one showed him with one eye open in light, the other lid lowered in shadow.

Henri had said to me only recently, "When I photograph with my little Leica, I feel that I am looking within with the one eye that is closed. With the other—the one that is open—I look without. I see the shapes, the living quality of what moves me to photograph. Without passion, without working in terms of the emotion of the heart and the enjoyment of the eye, nothing vital can be recorded. The relationship between the eye and the heart is of utmost importance. If I photograph people, their inner look must be reflected. I must reveal what goes on inside them as well as their relation to the outer world."

I realize that Henri's use of a Leica and his habit of having his minia-ture negatives enlarged represent the exact opposite of how Stieglitz worked. He is the leader of a new period in photography, yet he works essentially in the tradition of Stieglitz.

With the end of the war and the death of Stieglitz, in my own small way I face an entirely new period, just as the world does in colossal terms. The long drawn-out hostilities have had their climax in an event so staggering it is difficult to assimilate. What will the atomic bomb bring in its wake? Hitler and Mussolini are gone, but Europe is cruelly divided. Dreams of one world vanish.

Number XIV–XV of *Twice A Year* contains an "In Memoriam" section dedicated to those intrepid believers in freedom: Alfred Stieglitz, Paul Rosenfeld, Theodore Dreiser, Gertrude Stein. After a cruelly satirical George Grosz drawing and John Heartfield's devastating photomontages reflecting Europe's potential doom, an official photograph—the explosion of the atomic bomb on Nagasaki—is juxtaposed with a most exquisite, sensitive print: a delicate and loving sky *Equivalent* by Stieglitz.

After the war French existentialists exerted a pronounced influence on many American intellectuals. Richard Wright was fascinated by the concept. Thus far his primary concern had been race relations in the United States. His new preoccupation struck me as splendid—a broadening of vision. A natural connection developed between the ideas that interested us and the direction *Twice A Year* was taking. Dick spent so much time giving thought to the publication, it seemed inevitable and right that he should become an associate editor.

Each time I see Wright I am struck by his dignity and quiet demeanor. He is always impeccably dressed. The moment he speaks, his intensity—otherwise hidden—erupts. As he speaks eloquently, brilliantly, I have difficulty remembering that he was born in an anti-Negro South, that the vivid stories in *Uncle Tom's Children* and the whole of *Black Boy* portray the hostile world in which he grew up. They tell of a small, vulnerable boy who dared to rebel against smiling yes sir when his heart said no, of how he played the game to survive for just so long, until he could sell his soul for not one moment longer.

Some tell me Wright is paranoid, that he exaggerates, overdramatizes, distorts. Such unimaginative jeers are exasperating. How could he not be hurt, distraught, suspicious? Only once do I hear him report an incident that might be termed paranoid. On a trip to Chicago he felt faint at the terminal and asked a woman at the Travelers Aid desk for help. She gave him some little white pills, advising him to take one right away and another shortly after. He swallowed the first one, but as he walked toward a bench, he felt he was about to fall down. He reached the bench and took the second pill, which knocked him out. Recounting the story, he seemed convinced the woman had tried to trick him. Never again did he tell me of any comparable incident.

Jean-Paul Sartre and Simone de Beauvoir visited New York. Sartre phoned Wright, who in turn asked me whether he might bring both of them to the house. We inevitably spoke of existentialism. Sartre emphasized that it was a philosophy stressing the interdependence of man and the dignity of the individual. In part, he explained: "As existentialists we maintain that Descartes's 'I think, therefore I am' is totally inadequate. It's not only 'I' who think—and therefore exist—but my existence and my thinking are indivisible from the thinking and existence of everyone else in the world. 'I' am perpetually modified and influenced by everyone else. I cannot consider myself alone. I must respect the existence and freedom to decide for himself of every other individual. The choice you make for yourself is bound to affect the choice you make for the rest of the world. In other words: man must use his free will to establish a working basis for living collectively without destroying the dignity of the individual."

These ideas struck me as obvious rather than new. "We are born—alone. We die—alone. Each of us has responsibility for his own acts." I wondered how a diseased, subnormal, deranged person could be expected to have the same responsibility for his acts as one who was healthy, normal, of good fortune. I pondered, too, how anyone who sympathized with Stalinism could speak so glibly about respect for the individual.

Sartre—short, square-shouldered—is serious and concentrated. He obviously has trouble with his eyes, wears thick glasses, and looks rather diminutive in the presence of de Beauvoir. She has an expansive personality, her eyes are a glowing blue. She wears a bulky, ungainly knitted outfit that exaggerates her stockiness. None of this detracts from the impression she gives of being a handsome woman. While Sartre speaks, she is evidently restraining herself from giving her own definition of existentialism. Interrupting, she finally explodes, confessing without transition that she has an ardent desire to see Harlem. Will Dick take them? Because I detest visiting Harlem in this manner, dropping in on nightclubs as a sightseer, I don't go along. The expedition is a huge success, according to the visitors from Paris. Dick, I am certain, was excited about discussing existentialism.

Not long after, Albert Camus, whose temperament was totally different, arrived in New York. I asked if he was an existentialist, as rumored; he shuddered. "It is true that young people in France were in despair after the war, but you can explain nothing by way of ideologies. We must solve our problems through an active revolt against hypocrisy, brutality, lack of caring." His philosophy was clear from his anti-Fascist position and his writings.

"The hero of my book *The Stranger* is simply a man who refuses to lie. Society thinks it needs men willing to give only superficial signs of their feelings. If anyone dares to express his true beliefs, if he rebels against having to tell untruths, society will destroy him in the end. *The Stranger* is the story of a sincere man fighting against such a world. We must protest. Each of us. Not a mere abstraction of us. But each of us, concretely—in every act. Not in some 'other world' but in this one. Now. This moment."

He shook his head sadly about the ignominious way in which we treated the Negro. Disturbed by our attitude—as were most Europeans—even before he came to America, Camus had taken it upon himself to see that Richard Wright's works were translated and published in Paris.

I told the feature editor of the *Post* I wanted to interview Camus; he replied as he had about Sartre, "He's not news; no one knows about him." I explained that just because such writers were not yet well known but were important, they were news. He acquiesced—unenthusiastically—and I happily wrote about both men.

In New York Richard Wright tries to live in places that please him, in which he feels at home, and that he can afford. His way has been hard; he has worked diligently all his life, has had no patrons, has sought no favors. He is married to a white woman; they have a lovely daughter. No three people could be quieter, more dignified. Yet every time they must or would like to move, there are difficulties. The United States, in which Wright's works are on best-seller lists, has no place where he can live as a relaxed human being. The apartment in Manhattan to which he finally moves is more spacious, better planned, than previous ones. But there is always pressure, often unspoken. "You're a black man. Suppose you *are* Richard Wright. Your skin is black."

Because at last he has satisfying quarters and doesn't complain about the underlying tension, people say he has come up in the world and should feel at peace. But he doesn't. His new longing for Paris—his wish to experience another civilization, one that deeply attracts him—takes over. He speaks to me about his dream—to see Europe, feel it, become immersed in the cultural life there. Must his writing be limited forever to the Negro? Is he not a man—a full human being? I don't think of myself as a white woman. I simply travel around the world as a person, because I have that privilege. Why should it be denied to Richard Wright?

Dick suggests that he represent and promote *Twice A Year* in Paris. "I know they need it—I just know it." But then difficulties arise that I describe in a column entitled "Operation: Richard Wright," in the *Post* of June 17, 1946:

> One day early last winter, Richard Wright discussed with me the possibility of his going to Paris this spring. He said he would like to study, and to report on, cultural, social and political developments in France for *Twice A Year*. He felt also that the publication should be more widely known abroad. . . . It seemed important that Wright—certainly one of America's foremost writers—should see for himself what was occurring abroad and interpret it from his own experience. We agreed he should apply to the State Department for necessary clearance and documents and, as publisher of *Twice A Year*, I would write a letter stating the nature of his proposed assignment.
>
> From that point, the curious reactions encountered when the plan was subsequently mentioned to various key individuals are worth reporting.
>
> We were advised by no means to mention that *Twice A Year* or the authors to be contacted, or the movements and trends to be studied were "anti-fascist" or connected with the "resistance" or "democracy."

We were warned that trouble, suspicion, hostility might follow in Washington if we did!

We were warned it would be difficult for Wright to get a passport because he was a Negro. We were warned that the Government would not like Wright, in particular, to go abroad, because of the way in which he had always spoken out against injustice at home, and against racial discrimination.

I was asked why Wright, a Negro, would want to go abroad anyway. Wasn't it his place to stay here? What interest could he possibly have in Europe? Wasn't his subject matter the "Negro in America"?

I wrote an appropriate letter to the State Department, secretly fuming about the necessity to be so circumspect about mentioning the very words supposed to be our national slogans. I openly fumed at the attitude that Negroes should not be free citizens and be permitted to move about the world on bona fide missions like anyone else. I felt sickened that the function of the Negro artist was supposed to be limited, whereas that of any other artist could apparently be without bounds.

Weeks passed. No word from the State Department. Friends remained skeptical.

Meanwhile word that Wright might be coming to France had spread among some of France's cultural mission here. With almost lightning speed thereafter Wright received a telephone call that the French Government was issuing him an official invitation to be its guest and offering him his passage and a month of his projected stay at French Government expense. The invitation itself would be mailed to him forthwith.

Being shy, modest and utterly forthright, feeling almost incredulous at the unexpected honor and recognition, he replied in words approximating: "No, not really? I can scarcely believe it. Thank you more than I can say. I have tentatively booked my passage and already paid for it. Also, I have arranged to stay with friends if my passport is approved. I hesitate to accept reimbursement, but I thoroughly appreciate the honor that has been paid me. It is all too wonderful to believe. I thank you more than I can say."

Days went by and no invitation arrived. Wright began to worry. Had the invitation gone astray? It was rather a delicate matter to telephone and ask, but he finally did.

The French bearer of good tidings at the other end of the line, whose English was apparently sadly faulty, had imagined that Wright's exclamations of boyish disbelief had meant that he was not accepting the invitation.

Disabused of any such idea, the French authorities promptly mailed the invitation to Wright and he forwarded it to Washington. Again days passed. No word. It was almost time for his ship to sail. New accommodations would be difficult to get. Should the whole idea of going be given up? All the warnings were beginning to add up in the back of Wright's mind. Fears began to arise even about "communicating" with our own government officials.

Suddenly a telephone call came from the official American overseas radio division, inviting Wright to broadcast to France. An hour was set. Shortly before broadcast time Wright was again telephoned and told the broadcast was canceled. Why? Too many previous commitments. No time available now. Strange, since the invitation had come totally unsolicited to begin with.

Later it was discovered that Wright's former affiliation with the Communists had evidently been noticed and caused fear. Hadn't the officials read Wright's *Atlantic Monthly* articles repudiating Communism? Evidently not. Apparently once labeled, always labeled; one isn't supposed to grow—or to outgrow ideas.

More days passed. It was Saturday. The ship was to leave the following Wednesday. Friends, telephoned for advice, made contact with the State Department. Wright should ask directly what had happened.

He phoned and was told that the French Government's invitation had not been received. Offering to fly down with a copy, he was told to do so. Arriving with the copy, he was told it would not be needed. (Evidently the original had been there all the while.) He was handed his passport.

On his return to New York he was entrusted to take with him valuable paintings belonging to the National Gallery of Art.

On the appointed Wednesday he departed for Europe, a world emissary in behalf of the forbidden word "democracy," the first Negro writer to go abroad from America in just such fashion. Not as a Negro, not to do special work as a Negro, but as a first-rate writer, internationally recognized as such, to continue the same search preoccupying all artists wherever they may be—a search that finally benefits all alike—including the Negro.

Wright's reactions to France—to people, places, and the political situation—illuminated his letters to me from Paris with the acuity of his perceptions, his particular vision:

June 10, 1946

I love this country [France], yet I love it for what it is not, for being old-fashioned in a queer way. Their lack of experience in industrial living is what gives them their charm. They have a long, long tradition in thinking logically; indeed, one wonders if it is not precisely their love of their own peculiar kind of logic that shuts off the rest of the world for them. If you take them within the bounds of their own set of ideas, they cannot be beaten. But the world is just bigger than what the French think it is, bigger and richer and more varied. . . .

Yet there is a ferment of ideas here; everybody wants to have his say, regardless of what it is. There are 40 Paris daily papers and 200 weeklies!! Say, this ought to get a smile out of you. I've been talking to everybody, from bell-boys on up to the brainy ones, and everybody offers apologies for THINKING too much. "France is too intellectual," is the theme song now. I wonder who is putting out that line? Does it sound familiar? "We think too much, you know?" a porter told me with a solemn face. And that part of America that they like has to do with action, any kind of action; that is why they like our films. . . . They are sweet in their troubles. And they are beautiful. Is that what makes for tragedy?

I met a French woman who was telling me how she liked Negroes, how the CP would free them all, and I asked her about the Negroes in France and she told me without batting an eye that I was the first Negro she had ever met!!!!

We Americans are made out of something that these people know absolutely nothing about. They like our products, but they've no notion of the virtues or vices that made them.

I've met but one French Negro. I've seen quite a few on the streets, but oddly they are always walking together!!! I've been inside of 30 Paris cafés, and I've yet to see one Negro eating in one. I don't understand it. The same is true with the bars. Maybe the Americans and the Germans left behind some race hate, I don't know. I asked somebody if the CP was fighting for the Negroes and they said yes, of course. I said quietly that I'd find out soon, for I'd ask the Negroes themselves, and they just stared and said nothing. It was funny.

There is one fact though that ought not be overlooked; Willkie said that we have a pool of reserve goodwill in the world, well, our GI's all but emptied that pool. Boy, they left behind a bad taste in French mouths. I'm glad that most people take it for granted that I'm French, that is, until I open my mouth. It is not popular being an American in Europe right now. One minute these people think of us as Gods and the next minute they regard us as Devils. Which is not healthy.

None of what I've said is conclusive; I'm taking in new impressions each day. And don't let anything I've said obscure the fact that there is suffering here, and hunger. The girl downstairs who keeps the books is so hungry that she sways sometimes; her teeth are loose and she is scared of eating a hard bit of bread for fear that they'll fall out!!! That's life in Paris, 1946.

July 1, 1946

One learns slowly here. You are learning even when you don't know it, and then, all of a sudden, you wake up and find out how much you have learned. One thing I've learned thoroughly is that for some funny reason France and Paris have a way of wrecking Americans. I've seen some of the worst Americans in the world here in Paris. There must be some flaw in our national character back home that makes [people] go to pieces here. . . .

This is in the nature of a correction: I said in some letter of mine that I'd seen no Negroes in cafés or restaurants. That is true. Yet I am

196

going everywhere here and I see and feel no race feeling. I was puzzled. Was it because I am an American? I wondered. Then I met Senghor, the deputy from Africa [poet, later President of Senegal], and talked to him straight. I'd been assured that he was honest. Well, he told me that the Negroes were always together because they wanted to be. But few of them were born in France; most of them come from the possessions or the colonies. So they flocked together. That the Negro here is a kind of alien is strange. American Negroes are surely American. I'd forgotten just how thoroughly American. French Negroes have no social or political problems here, but they are French only in a superficial way. Surely not in the way that Negroes are Americans. (I'm sure that Senghor would be shocked to hear me say that; but it is true.) That is why there is no real great writing coming from French Negroes; you must be of the nation you write about, even though you are at odds with it, even though you are fighting with it. The Negroes here seem a little rootless; there is little of that strange strength that American Negroes seem to suck out of the air, in spite of oppression. What really worries the Negroes here, I suspect, is not that they are bothered, but that they are not bothered, ever. . . .

I've had some queer experience in writing here. I had an article in *Samedi Soir*; a story there; and a series of three articles in *Paris-Matin*. People were shocked. I asked them what was wrong; well, they couldn't say. But *good* writers just didn't write for daily papers. There is here a senseless snobbism which is ritualized and is utterly irrational. That is why French literature is so inbred, so foolish in some respects. [The French critic Claude] Magny is right when she says that they expect of writing something that writing cannot do. Literature here is a religion, and a kind of bad one at that. French lit. is really cut off from life, from the life that is lived each day. It is more important to keep up with tradition than to be true, honest, and real, and passionate. I don't quite know what one can say about correcting this; after all, it is the French who must do this and not me or you.

[French Communist poet Louis] Aragon has been wanting to see me like mad; have dodged him so far, but will have to see him sooner or later. Can't escape it without some good excuse. Political lines here waver, blur, and merge when you least expect it. He is a sort of priest among some people and if I deliberately refuse to see him it would be counted as an affront. But I want no tags here and I'm walking softly.

Your piece about the fantastic trip of mine was good, good. I'm letting the committee considering my application for food see it. There has been some question whether I came to do work or if I came as a guest primarily. Incidentally, when I got here, I refused to accept the French government's offer of paying my expenses for a month. I don't like folks to pay my way; I like to pay it myself, if and when I can. I think the French liked the idea, for they told me that they were very poor and what I would not use would give some poor French chap a chance to see something of life in these hard times here.

Gosh, I'm glad to be here; there is so much yet I want to see and learn. . . .

There is plenty of fear in Paris. People are afraid to say what they want to say; they say what is safe to say. They are scared of publishing where they want to. One does not write to say what one wants to say, but to say something that will make the people who count like one. The high degree of centralization of French culture has its points, but it also has its faults, its evils. It does not leave people alone enough. (For my part, I'm following the policy of putting my books and stories where I please; I'm not French and I'm acting on American assumptions. The other day I told a man that I'd not care if my stories were printed on billboards for all [to] read; he looked shocked and hurt.) Why write, though, if people can't read you? There are writers here who are counted good or great, but nobody reads them. They are known only in their small circle. Only luck takes their names beyond the prisons they build for themselves.

August 26, 1946

Dorothy, you ought to be here and see how the treatment of the Negro in America strikes these people. Each day the headlines blaze it forth. And, of course, when a Frenchman sees an American Negro, he is self-centered enough to feel that he has come to stay, to escape. That kind of an impression bobs up all the time and there is no sense in trying to explain to people. It is, in a way, a terrible criticism of our country; it is bad for a country when one of its citizens has but to show his face and folks think at once: Oh, he got away from that awful place. How lucky he is. But this is just so much an indication of the awful job we must do at home. Our poison has spread far and wide; and we give folks a stick to beat us over the head with each day on the Negro problem. Dorothy, it is bad, bad; from here it really looks terrible. I find myself even trying to explain how such a problem came about, find myself growing defensive a little. Indeed, my friends in the Embassy are sick of the phone calls from French people asking about Negroes being lynched in the USA. Of course, the CP here, having turned on the spigot of revolution because it suits their immediate ends at present, is helping the thing along, but of course with no real interest in the Negro and his plight. The Right press too has picked it up. I fear that Frenchmen who regard me sentimentally will get a shock from my books.

September 30, 1946

We, in the end, Dorothy, must be ready to accept the idea and fact that freedom as we know and hope, freedom such as Europe gave the world, is dead over here and will not perhaps return here in our time. The individual has been swallowed up into blocks, parties, movements, leagues, etc. The fear of one group creates another to balance it; then a third group feels threatened and organizes itself. And so on. Nobody is building here, or dreaming, or really creating; they are trying to defend themselves.

What makes for fear and what keeps it down? France has no fear of race, but she has much fear of other things. This interests me. Men were kind of happy in the Middle Ages when they had less to fear. They had poverty, illness, etc. But they were not as afraid then as now. Maybe, of course, they lived in illusion and we cannot and therefore we must live with fear. Maybe that is the human condition. Then, if it is, fear will certainly always keep us from thinking and acting rationally, acting in accordance with our best interests. The longer I live the more the reality of fear in life captures my attention. Do you know, Dorothy, we have more books about love, pity, hope, etc., than we have about fear, and fear is more, far more widespread and older. So little has been written about fear. So little is really known about it.

Wright returned to New York in January 1947; I could sense his idea of moving to Europe for good had become an obsession. Having a growing need to break out of his cage, the prison in which he felt inhibited, he was planning his exit every moment of every day. Several people who knew both of us begged me to try to change his mind. "Why doesn't he accept his place in America and write as a black man about the Negro? He will kill himself as an author, as a creative force, if he goes abroad to live."

I understood the argument, but couldn't agree with it. To be free is to be free. It isn't enough for a white person to say, "Yes, Richard Wright, you are fine. But you are black and that is your fate; you have no choice."

The disputes went on for weeks. I refused to attempt to dictate Wright's destiny. If he wanted to move to Europe, he should go. If he stayed here and was miserable, what good would it do? Would it improve his writing?

In July 1947 the Wrights set forth for Europe once more. I was the only one I knew who defended their going. Dick retained his interest and involvement in *Twice A Year*; we kept in close touch. He continued to record his reactions in letters to me:

September 10, 1947

I've found an alarming tide of anti-Semitism here in Paris. I don't quite understand it. It is powerless; there is no political force behind it. It is discouraging to find it though. I talked to Sartre about it and he thinks that the misery here is what is causing it; they want something to hate and the helpless Jew seems to keep himself in the headlines and they fasten upon him. This has made me think a lot. The hatred of the Jew today (and the Negro too) has something in it much deeper than merely finding a scapegoat, I fear. First, the Jew and the Negro are but tiny minorities and to hate them is easy, to fight them is easy, too, too easy. Then what kind of personalities are these that feel that it is all right to leap upon helpless and defenseless people and start fighting them? You see what I mean? It indicates a total lack of a healthy outlook on life. A real man with strength and courage would say to himself that I must find something *much bigger and stronger than Jews and Negroes* to hate; to hate such defenseless people is not worthy of me and my capacities. It is, in the last analysis, almost a matter of honor. And it means that all such subtle considerations have been lost to the common run of men today. In talking with Sartre about this I told him that there was something that I feared more than both Communism and Fascism, and that was the loss of the sense of humanity in men. He agreed. In our talk we did not see any form of action now today that could be of much use, save that of individual self-assertion. Even the acts of terror of the Jews [in Palestine], which are futile, are serving to keep alive somewhat the sense of what a man or a few men can do. From that point of view, I find myself in deep sympathy with the desperate acts of the Jews when they strike out blindly at their enemies. I've felt the same sympathy when Negroes do the same. I don't want to feel this way, but what other way is there to feel?

11

Unbearable tensions are mounting between Edward and me. I have begun to feel literally strangled when trying to take a deep breath. The first sense of anxiety I have known pervades my body. The anguish is beyond my comprehension and control. Not to be able to breathe! I have been breathing all my life; now I don't know how.

There are many beautiful interludes with Edward. So much that he does is noble—his record in the war, his work for cooperatives and Palestine, his efforts to battle anti-Semitism. He is my husband; I married him because I loved him; I don't want a divorce. I know the agony he goes through when he cannot control his temper or violence and then is abject. We deeply love the children, and the children love us.

Edward continues to be jealous of my modest activities. If I thought getting off committees or giving up *Twice A Year* and my *Post* column would stabilize our relationship, I would do so, but such acts will not truly help. Edward confesses he is upset by not being in a position of power although, in the past, he always belittled those who sought it. He has suppressed more than I suspected because of the early conflict with his father. Before our marriage he had willingly consulted a psychiatrist, though for only a short time. Now he bristles if the word is mentioned. All psychiatrists are hopeless; he wants to shoot them all on sight.

Since my father's death in 1945, I have had to take more responsibility for my mother and make frequent trips to Philadelphia. My eldest brother is ill in Hartford; I must drive there often. My health, my nerves, are at a breaking point. If I don't take some definite action, I shall fall seriously ill.

I go to a psychiatrist, a man somewhat familiar with our situation. I have advised many friends to seek psychiatric help after hearing their problems, yet I have never truly understood until now what anxiety is. I explain to the doctor my inability to breathe properly and tell him in detail about our marriage.

After a few sessions he looks at me with sharp penetration and says, "You have swallowed your rage too much and for too long." I feel as though a magic wand has been waved above me; some mysterious force relaxes my body; I can breathe freely. I say in wonder, "The knot has untied itself. How can I thank you?" I walk out of the office, my anguish momentarily relieved. But something warns me to take care: the sense of crisis has not disappeared.

Gradual changes are taking place within me. I remain troubled, but have no wish to withdraw, to seek a guru or protection from the real world. I accept struggle and conflict as inherent in life.

To be sure, I am a product of Western civilization, nourished and enriched by the Judaeo-Graeco-Christian tradition. Yet I cannot for a single moment identify with the idea of a covenant pledged between Israel and Jehovah thousands of years ago. My inability to look upon myself as a religious Jew, which has long confused me, no longer disturbs. That I cannot believe in a personal or a sectarian God is settled once and for all. The cosmos is too vast, mysterious, transcendent for any such limited view.

Nonetheless a gnawing hunger for the discipline of ancient tradition grips me; I long for ritual acts born of reverence, for a community of committed colleagues devoid of self-delusion. Above all, a world free from desperate poverty, violence, and bloodshed.

The recent death of Stieglitz has deprived me of the single channel through which my need for expression of the sacred in life could be released and shared. He photographed, communicated with awe and wonder, with dignity, devotion, and love. Each time we spoke, or touched, or he showed me a new print; each time I brought him a poem or one of my photographs that came through as I wanted it to—or sent him a flower—it was a ritual. Every time I saw him with others, bringing out their potential, it was a spiritual event. His *Equivalents* are still for me the most sensitive, reverential images of our era.

My first experience of traditional Indian art had been with Coomaraswamy; I take up his *Dance of Shiva* again, and feel the same excitement as before. I search out his later writings and find them even more penetrating. The fundamental wisdom of Eastern thought draws me to it with growing fascination. Yet even while this is so, I feel myself above all an American, privileged to live in a culturally pluralistic society.

I treasure the opportunity to have close relationships with those of diverse philosophies. No limiting bonds restrict my freedom to decide upon my own beliefs and I respect the same right for others.

I see much of Mai-mai Sze, asking her a multitude of questions about the Tao and Zen Buddhism. I am fervently curious about both. Mai-mai is writing a remarkable book, *The Tao of Painting*, to be published by the Bollingen Foundation. She quotes, "Tao cannot be conveyed by either words or silence. In that state which is neither speech nor silence its transcendental nature may be apprehended." She describes the Tao as the basic Chinese belief in an order and harmony in nature. Reverence and mystery are at its root. "There is evidence that the combination of *shou* (head) and *ch'o* (foot) symbolized wholeness, that is, spiritual growth. One aspect of the character *tao* thus represents an *inner* way, an integration of character with deep and complex psychological connotations (as to soul, mind and emotions). The idea of wholeness, literally from head to foot, of total harmony, like Heaven and Earth, is therefore the goal illustrated in the composition of the character *tao,* and *tao* is primarily an inner way toward achieving this aim."

To experience Taoism, Mai-mai tells me, is not something one can do swiftly—it takes time. Little by little an insight comes to one—alone, through talking, reading, living.

If tradition is taken seriously, is deep-seated, I know, it affects every act of one's life. The flow, equilibrium, discipline become the person. I respect the depth of what this implies and want to penetrate its possibilities more fully.

Mai-mai and I attended a lecture by the great Zen authority Dr. D. T. Suzuki. Understanding little of it, I decided to take his course at Columbia University.

Dr. Suzuki is small of stature and aging. His features are delicate; rimless spectacles are barely noticeable. He has the serious look of a professor, but if he is amused, his smile is gentle and responsive. He speaks in almost a whisper; I sit up front in order to hear him, but am not certain I always do. I watch his hands—beautiful, elegant. He never wears a kimono but always a Western suit, invariably well-tailored and of fine material.

He explains that unless one is at a point of crisis when coming to Zen, it cannot have full significance. Only if the need to attain enlightenment is a matter of life and death will Zen reveal its true meaning. I have come upon Dr. Suzuki at exactly the right moment!

The statement that spiritual power is gained through supreme enlightenment fascinates me, though I don't know exactly what supreme enlightenment is. I soon learn it has to do with the religious experience of feeling at one with the cosmos, the community, oneself. It is "an intuitive looking-into in contradistinction to intellectual and logical understanding." Enlightenment involves the unfolding of a new world hitherto unperceived in the confusion of a dual mind. The words of Coomaraswamy and Suzuki are almost identical. They bid us to rid ourselves of ego and illusion, of a sense of dualism.

One day in class someone asks what *Kokura* signifies. Suzuki replies: "Where there is no question of becoming or not becoming, that is where *Kokura* is. The concept of change implies that an object moves from one state to another—from what it is to what it is not. Moving from negation to affirmation implies becoming. *Kokura* is beyond both affirmation and negation. The very abode of 'isness' itself is where *Kokura* is. If one seeks *Kokura* it is not attainable. It is precisely in its unobtainableness that *Kokura* lies. It is only when we think wrongly that we assume that any word adequately can apply to *Kokura*."

Suzuki tells us that long ago a man named Daito Kuji was considered the right person to head an important Zen monastery. Daito Kuji learned of the plan but had no interest in it. He went to live under the Great Bridge where beggars gathered. No one knew of his whereabouts; a search failed to find him. Some suspected he might be hidden among the beggars. Fortunately, all knew he loved melons. Each beggar received a glorious fruit, but was told he must take it without using his hands. Only after one of the recipients answered, "Can you give me the melon without using *your* hands?" was Daito Kuji recognized. To "be put on a pedestal" by becoming head of the great monastery did not please him. Yet today the beautiful temple in Kyoto—Daito Kuji—is still named in his honor.

I talk with a popular exponent of Zen, who warns that the more we seek the secrets of the Tao and Zen, the further we move away from them. "What is Zen?" I ask. He looks at me. "Walk on," he answers, "Zen is everyday life."

Seeing Suzuki and his beautiful, brilliant young assistant, Mihoko Okamura, outside of class, I learn more from listening and talking to them than from lectures. I ask Mihoko what she thinks enlightenment signifies. Her reply: "The discovery of one's own limitations." What a blessing she is!

I learn from Suzuki that we must rid ourselves of the tyranny of intellect, of theory, of conceptualism. Zen has no God to worship, no ritual, no ceremonials. Even though I had come to it hungry for ritual born of reverence, Zen rejects the idea of soul, philosophy, religion. It affirms affirmation, and freeing the mind of all obstructions. One's intellect must be its own master. Neither polytheism nor monotheism has meaning for it. "Search out the depths within," says Suzuki. (He deplores the complexity of Indian thought, which I do not. Neither can I deny the rationalism of the West.) But my experience of Suzuki and Zen challenges, crystallizes, and unclutters much for me that at the moment I need most to have put in order.

When I visit Suzuki and Mihoko, they offer me Japanese ceremonial green tea. Mihoko whisks it in a dark bowl until it froths. Small slabs of a jellied sweet are served, to be eaten just before drinking the at first rather bitter liquid. I am converted to green tea at once. Mihoko is certain she can get me some from a nearby Buddhist society which imports it from Japan.

The enchantment of the tea ceremony stays with me for days. Mihoko presents me with a whisk—a scoop for measuring, with a long, graceful handle—and obtains the green powder. It looks best against a dark surface, not, as with Chinese tea, against white. Where to find a bowl that is just right?

I remember a Japanese shop on Eighth Street: there, on a shelf, stands a dark brownish-black bowl of the right size and shape. I smile at the man in charge. "Do you consider this correct for Japanese green tea?" He smiles back. "Yes, exactly." Unfortunately he has only one bowl, but expects soon to have another like it.

"How do you prepare the tea?"

The man tells me his wife brings the water to a boil, then pours it over the tea at once. I thank him for his advice and buy the single bowl.

Practicing by myself, I pour the boiling water into the bowl from the beautiful, long-handled wooden measuring scoop, and whisk and whisk. The liquid neither bubbles nor froths as it should; I drink it without pleasure and decide to try again before daring to offer the tea to others.

A short time later I revisit the little store; the owner shows me another bowl. I buy it and recount my sad experience. The man advises me not to follow his wife's example but, rather, to permit the water to continue boiling for a few minutes. I thank him again.

A friend comes to see me who also has fallen in love with ceremonial tea. I have on hand the proper sweet bean jelly, offer to make the tea, put the kettle on and, leaving the water to boil, return to my friend. As we talk, I forget the kettle and then, with horror, remember it. I rush to the kitchen: the water is almost boiling over. I pour it into the bowls and start whisking madly, like one possessed, first in one bowl, then in the other. The tea froths exactly as it should. Carrying the tray with the bowls and plate of bean jelly to my friend, I am flushed and excited, admitting that this is the first time I have prepared the tea properly. We relish our sweet and sip our tea from the beautiful bowls. I have put my whole heart and soul into the whisking. The length of time the water boils makes no difference. Clearly the way to whisk is to do it with all of oneself. A perfect Zen story.

One afternoon Mai-mai Sze takes me to meet Natacha Rambova. In a small, simply furnished, book-filled apartment opposite the City Center, I find a few Far Eastern gilded statues, but no other art. Mai-mai has told me little about Rambova, who clearly is a very private person. Married to Rudolph Valentino during the height of his career in the twenties, she was a designer at the time and was involved in Hollywood activities. She left him after a few years and now lives a secluded life, dedicating herself to studies in Egyptian symbolism and to editing books on the subject for the Bollingen Foundation.

On first meeting Rambova, it is said, Valentino found her the most beautiful woman he had ever seen. She is still handsome, but pale and fragile; she has the look of an intellectual Garbo. The suit she wears is gray, severe, plain; she sits at a table on which typed pages are neatly stacked. Occasionally she sips water from a glass before her.

Her words and tone of voice reveal a vast impatience with the present-day world. "We are decadent. We have forgotten the great traditions, the meaning of symbols, the need for inner discipline. We ignore the sacred. We are lost children, surrounded by ugliness. Great civilizations create great beauty. People today have respect for nothing, conduct themselves without dignity." The voice is tired, expresses dismay. I don't know how Mai-mai is reacting.

Rambova points to the papers before her. "I have been working on the symbolism of numbers, body parts, animals." I don't know what she means. "Until people understand these ancient symbols and the labors through which each of us must go—until they comprehend the great myths—they will continue to be lost." She looks at me intently. "We can't skip over any experience and expect to comprehend our lives. We have to undergo periods of absolute darkness, blindness, before we can be transformed and ready to see." This serious, dedicated woman knows something to which I should pay attention.

As Mai-mai and I leave, Rambova says to me, "We must meet again. Telephone any time you like." She speaks with great kindness. We make another appointment; this time she talks about herself, her early background. She does not mention Valentino, or the fine actress Alla Nazimova, or anyone else with whom she was closely associated in Hollywood.

Born Winifred Shaughnessy in Salt Lake City, the daughter of a Catholic father and of a Mormon mother who became a Christian Scientist, she grew up in San Francisco, before being taken to Europe to complete her education. Her excitement about myth led her to the British Museum and its nearby bookshops, where she immersed herself in Eastern thought. She ran away and studied ballet in Paris. (Her Russian ballet master suggested she call herself Natacha Rambova.) Later she became interested in Theosophy.

She returns to our previous talk. "Dorothy, we must progress through many stages, we cannot avoid them. If we are trapped into being fascinated by glamour and are then disillusioned, it isn't necessarily so that all we have to do is put it aside. We must recognize why glamour has attracted us and why it no longer does. We should examine everything that has happened in our lives, so we can learn from our mistakes and discover what our next steps should be. That is what myth is telling us, but in the modern Western world we pay no attention.

"There is no true religion. Everything is institutionalized—both the material and spiritual. Having reached the lowest ebb of a material cycle, we are not in tune with nature; we are concerned with only part of the cosmos—the material. Slowly our civilization is beginning to break out of its imprisonment into an awareness of nature and one world, although narrow considerations—nationalism, racial prejudice, and other destructive forces —are working against us. Yet I have faith that higher concepts are bound to persist."

Rambova continues with her monologue: "The essence of the great teachings of the past is contained in symbols. It cannot be expressed in words. Symbolic imagery in early texts and in the arts became the means of naming. To name is to bring into existence. The more symbols are understood— become part of ourselves—the more easily the pattern of how we must live, and toward what end, is shown in all its fullness. Such comprehension adds power to the carrying out of our everyday tasks; to the way we write, create art in whatever form. Ancient symbols which release consciousness and relate to all human experience are to be interpreted at every level and in their negative as well as positive aspects.

"Myth and symbol reveal the complex nature of our relationships, harmonies, contradictions, ambiguities at the deepest level. Problems can be solved only by righting the psyche, setting it in order, not through withdrawal and hiding. I am talking about not an intellectual exercise but a process of growth, awareness, training. If we concentrate profoundly, through repetition and meditation, we create tradition from within; we become one with it."

Rambova leaves ancient tradition for the moment. "The modern West has ignored these considerations. Only Jung and a few followers in our time illuminate the positive role that dreams play in the making and understanding of myth, while Freud has brilliantly grasped the negative or repressive aspect of our psyches. Jung explores the inner man, not simply to reveal our illusions and delusions, masks and aggressions. We have to recognize our lack of control, our will to power, our inability to feel in harmony with ourselves, with others, with the cosmos. We must get at the root of our anxieties, false ambitions, fears. Only in this way can we awaken to real values; only so can psychic energy be released and consciousness acquired. Just to be aware of these truisms is not enough; we must use ourselves constructively. This is what the ancients did through their training and disciplines. To penetrate the significance of symbols is itself therapy; it is the only true knowledge.

"We can understand these principles only after a period of crisis. To become an ascetic, a devotee, or an intellectual follower—to think one is 'spiritual'—won't help. We must go through the process of learning, but also through the 'labors' of myth. We must pay the price for our errors. We cannot escape. We can help each other only if those who are seeking feel a real need. Otherwise there can be no true communication."

I am enthralled. Again I have found the very person whom I should listen to at just the right moment. My deepest disturbances are being brought to the surface; proper demands are being made of me. I have needed a great shaking up. Natacha is giving it to me.

The next time I go to her she starts at once to tell me the provocative tale of the beautiful maiden Psyche, and Eros, god of love. It is a relief to hear a concrete description of specific experience rather than abstractions.

Psyche has two older sisters who typify the same flaws as their counterparts in *Cinderella* and *Beauty and the Beast*. They are envious, greedy, and mischievous whereas Psyche—younger, innocent, lovely—is the promise of the future. Eros forbids her to look upon him even after their marriage; she must have faith and be free of desire. The sisters nag her into disobeying, whereupon Eros vanishes. In order to find him again, Psyche must undergo a series of labors.

Natacha elaborates: "Think about the jealous sisters, Dorothy—they are grasping for material advantage, for illusory goals, desires which they should have outgrown. When Psyche gives in to their vicious incitements, she loses Eros and all the riches he has bestowed upon her. The labors she embarks upon—which test her courage and faith—do not destroy her, but instead restore Eros to her and bring her to maturity."

I tell Natacha that our talks are of inexpressible value and confess that I have been in an anguished state of crisis. My marriage has been disintegrating for some time. "I went to a psychiatrist because I was so upset I couldn't breathe. He helped me temporarily by saying I had swallowed my rage too long. For a while I could breathe freely, but now I can't again."

She replies calmly, "Lie down on the floor." She, too, lies down. Her voice is impersonal. "Shake your arms to relax. Lie perfectly flat and still. Don't do anything for a moment. Now breathe in. Slowly." She tells me to take longer breaths, but I can't.

"Lie on the floor at home and try to breathe in and out, slowly. Don't force anything." I feel like an idiot, but Natacha handles the situation with a professionalism that puts me at ease. I stand up; we bend and stretch for a few minutes. "That's enough for today. We'll do more the next time you come."

Natacha's exercises teach me to control my body in a new way, not quickly and vigorously—a result far more difficult to achieve than my earlier ability to throw a basketball into a basket, or hit a tennis ball so hard it couldn't be returned. Progress is slow. To control even a single breath—breathing in, holding it longer each time, breathing out—is tantalizing. Knowing we are on the right track, I follow instructions, although earlier I would have rebelled against such seemingly inactive procedures.

Our exercises grow increasingly complex and then one day Natacha says, "Dorothy, it is clear you have been living a largely extrovert life. That is what the psychiatrist was probably telling you. Your crisis is warning you to pay attention to your inner life—the inner self you've been repressing. I see you as a very feminine person, essentially an introvert. You have much to give, but you aren't using your full creative power. You have felt rage at being deprived of that opportunity. There comes a time in our lives when we must use our real selves to the utmost. This means giving up many things to which we have become accustomed and cling to mistakenly."

To my surprise, she adds, "I would like to do your horoscope. I am certain it will tell you much about yourself." I confess I can't take astrology seriously in personal terms, but Natacha goes ahead. I tell her I was born on March 28, 1905, I think at four o'clock in the morning. The next time I see her she is excited, her face radiant. "You came into the world under the sign of Aries, with Taurus in the ascendency, and Libra rising. You have been an extrovert—active, a leader—during the first part of your life. You have the clarity of Aries and the power of Taurus. Now you must go on to the next step. Libra is rising. This is telling you to use your feminine creativity, your inner self. Listen to what is being told to you."

Despite my skepticism about astrology, what Natacha says somehow has the ring of truth. "You're doubtless right, yet I never look upon my work for social causes as extrovert; I feel I have a responsibility to society. I try to strike a balance between activities helpful to those less fortunate and those necessary for my own development or equilibrium. Still, I'm truly grateful for what you've told me. I said I was born at four o'clock in the morning. But my mother now tells me I was born at four in the afternoon."

Natacha is pleased. "I thought something was wrong with your having been born in the early morning." This amuses me, which Natacha notices. "If you don't believe what I've told you, I beg you to have a Rorschach test. I can send you to a friend—an expert—who will do one for you, unofficially, and give you the results."

I take the test, which shows I am using only one-third of my capabilities; I should be doing more creative work of my own. Natacha is jubilant.

Although I don't believe in horoscopes or astrological analogies at a personal level, the inner patterns of development they describe have great meaning for me. The significance of each sign or symbol leads logically to the next. With uncanny accuracy our psychological growth is traced. The signs, body parts, animals, and seasons give clues and warnings about who we are, where we are in our development and what we must become.

Natacha has opened a most important door for me. Instead of lecturing about how to behave, she has shown, through elucidating one myth after another, the road we must take and the price we must pay for our youthful unknowing conduct. It is from the symbols of many cultures that I learn what commandments have failed to communicate. The great legends hold secrets we must slowly and constantly unravel. Tradition is the handing down of these secrets by those who have penetrated them, to those who are ready to understand. In eternal succession.

Art and Action—583 pages! The contents are so rich they are almost too overwhelming for a single issue, but unfortunately it is the last number of *Twice A Year*. The financial drain is too great, and I refuse to change the breadth of the publication.

Curious that there should be the greatest demand for the final, as for the first number. I cannot afford to print a second edition of *Art and Action*, which, oversubscribed, would certainly sell out, as did the first. It is a sad moment, but I must stop publishing. I look at the volumes as they stand side by side and cannot quite believe they exist.

I salute those whose thoughts have been recorded. The dream I had of creating a journal may not have turned out exactly as planned, but perhaps the result is better than I had envisioned. Something essential in Mary Lescaze and myself—as well as in Richard Wright and Brom Weber—has taken form. Like a plant, any creative work has its mysterious seed; what eventuates cannot be foreseen. The growth of an individual follows its own laws, its own inevitability of development. No prevision can compare with the concrete testaments of living, breathing men and women, whose pages have come to us like so many treasured guests bidden by an invitation born of undeniable faith.

The publishers Pellegrini and Cudahy ask me to edit a volume of Marin's letters and writings. Herbert J. Seligmann's 1931 edition is out of print and Marin has written much in the interval—mainly letters and forewords to catalogues. I am delighted. After I have begun to organize the book, symptoms develop that indicate I may have cancer; I must have an immediate exploratory operation. Fortunately there is no malignancy, but because I am overtired, my doctor insists I go to Florida to recover. My friend Maggie Dunham suggests joining her in Sarasota, where she is about to visit Chick

(A. Everett) Austen, former director of the Wadsworth Atheneum in Hartford, now director of the Ringling Museums. I finish Marin's *Selected Writings* and remain in Sarasota for further recuperation.

It is comforting to be with congenial friends and be included in the undemanding activities attendant upon the arrival of the British poets Dr. Edith and Sir Osbert Sitwell. Austen has invited them to read their poems at the Ringling Mansion. He has redecorated the living room of his splendid house on the Gulf of Mexico as a fitting setting for a reception after the reading.

The winter colony can speak of little else but the Sitwells. "What are they like?" "Have you read them?" "Aren't they frightfully difficult to understand?" "What did you say his name was? Oswald?" "No, Osbert." "Is she really a doctor?" "Naturally we shall dress."

I am asked to Sir Osbert's press conference. Dr. Edith is resting. He appears punctually at four. While admitting he is fatigued from the train journey south, he is polite and considerate, seeming to give his undivided attention to those gathered around him. He apologizes that he must be on his way before too long to retrieve his suit from the tailor for the evening's reading.

A reporter, shyly: "Do you mind the heat?" Sir Osbert: "It is never too hot for me. The temperature of the next world, I should imagine, will be just about right."

Question: "Where have you been lecturing?" With patience, sweetness: "New York, Boston, Montreal, Toronto." No notes are taken.

Painful pause. "Where else?" "Hamilton, Lynchburg, Yale." Still no notes. Longer, even more tense interlude: "Where else?" "Baltimore, Buffalo."

At last a timid query ends the nightmare. "Which American authors do you admire?'"

"El-yutt, of course." The answer is prompt, assured, courteous. "But then after all, El-yutt is an Anglo-American, is he not?" The speech is too fast, the accent too British for the words to be caught. Still no notes.

"Who else?"

"I would say Henry Millah."

"Who?"

"Henry Millah."

"Who is Henry Millah?"

Skillfully elusive, Sir Osbert blithely continues with his list: "I like very much some of your Southern writers. William Faulkner, Eudora Welty. And then, of your poets, E. E. Cummings, Marianne Moore. Some of John Crowe Ransom. José Garcia Villa. The early Pound. Frost."

No response.

Question: "Do you think all experimentation in the arts is necessarily good? Hasn't it led—in the main—to the creation of a great deal of work that is unintelligible? As in the case of Gertrude Stein?"

Sir Osbert (the flicker of a smile): "Gertrude Stein—unintelligible? I should say, on the contrary, too simple."

No response.

Sir Osbert: "Do not forget all poetry is unintelligible to some readers. It is not a question of poetry (and by that I mean only good poetry) being unintelligible when it is not understood. Rather, those who read it are un-intelligent if they do not understand. In the arts, experimentation is in-evitable."

The evening of the reading is soft, warm. The Ringling Mansion, enormous, ornate, was erected by circus magnate John Ringling in imitation of a doge's palace (some say in imitation of an imitation). Like an interloping ghost, it rises on the outskirts of the unpretentious twentieth-century winter resort Sarasota.

The towering great room in which the poems are read is dimly lit. Marble floors with huge black and white squares. A festooned gilded column in a corner. As I walk toward my chair, I note deep, dark red velvets, damasks, gold braid, rock-crystal chandeliers, candelabra, tapestries, a pipe organ. I overhear a proud comment: "Mrs. Ringling made that lampshade herself."

The audience is large, keyed up. A hushed voice: "There hasn't been so spectacular a welcome for any British author since—since Dickens!" A well-dressed man introduces the Sitwells, confessing that the only thing more difficult to describe than one such genius is two.

Sir Osbert enters. After the enraptured applause subsides, the musical voice communicates with utmost simplicity. He reads for twenty minutes, whereupon Dr. Edith glides toward the audience, also to read for twenty minutes. She is tall and queenly, described correctly as gothic in appearance, gothic enough to hang bells in!

Her hair is the color of honey. She wears a honey-colored brocaded cloak over dark green satin. The head is that of a great regal bird. A honey-colored lion's power lurks within.

Dr. Edith finishes her reading. The high priestess has cast a spell over the great hall; prolonged applause. Dr. Edith then asks whether she should read something light now or something more serious. A woman's voice implores: "Read one of the terrifying ones!"

After the last poem, members of the audience crowd forward. A young woman: "You go in for the heavy and the religious, don't you?" Dr. Edith, freezingly polite: "For the religious, yes. For the heavy, no."

Another woman hovers about Dr. Edith, soulfully begging to converse with her whenever convenient. About what? About stresses. "About what?" asks Dr. Edith, dumbfounded. Woman: "About stresses." Dr. Edith is at a loss. "Stresses in poetry, of course," explains the lady. Dr. Edith maintains her distantly gracious manner.

During the next week, in the torrid afternoons (it is May) I drove the Sitwells through the flat, desolate Florida countryside in a rented sedan, the only car available. Dr. Edith wore her usual heavy robes: a velvet cloak over a long satin tunic. Her hat was felt, her gloves woolen. I was certain her boots were fur-lined. Over the cloak was wrapped a bulky woolen sweater. I had on a short-sleeved cotton dress. As we climbed into the car, I surreptitiously rolled down the window next to me approximately half an inch. An immediate reaction: "Dahling, isn't there a bit too much air?" I had already turned the window up at the first syllable. The comedy was repeated again and again.

Dr. Edith agrees with everything everyone says, so long as a conversation is concerned with a relatively unimportant subject or when good manners are the height of what is required. The moment a discussion turns in a direction about which she has strong feelings, the finely drawn lips quiver. The eyes appear as from behind protectively receding slits. A heavily iced curtain drops hazardously before those who arouse her ire. She is even more beyond reach than when normally polite; her voice takes on an overwhelming authority.

Sir Osbert's eyes become large and glowing when he feels cut off or wishes to be. He hides behind a thinly iridescent veil he can at will transform into a cold and solid wall. At first, he appears more accessible than Dr. Edith.

The subject of being shy arises. Dr. Edith: "We are shy through fear, when curtains are lowered, shutting us out." Does she realize she induces comparable diffidence in others? Sir Osbert: "That dreadful feeling—especially when you are young—wondering how in heaven's name you are going to be able to withdraw from a room. Even today I am frightfully timid. Frightfully. I suffer agonies every time I must read my poems." Dr. Edith: "So do I."

Of fame: Sir Osbert, with disarming candor: "I simply love it. Every minute of it."

Dr. Edith: "Fame? If you achieve it during your lifetime, as it grows, it leaves you less and less time for yourself. And then, after you are dead, all anyone really cares about is digging up the details of your private life."

12

I met Coomaraswamy for the last time shortly before his death; he looked alarmingly frail, but seemed as eager to talk as ever. He told me with great feeling of a book he was anxious for me to read, *Capitalism, Socialism or Villagism?*, by Bharatan Kumarappa.

To Coomaraswamy the ideal of villagism in the Gandhian sense represented a goal higher than that of capitalism or socialism; a goal higher than that of either mere individualism or mere centralization of power.

He spoke that day, too, of Meister Eckhart, with particular warmth. In his last years he merged more and more intensely in his own thought the great tradition of the West and the great tradition of the East, just as he felt such a merging must take place in the world at large.

As we said goodbye he shook his head sadly about how few Indians seem to realize the meaning of the great tradition they have inherited, or to live in its image, and spoke with even greater sadness of the way in which America has lost all sense of it. But, he remarked, because India still clings to her great tradition, at least to some degree—though sometimes wrongly— she represents a greater hope for the world than does any country in the West. The revival of a positive attitude toward villagism and the possibility that an enlightened cooperative society might be created in India filled him with great hope. He tapped Kumarappa's book with the same reverence he might have displayed in handling a piece of great Indian art.

There was something deeply moving about hearing the faraway voice sharing the quintessence of what the long and dedicated life had taught. But I left with a heavy heart. The skin was a shade too transparent; the voice a shade too weak. The body seemed alarmingly fragile. After I left him, I said sadly to those whom I joined, "I shall never see him again."

Within a short time Coomaraswamy died.

After painful years of struggle India had won her freedom, but Gandhi, unique symbol of nonviolence and love, was struck down by a fanatical murderer in 1948. Nehru's sister Krishna wrote to me from Bombay after the tragedy:

March 12, 1948

The last time I met Mr. Gandhi was on the 29th morning. He was so full of life and fun. I had not seen him so bright for ages. He looked so well too. He asked me about our boys—about my writing—about our next trip to America. He teased me about a hundred little things and I returned home thankful that he had survived the last fast for we needed him so badly. I little knew his span of life was running shorter and shorter each minute and in another 36 hours he would no longer be with us.

Since we heard the ghastly news we lived in a daze. We saw him dead—we saw his funeral and yet we could not believe he was gone. India was stricken of course but nothing could have been more heartbreaking than my brother's face—the anguish written all over it. In one night he aged 15 years—in one night his straight shoulders became bent as though suddenly and without warning a terrible burden had been placed upon them. We who loved him and stood by could do nothing for his grief was too personal to be shared even with me or Indira his daughter. Since Mr. Gandhiji's death, I fear for my brother all the time and I can't bear to be away from him.

October 1949: "India hands," as those of us who had worked for Indian Independence through the India League were called, together with members of the Indian community in New York and the appropriate government officials were huddled together in a huge hangar next to La Guardia Airport. We were waiting to greet Prime Minister Jawaharlal Nehru, who, as an official guest of President Truman, was paying his first visit to the United States.

The red carpet—to my disappointment, pale and not truly crimson—was rolled out. The great plane landed. Cameras rolled and clicked. The military seemed inappropriate, but were inevitably on hand with martial music. Nonviolent Nehru descended, elegant and handsome. None of his photographs had given any inkling of his radiance. He walked toward us with easy grace, looked bemused, unofficial; he seemed even shyer than I felt. One by one, we were introduced to him. He was warm and affable, but gave no evidence that he was paying attention to or hearing our names—even those of people who tried to show how well they knew him. His daughter, Indira Gandhi, was small, fragile, looked tired. His sister, Mrs. Pandit, now India's Ambassador to the United States, looked modest and distinguished. While Indira tried valiantly to smile, Nehru couldn't quite smother his own somewhat bewildered amusement.

Those who came to the hangar had to move swiftly into long, sleek limousines in order to return to the city with dispatch. What a waste of time, I thought. Then second reactions crowded out the first. Nehru! Who else at the airport had spent years in jail in a noble, nonviolent struggle for freedom? Had I witnessed no more than how unimpressed he was with himself—how amazed he was that so many people had bothered to welcome him—it would have been reason enough to celebrate him.

Pearl Buck and Richard Walsh have an evening reception for Nehru at the Waldorf-Astoria, where he is staying. I cannot quite imagine him there. Edward and I arrive at the appointed hour. Nehru stands in the middle of a large room. His expression is the same as at the airport. He speaks to no one, except to acknowledge introductions. I feel again that he hears no names, sees no faces. Is it because he has been alone in jail so much that he pays little attention to what is going on around him? Has he become dependent on nothing other than himself? Or, now that he is Prime Minister, do his burdens so preoccupy him that his visit to the United States is simply an irksome interruption? He continues to look unofficial, natural, boyish, in spite of the bald head. He has written that he has a private face, and he has.

I am taken to Nehru and introduced again. No one nearby is speaking. As usual on such occasions, I am tongue-tied, but I loathe a vacuum. In desperation I say, "It is wonderful you have come to the United States." My eyes meet Nehru's. His quizzical look is still there, challenging, baffling. I blush, feel absurd at having made so banal a remark. The faintly bronzed face breaks into a winged smile. I add as quickly as I can, so that then I may remain forever silent, "I do hope that as you travel throughout the country you won't speak only of your political ideas, but also of your philosophy."

The dazzling head is thrown back, the luminous eyes flash. Nehru's body vibrates with full laughter. "*My* philosophy?" The clipped British accent, the unexpected, self-mocking, rhetorical question breaks the ice, but it makes me want to run away out of sight.

I expected Nehru to wear his white Gandhi cap and Indian jacket. His Western suit is of a fine gray wool, well-cut; his tie is plain gray, of heavy silk. He has the bearing of a prince. In any civilization he would stand out as an exceptional man. His eyes are those of a searching, visionary intellectual. His baldness accentuates the noble cast of his face with its high cheekbones, generous mouth, and sharply sculptured nose.

The evening is glamorous, yet painful. Everyone is eager to converse with Nehru, to impress him. Few are able to say more than a sentence. He listens most politely but continues to speak almost not at all. I hate to venture far from where he is; I should love to hear whatever he might say, but make no attempt to talk with him further.

Toward the end of the reception I see him whisper to Nan Pandit in what I imagine to be Hindi. She beckons and asks me please to remain after the others have left. Her brother wishes to tell me something. I am startled; I had no inkling he had any awareness of my existence.

Edward and I step aside and wait. Nehru explains to me that on the following day a literary tea is being given in his honor by the Walshes, who are standing quite near, bidding tonight's guests farewell. Nehru drops his voice: "I have examined the guest list. I see only names of authors I have either read or heard about. And a few old fogies. But no younger, progressive writers, editors, publishers." He asks if I would be so kind as to see whether the list might be expanded. Would I call him promptly at nine-thirty in the morning and tell him what I have been able to accomplish?

He glances at a formidable minute-by-minute schedule he holds before him. "I shall be able to talk at that time only. If there is no way in which you can have appropriate names added, would you terribly mind inviting those you think would interest me to your house the day after tomorrow? Nan tells me you know everyone. I will have no more than three-quarters of an hour free, beginning at three-thirty in the afternoon."

I am baffled. I wonder whether Nehru has any notion of what he is asking me to do—of how outraged the Walshes will be at my interference. I have not been invited to the tea, and even if I had been, how dare I try to rearrange what has been planned. I explain the awkwardness of my position. Both Nan and Nehru are reassuring. "Blame it on us. There will be no problem at all." I foresee only difficulties.

Nan says something in Hindi. I pray she is telling Nehru that the entire idea is out of the question. Nehru turns to his schedule again: "Oh, yes, there is one thing more, I fear. Nan says you know the Mayor well. I wonder would it be possible to have him cut the morning ceremonies to a minimum. I note that a good deal of time is to be spent on formalities." He smiles, winces. "Perhaps when you telephone me, you might let me know about that, too?"

I am torn between feeling that what has been asked of me is impossible to carry out and wanting to laugh. But then, as I visualize a somber-faced Nehru confined in jail, my resistance and hesitation vanish. Nehru bids us good night: "I shall hear from you promptly at nine-thirty, then?" He bows and presses the long, graceful, tapering fingers of his two hands together in India's prayerlike hail and farewell.

I reach Mayor O'Dwyer on the phone promptly at eight-thirty. O'Dwyer: "Of course I shall shorten the ceremonies. I'll do anything for that man. He's great. What do you suggest?" "Just leave out as much as you can. But I feel Nehru will want to know exactly what the timing will be, and I have to make another inquiry before calling him." O'Dwyer's proposed cuts are sensible and I thank him quickly, as much with relief as gratitude.

By nine o'clock I decide it is not too early to telephone Pearl Buck. I feel apologetic about my mission and imagine her exhausted from the reception of the night before. Pearl suggests I take the matter up with her husband, to whom she hands the phone. I succeed in having Lewis Mumford, W. H. Auden, and a few others added to the list. Our conversation comes to a halt with a thud when I suggest asking Max Lerner. I cannot imagine that Walsh considers Lerner too radical, but I can think of no other reason for his refusing to invite him. There is no time to plead or argue.

The Walshes cordially invite me to attend the tea, and request me to help them take care of Nehru. With trepidation I dial the Waldorf and reach Nehru at once. He expresses warmest appreciation for the excised routine of the morning. I explain about the tea. Nehru sighs and begs me please to arrange something myself for the following afternoon. I ask whether there is anyone he especially wishes to meet and how many people I should invite. Nehru: "I leave everything to you."

Edward and I are due at the Mayor's welcome for Nehru at City Hall before eleven, and are also asked to virtually all the other special events throughout the day and evening. I must rush now and find a taxi for the long ride downtown. How am I, with twenty-four hours' notice, to gather a group of choice intellectuals at the unlikely time of 3:30 P.M.? In the cab I scrawl the most suitable list of people I can concoct, then write out a telegram of invitation.

What do you serve at three-thirty to honor a Prime Minister? No intoxicants are in order for Nehru. How shall I find even a moment to hire extra service, order food, make proper arrangements? I feel frightened, but keyed up. Shall I be able to pronounce "Jawaharlal" effortlessly when I introduce him? Never before have I had to arrange or preside over such a gathering. I want it to be not just a social event, but meaningful.

Edward meets me at City Hall and we are asked to sit at the top of the grandstand. I am placed between the Mayor and Nehru. The Sanitation Department band plays and a chorus of policemen is about to perform. O'Dwyer: "Members of the Police Department are not selected for their voices. But they are going to sing!" He then quips, as nearby sirens scream, "They are expressing will and warmth." I find myself smiling, yet filled with a sense of horror. Why can an official welcome for one of the world's most distinguished figures not be as distinguished as the guest himself?

Nehru leans toward me and asks whether I see what he does. A leading member of free India's official entourage, who never was a follower of Gandhi, or a participant in the fight for freedom, but was long an important emissary for the British before independence, sits a few rows below us. He wears a gleaming, fresh white Gandhi cap, obviously for the first time. Nehru shakes with laughter, yet seems in perfect control. I, who always laugh too hard at such moments, put my hand over my face, but am convulsed by what is occurring everywhere around us.

An official approaches Nehru to congratulate him for attaining India's independence. Nehru (indignant): "It is not I who freed India. It was Britain's Labour Government." The official disappears. Nehru turns and asks me whether the "pool" about which Thoreau wrote still exists. I assure him happily it does.

The following afternoon the block where we live on East Seventieth Street is roped off. Sirens blare. The Prime Minister and his party arrive punctually. Edward and I go to the curb to greet him. Our living room is crowded. I have invited not only writers, editors, publishers, but a cross-section of opinion molders and intellectuals who might not otherwise see Nehru at close range during his visit. Also members of the Nehru family and a few of their close friends.

I announce (as agreed) that Nehru prefers not to make a speech but will answer questions. He adds, to my surprise, that nothing said will be off the record. I introduce him to each individual so that there can be at least some personal interchange, then suggest that all sit down (many must sit on the floor). There are approximately seventy-five guests. Nehru looks relaxed, friendly, stimulated. After he expresses his pleasure about being in America, a hush falls over the room. Cameras click. A *Life* photographer and a few others are present. Everyone is too awed to speak. I explain again that Nehru has only a short time free.

An editor observes with respect how spiritual India is, as opposed to America with her materialism: "You are such a great spiritual leader, Mr. Prime Minister." Silence. The editor asks Nehru please to comment on the point. His warmth recedes. He bangs a hand on the arm of his chair. "What nonsense! India is no more nor less spiritual than any other country, and I am *not* a spiritual leader. People who say they are 'spiritual' generally have no concept whatever of how to cope with the realities of life." Nehru has become tense, but everyone else is delighted. There is spirited applause. All laugh with relief, and so does Nehru. As people unwind, questions flow.

A writer: "Why have you been critical of the United States, comparing us with Soviet Russia? You say we are both great proselytizers, that we are both positive we have all the answers." Nehru is amused. "I quite understand about being a proselytizer. I'm one myself." Again an outburst of laughter. Another question: "Is India hoping for Marshall Plan–type aid?" "We do hope for a loan, yes. But without having to ask for it." Again, laughter. No one expected Nehru to be humorous, especially about so sensitive a subject, but I sense raw nerves beneath the bright surface.

I decided to serve the most delicate melon and other fresh fruits still available, crushed and iced, as a beverage. I fear it will turn out badly, but what results is one of the most delectable cold drinks I have ever tasted. The best and lightest *petits fours* were hastily ordered, tea sandwiches have been made at home. The chrysanthemums and autumn leaves look colorful and festive. Everyone has worked diligently and devotedly so that the afternoon will be a specially beautiful one. Nehru's presence in New York has evoked an extraordinary response.

He stays nearly an hour and a half, instead of the allotted forty-five minutes, which makes him late for his next appointment—for him, most unusual. He looks flushed and happy, smiling warmly as he stops to speak with each person, before departing.

When Edward and I take Nehru down to his car, he asks why I don't come along the next day to Boston. For his one unofficial trip he is being given a plane by Washington—the Dewdrop, named for Thomas Dewey, to whom it would have been made available had he instead of Truman become President.

"The plane will leave New York," Nehru explains, "at eight-thirty in the morning. You'd have to be at the Waldorf promptly at eight. Nan and Indira are going along. You can leave a message for me at the hotel or tell me later at dinner this evening whether or not you can go. I hope you can. We shall be back in New York the day after tomorrow."

Edward agrees I should accept Nehru's invitation. I have never flown before, am terrified of airplanes. But now I succumb to the irresistible request, so that my first flight takes place on a beautiful, wind-still October day, with Nehru.

We are to attend a luncheon in Nehru's honor at the residence of Harvard's President, James Conant. Visits are scheduled for the University Observatory and the Fogg Museum; for Wellesley, where the Pandit girls have received their American education; and for Boston's two Ramakrishna centers. The single event, I am told, in which I am not to participate, since it will be a diplomatic affair, is a dinner for Nehru to be given by William Phillips, Roosevelt's representative in India prior to independence. I telephone our son, Andrew, at Harvard, and we arrange to dine together at his favorite Chinese restaurant.

As we enter the plane in New York, Nehru, Nan, Indira, and I are ushered into a spacious section resembling a large living room. The Indian officials accompanying Nehru disappear into another part of the plane. Indira looks weary and lies down on a sofa. Nan sits opposite her and opens a newspaper. Nehru approaches an armchair and motions me to the one next to it. Since no one tells us to fasten our seat belts and I don't even know what they are, we are bumped up and down a bit after we take off. A steward appears who looks worried. He suggests to Nehru that we fasten our belts, which notion Nehru brushes aside. Since he doesn't use his belt, I ignore mine.

Nehru sits blithely on the arm of my chair as we look out at the lovely, lush green earth below, the glistening deep blue ocean beyond, and the billowing white clouds in an intensely cobalt sky. Within a matter of moments, I point to our summer home on Cape Cod. How minute, yet arresting, are the Cape's delicate curves.

We discuss Hinduism and Buddhism. Nehru: "It is curious, the eternal spinning of the philosophers' web; the endless effort to penetrate the meaning of what forever eludes us. One constantly is asked what one believes about God; to tell one's view of immortality—all within a moment." We fall silent. Four eyes intently study the skyscape, landscape, seascape. All life, all time, all space seem compressed into the size of a windowpane focused on a split second in time, and on eternity.

"Our traditions are so ancient," Nehru continues, "I always think of India as something of a palimpsest—a manuscript first written upon long, long ago. And then, over the faded original writing, throughout the centuries, people have tried to put down again and again what they thought was there to begin with. So that by now no one can be certain what the original traditions were.

"Do you know what the Buddha replied"—Nehru speaks as though of an intimate contemporary with whom he has only recently conversed—"when asked what he believed about the hereafter?" I do not. "He said he never had quite gotten around to the subject, there was still so much he didn't know about this life." We smile. Nehru: "It is written that someone inquired of him how many leaves there were on all the trees in the world. He noted the difficulty of counting even those within his own horizon."

Nehru looks so modern, dressed in Western garb; his voice is so contemporary in spirit, emphasis, intonation, with its splendid British accent; and his approach to life is so cosmopolitan, that at moments it is difficult to remember that he comes from a distant and ancient civilization.

Nehru: "I have a strange feeling, as people have been talking to me here, that everyone has a secret wish to change my direction, my view of the West, India's foreign policy." A pause. "I sometimes wonder whether it ever occurs to others that I might alter their direction." The jest is a modest one, coming from the most influential non-Western writer of world history.

He shifts the conversation. "Often I find myself saying to those who arrive in India—especially Americans—'You will discover here just what you bring within you.' Recently one of your well-known writers traveled to the city of Benares and reported that all he could see there were the most horrible and disgusting conditions. He found only evil smells, dirt, filth. I dislike such things as much as anyone. Yet if you notice no more than that, you will not truly have experienced Benares. When I go there, a thousand pictures come to mind: I recall how it already was a living cultural center some three thousand years ago, how even then people gathered from far and near to discuss new ideas. It was, you know, at Sarnath, in Benares, that the Buddha gave his first sermon."

Newspaper headline: "Nehru Arrives in Hub in Snappy Homburg Hat. Gold-plated Plane Carries Premier Here."

We are late arriving at the Fogg Museum. A curator I know catches my eye and moves up beside me. He confides: "We were lined up down here to receive Nehru earlier, but because your party was detained, we were told to return to our offices and get on with our work until he arrived. Soon there was a loud knock at my door. The caretaker appeared, looking elated. 'Nero is here,' he shouted, 'Nero is here!' So I came down to see if he was fiddling," concludes the curator.

Later in the day we visit Boston's two Indian spiritual centers. At the first, the name of virtually every religious denomination in the world is printed large upon the walls. In almost a whisper Nehru reads out softly: "Hinduism, Mohammedanism, Buddhism, Christianity, Judaism, Zoroastrianism . . ." On and on. As he comes to the end of the list, the winged smile appears. "I do hope they haven't forgotten anyone."

At the second center, an Indian swami introduces his distinguished Prime Minister: "How gratified we are to have with us today the great Jawaharlal Nehru. We are only sad that we cannot have with us also his beloved wife." (She died in 1936.)

As we climb back into the limousine, Nehru remarks, "You should be glad, Dorothy, that we don't have *three* spiritual centers in Boston!"

In the evening, I set off happily with Andrew. When I return to the Copley, there is a huge pile of messages: 8:00 P.M.: "Where are you?" 8:30 P.M.: "You are seated next to the P.M. Your chair is empty. Come at once." Wrong information, unfortunate result.

At the Boston airport, as we are leaving, a dignitary tells Nehru of his admiration. "It must be wonderful to be the unanimous choice of your countrymen." As we walk toward the plane, Nehru laughs. "To tell you the truth, Dorothy, my colleagues can't figure out how to get rid of me, but they'd like to. Every time we have a crisis I threaten to resign. Then, because the masses are with me—or I am with them, and everyone knows it—what I want to do wins out." Although certain of Nehru's phrases might make him sound self-satisfied, the more I hear him, the more I realize he speaks as a serious scientist describing stubborn realities, often with humor. He analyzes impersonally insoluble situations that no longer fail to astonish him. He has lived with them too long.

It is still early in the morning when we arrive back in New York. Nehru invites me to stop off at the Waldorf before I return home. He hands me a book of his—*The Unity of India*—which he inscribes. He calls my attention to one particular passage:

> I tried to give my mind to the activity of the moment, and perhaps, in a measure, succeeded. But my mind was largely elsewhere, and I went through my engagements and the day's programme, and functioned on the public stage, like one who is absorbed in some other undertaking or is on a secret errand whose object he cannot disclose. The loveliness of the land enthralled me and cast an enchantment all about me. I wandered about like one possessed and drunk with beauty, and the intoxication of it filled my mind.
>
> Like some supremely beautiful woman, whose beauty is almost impersonal and above human desire, such was Kashmir in all its feminine beauty of river and valley and lake and graceful trees. . . . It had a hundred faces and innumerable aspects, ever-changing, sometimes smiling, sometimes sad and full of sorrow. The mist would creep up from the Dal Lake and, like a transparent veil, give glimpses of what was behind. . . . I watched this ever-changing spectacle, and sometimes the sheer loveliness of it was overpowering and I felt almost faint. As I gazed at it, it seemed to me dream-like and unreal, like the hopes and desires that fill us and so seldom find fulfilment. It was like the face of the beloved that one sees in a dream and that fades away on awakening.

Our eyes meet; his reveal a tenderness I have not seen before. I cannot conceal my own emotion; I burst into tears.

While in New York, Nehru must make several formal speeches. He tells me he is accustomed to addressing thousands of peasants spontaneously at gatherings all over India, not a few hundred upper-class individuals at a formal dinner in a hotel ballroom, as in New York. Only when in jail, or speaking to masses of Indian villagers, is he able to collect his thoughts, clarify his ideas. "You see, at heart I'm not a politician; I'm a teacher. I'm always eager to share what I am learning."

The most important New York event in Nehru's honor was arranged by the East and West Association, the Foreign Policy Association, the India League, and the Institute of Pacific Relations. The audience was clearly excited and in a gala mood. After warm introductory remarks, Nehru apologized for not having written out a speech, which he discovered he was expected to do. He hadn't prepared one, he explained, partly because he disliked writing down in advance what he was to say, and partly because, "If I may confess it with all humility, I just forgot about it."

Some were amused, some even delighted, by Nehru's frankness, but for others his confession was unforgivable. After dinner I heard grumblings, too, that he had rambled. I was amazed by the audience's relative coolness; it was a relief to hear a public figure speak so thoughtfully, honestly, and with refreshing spontaneity.

Nehru made a special effort to talk with the labor leader Walter Reuther after dinner, and then was taken up to the top of the Empire State Building. Other Nehru events in the New York area included his receiving an honorary degree from Columbia University, and addressing the Overseas Press Club, the National Trade Council, and the Council on Foreign Relations. He stopped in, by choice, at a dinner honoring the educator-philosopher John Dewey, and spoke extemporaneously in his honor. He went to Princeton to meet Albert Einstein.

Nehru told me he had expected American businessmen to be hardboiled: "I'm surprised to find they are, on the contrary, extremely soft-boiled. I must confess, though, that one thing rather shocked me. I was told with great pride at a businessmen's lunch that those around the table represented two billion dollars. That really horrified me!

"But I look into the eyes of people here and see kindness everywhere. I am amazed by the friendly, hospitable, generous approach of the Americans. Even though, throughout the West, life is viewed as an either/or affair. In India the Hindu admits to knowledge of both good and evil; he knows he behaves in both ways. Perhaps, because the East is older and has gone through more, it has greater tolerance and understanding."

Seeing so much of Nehru during his visit, I realize he has no public relations machinery and that he composes his own speeches, whether or not they are written out. Again and again he dispenses with the pompous. Someone asks what will be the subject of a talk he is to give that evening. "I have no clear idea as yet," he replies with a smile. "All I know is I hear it will be my most important speech, and that I'm to make a most significant political pronouncement."

I sense throughout his stay in New York how widely Nehru is suspected of being pro-Communist, even though it was he who—against the wishes of many of his colleagues—insisted that India adopt a democratic constitution. He consistently speaks out against the Communists at home. But he explains that, in view of India's proximity to both Russia and China, it must maintain a policy of nonalignment.

It is readily forgotten that the legacy of imperialism has not endeared the free world to colonial peoples to the degree the West would desire. Nehru seems fully aware of and opposed to Stalin's ruthless use of power and his threat to democracy, peace, security, and decency throughout the world. That he does not speak out more forcefully against Russia, as he did from the first against Fascism and Nazism, puzzles and disconcerts many. But as he elaborates on the question, I fully understand the dilemmas he faces as head of a new, militarily weak, poor nation, flanked by Russia and China.

Rumors spread that, while in Washington, Nehru became angry when President Truman and Secretary of State Dean Acheson offered India aid if it would follow our foreign policy. Nehru insists this is a fabrication. I ask Eleanor Roosevelt to check the rumors; she assures me Nehru's account is correct. Yet reporters consistently question him about his stand on Communism, implying he is pro-Russian and anti-American. Stories continue to circulate that he rebels against America's tying strings to possible aid.

The official visit in New York came to an end. No formal delegation was on hand at the airport to bid Nehru farewell. A voice: "You may not like attention, sir, but surely you must miss it, when there is none." Nehru, candidly: "Yes, of course. If I see a crowd at an airport to greet me or to say goodbye,

I react at once, 'Why all the fuss?' But then"—a smile—"if no one is there, I do miss it."

Nehru moved forward to his plane. The red carpet had again been rolled forth in his honor, but this time, I noticed, it was upside down.

13

After Nehru's departure, Nan Pandit and Krishna Hutheesing tell me he is inviting me to India for the Founding of the Republic celebrations in January 1950. I am to stay at the Prime Minister's House in New Delhi.

Nan, too, is attending the official ceremonies. Why, she asks, don't I fly over with her? I make certain I shall be permitted to pay my own travel expenses and am assured someone on Nehru's staff will make all arrangements for me in and out of Delhi. I shall be free to go where I choose, to visit whomever and whatever I wish.

Having seen so much of Nehru and Indira in New York, I feel deeply attached to them. Indira's shyness and intelligence have made me reach out to her. I know she has had a lonely childhood and that older members of the family are better known. I like her and feel at home with her. Others tell me she is difficult to talk to, but they say this of Nehru, too.

I have not been abroad since the children were born, not wanting to leave them, whereas Edward has traveled extensively. Now Nancy and Andrew are grown up. I no longer publish *Twice A Year*; I have been resigning from committees and plan to take a leave of absence from the *New York Post*. Happily, Edward agrees to my going.

Louis Fischer encourages me to make the journey, but advises me not to dress the way I do normally. India is a poor country, he admonishes.

I reply that I dress simply, know very well about India's poverty, and ask what I should do—buy a new wardrobe? In spite of their country's condition, the Indian women I know have more sumptuous clothes than anyone else. My own are modest by comparison.

At the time of our marriage, my wardrobe consisted of classic, simply cut dresses from Paris, and a few made in Philadelphia by an excellent dressmaker. In New York, surrounded by so many expensively overdressed relatives and their friends during the Depression, I felt a wave of revulsion against elegant clothes. My rebellion took the form of wearing Shetland sweaters to the Philharmonic, the opera, concerts, theaters, family gatherings—much to the Normans' dismay.

As my trousseau began to wear out, I attempted to save money by buying inexpensive clothes, but found this represented no economy. My secret desire was to possess a single simple Valentina dress that I could wear on every occasion, and that would last forever and never go out of that despicable word "style." Valentinas, however, were so outrageously expensive that my dream was shattered. Although I considered her creations works of art, they could cause only trouble in the family. Her deceptively unobtrusive clothes would shock even Edward and make me feel too guilty to enjoy them.

I stopped often before Valentina's little show window wide-eyed, even while finding no solution to my problem. At the same time, while walking down Lexington Avenue or through Greenwich Village, I fell in love with hand-woven, inexpensive "peasant" blouses. But clothes from Mexico or South America embarrassed Edward. I allowed myself to buy only occasional bits of colorful folk art—short lengths of material, small handbags or handmade belts. At least I had something to wear I loved.

As more and more exquisitely dressed Indians appear on the scene and give me presents of gloriously hand-spun, hand-woven fabrics or an occasional sari, I feel ecstatic. Curiously, I observe, the loveliest clothes are worn by those from the poorest countries. I learn slowly that traditional objects made for personal use attract me most. The effect of the touch of the hand—often the involvement of a single person with a single piece of cloth—is at the root of my delight.

Noticing the clothes Indians wear and their gifts to me, and seeing the fabrics at Coomaraswamy's house, I am drawn more and more to hand-woven materials—to their earthiness, their nonmechanical beauty. Mary Lescaze introduces me to the work of Fred Gwinn, who had been an assistant of the talented designer Elizabeth Hawes. With trepidation I order from him my first suit of Rabun wool, hand-woven in our own South.

The war ends; shantungs arrive from China and Italy. Their texture and color overjoy me. Edward remains only mildly approving. He confesses he lacks the sense of security to wear things that are different. I cannot turn back. I want to please him but am caught by my own complexity. It is the same with food, people, everything. I am exposed to and learn about exotic dishes from foreign lands and try to improvise and order them at home. Edward, who says he is a meat-and-potatoes man, doesn't respond, though if we were traveling he doubtless would. In daily life he is much more adventurous than I, rides beautifully, sails under conditions that frighten me. Yet in matters of taste, where physical courage is not in question, I go my own way in a manner that astonishes him. I cannot understand his petty fears, in view of his general fearlessness.

For my trip to India I acquire two nondescript, inexpensive, black jersey blouses and a long, black, dreary skirt to wear with them. Otherwise my bags contain two dresses suitable for evening events and several for daytime, for both warm and cold weather. Luggage weight is limited, in any event.

Since Nan Pandit plans to take a plane that touches down in Iraq—the quickest route to India—I shall require a transit visa. It is refused because I am Jewish, though I wouldn't even have to leave the plane. I tell Nan, who cables Nehru; he intervenes in my behalf, but without success. In consequence, we must fly to London and change to an Air India plane that stops in Cairo—a much longer flight.

Arrival at Bombay airport: a pleasant, human-scale building. White. Flowers blooming in bright profusion. The shock of the too-thin dark bodies on the roads and in the surrounding countryside, as we drive toward the city. And then the sharp contrast of prosperous Indians in their fine cars, and beggars haunting the streets.

At night the necklace of lights strung along the coastline hides a thousand signs of misery and degradation. Certainly there is poverty in America, poverty everywhere. But I, like the other occupants of the Taj Mahal Hotel, whether Indian or foreign, am well-fed, well-dressed, privileged. A gnawing sadness.

I decided to rest for two or three days before proceeding to Delhi and was placed in the care of a Parsi couple—Mr. and Mrs. D., friends of friends—who were exceedingly kind to me. She was European-born, he a wealthy Indian businessman. Both were pro-Communist.

Mrs. D., eager to inspect my clothes, came to my room, where I showed her my dreary black evening blouses, skirt, and dresses. She was shocked; I couldn't possibly wear them to the festive evening events to which I would be invited as a guest of Nehru. No one had told me the ceremonies in Delhi involved state dinners and the like. Mrs. D. suggested I have the English dressmaker in the hotel make me at least one splendid brocaded jacket to wear with my dismal skirt, which I did.

Before leaving Bombay, I was handed a message for Nehru asking that he free the Communists who, the D.'s told me, were unjustly in jail; also a sentimental, admiring poem to present. A curious prelude to my Delhi visit.

New Delhi. The Prime Minister's residence. The atmosphere is charged with excitement. Servants in colorful dress, sashes, and turbans behave with great decorum; they add a touch of formality both fitting and exhilarating. Something very special is clearly taking place and I am delighted to be able to witness it.

Under the British the P.M.'s house, whose architecture is nondescript, was occupied by the Commander-in-Chief. A cannon in front of the building—a military relic of colonial days—seems out of place, but no one pays any attention to it. I find no bitterness about the past, about the British, at any level. Far more urgent problems demand time and energy. A large rectangular plot of wheat grows on what was once mere lawn—an example, it is hoped, that will be followed by others.

The great hallway on the first floor of the P.M.'s house is in no sense imposing, but the garden beyond is enchanting. Fine trees, masses of roses, and a vast expanse of green; the sky an intense, clear blue. After Bombay, the crisp air is a relief.

My room—large, inviting, comfortable—is filled with flowers. Bearers walk in and out without knocking. The door does not lock. I must get used to the lack of privacy. Anna Ornsholt—Danish-born, a lovely woman, outgoing, efficient—is in charge of the staff. She comes to welcome me, at once makes me feel at home.

I have no idea how my time is to be allotted, what I am expected to do, in which events I am to be included, what would be appropriate to wear on what occasion. One look at my desk reveals an imposing stack of invitations, next to which is a detailed program listing an overwhelming succession of appointments with cabinet ministers, heads of museums and social welfare agencies, government officials.

Before I retire the first evening, Anna asks whether I would like breakfast on a tray in my room, or prefer having it with Nehru, Indira, and the others downstairs. I ask what she thinks; she says I must follow my intuition. In view of the enormous pressure of events, the family might care to be alone for at least one meal. I ask for a tray in my room at 8:00 A.M.

At 6:00 A.M. a bearer brings morning tea. Because of the language barrier, I cannot tell him I am tired, want to sleep, require no tea at this hour. I smile and say, "Thank you." Soon two other bearers enter with buckets of hot water for my bath. (The tub has recently and generously been installed for my convenience.) At 8:00 I am served orange juice, porridge, an egg, toast, and tea. At 8:30, while I am trying to finish the to me enormous breakfast, Anna comes in. The Prime Minister has sent up word asking where I am. Breakfast downstairs is served at exactly 8:30; no one has told me I am expected. I fall into my clothes and rush to the dining room, much embarrassed at possibly having disrupted Nehru's schedule.

He leads me to the buffet where breakfast is laid out and insists, in his gentle way, that I eat properly. He suggests I take just what I already have consumed upstairs. Only the family is present; breakfasting under such conditions is lovely. The day is again glorious—as is every day. Such perfect golden and blue weather is a miracle.

Because of the sun, the middle of the day is warm but the shade is cool;

the afternoon is still cooler, the evening cold. Throughout the day my room is chilly; the windows are open, so I close them. They are reopened at once by an attentive bearer. I find no way to communicate or change procedures; all I can do is smile. Attendants continue to carry in roses or tea, to perform one task or another. I value privacy above all and dislike the cold. But I am so elated by the rush of events and by seeing Nehru that nothing else matters.

I tell Anna that, since I am expected to go down to breakfast, perhaps she can make certain that a tray will not be brought to me in the morning. Also, I don't need morning tea at six; I sleep badly and would appreciate being called only in time for breakfast. The following day, morning tea arrives at six. The buckets arrive. My tray of breakfast arrives promptly at eight. Every evening I say I don't require morning tea or a breakfast tray, but every morning the ritual is repeated. Afraid of offending, I drink the tea, eat some of the breakfast quickly, then stagger down to the dining room just before 8:30 A.M. Nehru is obsessively punctual and continues to watch over my meal with the grace of a prince. I have two breakfasts a day throughout my more than six-week stay at the P.M.'s house.

Each evening, we gather before dinner in the large drawing room on the second floor. Everyone must arrive before Nehru. A tiny, movable electric heater stands in a corner, far from the entrance. As always, I am cold at this hour. While waiting, a few of us huddle around the feeble heater. Nehru stops at the door as he enters, sniffs, and says, upset, "Someone has turned on that blasted heater again!" We scurry away with regret; it is immediately turned off. Those of us who have been standing near the pitiful mechanism have felt almost no heat, yet Nehru, at the opposite end of the huge room, is both aware of and hostile to it at once. An extraordinary man.

A printed card in my room lists the other house guests: Mrs. Pandit; her daughters Nayantara and Chandralekha, and their husbands, Gautam Sahgal and Ashok Mehta; and Padmaja Naidu, daughter of the famous Indian poetess Sarojini Naidu. His Excellency Dr. Sukarno, President of the Republic of Indonesia, and Madame Sukarno have not yet arrived.

The day after I reached Delhi, a luncheon was given by Nehru in the garden for a group of scientists attending an international conference. Next to me at the table was a Russian scientist, nearby a British professor I had met in Woods Hole. The British professor, like my hosts in Bombay, was extremely sympathetic to Stalinist Russia. As we left the table, the British scientist approached me. "As a guest of Nehru's, you can do a great service. He is practically a Fascist. All of India's Communists are in jail. Do persuade him to free them."

How ironic to be asked twice within so brief a time to act in behalf of India's Communists. I had no intention of suggesting any action to Nehru. But I quickly realized that if I wanted to interview any Communists while in India—to learn something of their attitudes and situation—this might be my one opportunity to find out with whom I should get in touch. My British acquaintance took me across the lawn to meet an Indian scientist, who assured me that when I came to Calcutta he would introduce me to any Communist I wished to meet. He gave me his card; we shook hands like old friends.

Free India's Republic Day, January 26, 1950: Indians mass on New Delhi's broad thoroughfares; on her spacious maidans, or open spaces. To my Western eyes, the vastness of the crowds is overwhelming. Glowing before me are gaily colored saris, turbans, shirts, but oppressive signs of poverty are ever present. The sun heightens the brilliance of the sky. The pinkish-orange government buildings look especially splendid today. I sense the pent-up emotion of the populace, which at any moment is sure to burst forth in some exultant fashion.

We arrive early at the great Durbar Hall, well before the swearing-in ceremony of the country's first President. The hall is empty, except for officiating attendants. Nehru at once inspects the seating arrangements, finds them not to his liking, and reorganizes everything so that, although he observes protocol, people will feel more at ease.

Promptly at 10:15 A.M. the Governor General, Chakravarti Rajagopalachari, and the President Elect, Rajendra Prasad, arrive. The noble national anthem, composed by Rabindranath Tagore, is played. The Governor General reads a proclamation in honor of the birth of the Republic and a letter from the Constituent Assembly naming the President. The latter, in the presence of the Chief Justice, takes the oath of office. The Governor General's flag is brought down, the President's flag hoisted, a thirty-one-gun salute fired. After a short Presidential address, the Prime Minister and other important government officials are sworn in and presented to the President.

Everything has proceeded with dispatch, yet with great dignity. The formality seems entirely fitting. Everyone looks regal, in spite of the simplicity of the Gandhian tradition. The proceedings reflect a mixture of British and Indian custom. Even devoted female followers of Gandhi are dressed in exquisite, delicate silks. One of them wears precious stones as well as a glorious thin, white sari, shot through with the finest of golden threads. She whispers that she made a solemn vow to her beloved Gandhiji that she would wear only hand-spun, hand-woven Indian fabrics, which in fact meant thick khadi, cotton. She assures me, too, that Gandhiji did not object to jewels. I am reminded of Sarojini Naidu's remark that it took millions of rupees to permit Gandhi to live so simply. (It surprises me that fabrics hand-woven by peasants, which I admire above all, are exceptionally costly.)

In spite of the solemnity of the occasion, I am secretly amused by Nehru's having rearranged the seating plan the moment he entered the Great Hall. Even while functioning as head of state, he intuitively plays the role of host, wanting no one to be offended or belittled. Wherever he goes, he cannot resist making certain events proceed promptly, efficiently, yet also humanly. He respects tradition, but refuses to be frozen by it.

Later in the day an official teases him: "When you reach heaven, my dear friend, you will get busy at once, I'm sure, to see that all is in order. I can hear you complaining to God if everything isn't run efficiently." To which another high official adds: "And you'll be certain to read the press notices, to see that nothing has been misrepresented."

Flags, pageantry, uniforms, color, movement enliven Republic Day. At 2:30 P.M. on the dot the President, driving in state, leaves Government House. He rides in an impressive horse-drawn coach; a ceremonial umbrella is held above his head. At first glance this looks more British than Indian. Yet according to Indian tradition, the umbrella has been carried in connection with deities, kings, and heads of priestly orders in Hindu ceremonials over the centuries.

To see troops marching in Gandhian India is something of a shock but, as so often, I remind myself that the country must function in the everyday world, in spite of Gandhi's vision. He himself was fully aware of the nation's need to be realistic. Though he never agreed to be head of state, he understood and respected the responsibilities of those who must govern in an imperfect world. Even Nehru has said: "I prefer the organized violence of the army to the unorganized violence I have seen perpetrated by so many who give lip service to nonviolence and pacifism." And he added, somewhat surprisingly: "The army raises standards of efficiency, so badly needed in India."

The majesty of Republic Day ceremonies is difficult to describe. The new President is a simple man; he has no desire to live in the huge Government House, formerly the British Viceroy's residence. It is Nehru who constantly looks the prince, no matter how simply dressed. Yet never for a moment is he ponderous.

The same evening a formal dinner is held at Government House, in honor of the birth of the Republic.

After dinner President Sukarno, Nehru, and I converse. A photographer comes up and suggests I stand closer to the two men so he can take our picture. An Indian notices the episode and later whispers to Nehru, asking who I am. I cannot help but overhear. Nehru: "Mrs. Norman is an American. You can tell, can't you, from the high forehead and intelligent face that she is Jewish? Jews so often have a special sensitivity."

I blush yet also feel an irrational joy and wish the whole world could hear Nehru's words, not about me, but as an antidote to widespread anti-Semitism.

Nehru takes the Sukarnos and me to Old Delhi, to the majestic twelfth-century sandstone Qutb Minar. As we drive through New and Old Delhi, we see at close range the magnificent circular Parliament House, the Central Secretariat, and enormous Government House—Rashtrapati Bhawan. The pinkish sandstone glows in the bright sunlight.

New Delhi reminds me of Washington—also a planned city—with its wide, tree-lined avenues and parks, but here the government buildings are far more regal, having been built for the British Raj. Old Delhi is of another world. The striking, massive Red Fort built by Shah Jahan in the seventeenth century bears on its walls the inscription: "If there be a Paradise on earth, it is this—it is this—it is this!" The famed Jama Masjid or Great Mosque is a marvel, with its granite paving inlaid with marble. Ruins, at this moment, become an acquired taste for me. If none are to be seen on the landscape, I miss their weathered, ancient, reassuring presence.

A plane is made available to take Sukarno and his wife to the Taj Mahal in Agra—for nearly a century capital of the Moguls. Also to Fatehpur Sikri, a sixteenth-century Mogul center of culture. I am invited to accompany them.

Sukarno talks to me about having been brought up on Whitman and Lincoln. He assures me with pride that his training has been far more democratic than that of Nehru or other Indian leaders. The Indians, he says with rather a superior air, have been nurtured by British tradition, he by American. In his khaki uniform, he who played a most important role in helping to win Indonesia's independence seems unpretentious, sincere, idealistic. Madame Sukarno smiles sweetly but we cannot converse. She knows no English; I am ignorant of her language. She is as delicate as a butterfly.

On our return to Agra, the government car in which we are driven breaks down—the first of many incidents I witness. Villagers from near and far gather around the car. Sukarno makes a festival of the occasion, borrows a peasant's bicycle, and merrily rides off on it. I photograph him. Madame Sukarno and I are given Nagpur oranges—glorious, delicious—the best I have ever tasted. She and I, smiling at each other, sit by the roadside. Efforts to repair the automobile yield little result for quite some time.

The countryside is both beautiful and disturbing. So much of India's land is divided into pitifully small lots, their soil infertile, dry, unyielding. Often, throughout India, either floods or drought destroy harvests. How can such tired earth provide sufficient food for the country's millions?

One day we returned to the P.M.'s house after a succession of ceremonial events. Nehru and members of the household walked through the large entrance hall toward their offices or private rooms. For a brief moment Nehru stopped and stood on his head. Those walking in front didn't see what he had done. I felt he had relieved the tension of sitting through endless formalities. He cast an amused look to see whether I had noticed. I caught his eye and, as usual, had to use all my will power not to laugh. Nehru walked straight ahead as though nothing out of the ordinary had occurred.

Pilgrimage to Raj Ghat, where Gandhi had been cremated only two years before. Flowers were piled high. Everyone was silent, prayerful. A loudspeaker squeaked throughout the chanting of the Bhagavad Gita. During a further ceremony in a large tent, Nehru sat spinning, looking gloomy. He spoke in a low voice to the President of India, next to him on the floor, also spinning: "How horrible to have that radio squeak during the Gita."

As I watched the mass of Gandhi's devoted followers and saw India's leading political figures squatting and spinning, I wondered if such a phenomenon could occur anywhere else in the world with equal calm, dignity, reverence, and devotion.

Liaquat Ali Khan, Pakistan's Prime Minister, arrives in New Delhi for talks with Nehru about disturbing tensions arising from partition: the canal waters dispute, the exchange of minorities, financial settlements. Liaquat is staying at the President's house, where an official banquet is to be held in his honor. He is Nehru's guest at lunch.

During breakfast a large packet of enormous, ripe guavas is handed to Nehru. The first of the season, they have been sent as a gift from the United Provinces, where both Nehru and Liaquat were born. Nehru says to Anna, his conscientious Danish head of staff: "I doubt that Liaquat will have received any guavas as yet in Pakistan. Probably he has been fond of them since boyhood, just as I have. Please take a goodly portion of these to him, nicely packed. You must go directly to his suite at the President's house. By no means leave the guavas at the entrance with an attendant. Anything can easily get lost in that enormous building. Take the guavas to Liaquat's rooms and give them only to his personal assistant, so he is certain to receive them. Be sure to say the guavas are a gift from me, so that everything will be clearly understood."

At lunch I am seated next to Liaquat. He berates me for spending over three months in India and planning to stay little more than three days in Karachi, Pakistan's capital. He promises to take good care of me; he will make anything I desire available. I must send him the exact dates of my proposed stay, so he can help me procure a room at the new Karachi hotel still being built. We shall have good talks in Pakistan.

As the luncheon—routine, official, but friendly—is about to end, Liaquat whispers to me sarcastically, "Don't you think this is rather simple fare to be served by a Gandhian?" I bristle. Nehru has attempted, in his usual unpretentious way, to have a proper but by no means elaborate luncheon for a visiting head of state. Considering it is given for the Prime Minister of an unfriendly neighboring country, it is difficult to imagine how any occasion could have been handled more appropriately or graciously.

The morning following the President's banquet for Liaquat, Nehru comes to breakfast looking as though a thundercloud has descended upon him. To Anna: "What happened to the guavas?"

Anna: "I did just what you asked. I took them directly to the P.M.'s suite and left them with his assistant. I said, as you told me, that the guavas were a gift from you."

Nehru: "Most odd. I believe you, of course. But Liaquat mentioned nothing to me about them all evening. As I was about to leave, I told him I had been especially eager for him to have the guavas; had he not received them? He said no, there was no gift from me. He had seen no guavas."

Only the family is at table. Someone calls out: "Of course he received them, the liar." Nehru, sternly: "Why should you doubt Liaquat's word? If he said he did not receive the guavas, he did not receive them." Everyone scoffs. I find Nehru's conduct in the midst of delicate and difficult negotiations illuminating. His inability to mistrust even an enemy moves me; it explains much about him.

A member of the household tells me, "Nehru is so good, he cannot believe that anyone else is dishonest. People often cheat him."

No one I meet in India chides Nehru for not living as austerely as did Gandhi, nor thinks it anything but correct that he should function in a manner befitting a Prime Minister. If he were lavish in his habits, if he did not dedicate himself totally to his country, that would be a different matter.

Nehru has even reduced his minuscule salary. Almost the only funds he has of a personal nature come from Western publication of his writings. I find two pirated editions of his recent *Visit to America* in Delhi bookstores and show them to him. He shrugs and looks pained, but says he intends to do nothing about the infringements.

A warm and relaxed friendship with Indira Gandhi deepens as I see her at mealtime, in interludes between appointments, and at formal events. She, her husband, Feroze Gandhi (no relation of the Mahatma), and their two small sons, Rajiv and Sanjay, live down the hall from my room.

The harmony engendered between us in New York intensifies. I like her independence of spirit. After a dance recital in honor of the Republic's founding, Nehru suggests we go backstage to congratulate the performers. Indira's reply is decisive: "I refuse to congratulate anyone who has danced so poorly!" We head straight for the P.M.'s house.

Daily incidents strike us in the same way, whether moving or amusing. The Agha Khan, garbed in a Western woolen suit with vest and wearing a fedora on an intensely warm, sunny day, came to lunch, which was served on the lawn. At the end of the meal, as we moved toward the house, he asked to see Indira's children. She brought them to him. Aged three and five, they wore scant little sunsuits. The heavyset, heavily dressed figure—one of the world's richest potentates—leaned toward the boys and exclaimed, "Poor little things. They'll soon be having to work." After he left, Indira and I shared our amusement.

Early one morning I am to accompany Nehru on a trip to Pilani, where a new university is to be dedicated. I wake up with a sore throat, but to change plans at 5:30 A.M. would be difficult. It is extremely cold. I wear a sweater, woolen suit, and topcoat. Also a tight-fitting velvet cap. I feel chilled on the plane but know I must see the day through.

We arrive at Pilani in Rajasthan, its new buildings shining and white. Nehru is asked to mount a beautiful horse and rides through the town to a tumultuous welcome. We attend ceremonies, watch young girls perform traditional dances, visit a Montessori school and various parts of the new university. We are escorted to luncheon at the splendid home of a member of the famous and wealthy Birla family, who helped found the college. During a prayer meeting held at the Delhi home of another Birla—G. D., a great supporter of Gandhi—the Mahatma was assassinated.

Nehru is to speak at a cattle fair after lunch. I whisper to Birla's daughters that I don't feel well and ask whether I might lie down for a bit and catch up with the party later. They say, "Of course," and take me to a bedroom and disappear. Within a matter of moments they return to present me with a magnificent old South Indian sari. Ignoring my desire to collapse on the inviting bed, they plead that I try it on, saying I will look marvelous in it. All I want is to rest. I explain I do not have the lovely, flowing figure of an Indian woman. The sisters insist. Finally I agree to allow them to drape the length of exquisite silk in traditional style over my bulky suit while, shivering, I ache for their bed and my topcoat.

Moving toward a mirror, I see so ludicrous a figure, I laugh and quickly put my coat on again—over the sari, suit, and sweater. Word comes at once that the car in which I am scheduled to drive is ready to depart. I have no time to remove the sari and we hurry to the front door.

By the time our car arrives at the high grandstand from which Nehru is to address thousands of peasants, he is just rising to speak. As he catches sight of me with the sari hanging below my coat, he stops short for a moment, his eyes following my ridiculous figure as I climb up the steep stairs. He looks at me open-mouthed, then proceeds with his speech. I sit through the ceremonies quietly freezing and fearful to meet Nehru's amused eyes when the speeches are at an end.

Throughout the day I have admired the folk art of the district, particularly the tie-dyed, colorful cotton saris its village women wear. Reaching our plane, I find the Birlas have arranged for someone to buy a stack of them for me. And so we depart, I still wearing my elegant, ill-placed sari, my hands laden with a host of beautiful local ones.

246

Twenty-four hours later, I visit a village consisting of the usual poor mud huts. A group of ill-fed children have gathered in a vacant space that is pure dust. The sun beats down. A fine young man from a nearby town arrives to demonstrate exercises he wants the children to perform, explaining to me that in the afternoons they wander about aimlessly. He is eager to help them develop.

The children follow his instructions, but the movement of their feet creates such an enormous cloud of dust that I find myself choking. Everyone coughs. The situation is agonizing. Tears come to my eyes. After catching his breath, the young man tells the children to stand quietly for a moment until the storm subsides. He calls over to me in undisguised anguish, "They ought to blow the whole place up and start over again. It would be much better." I have never heard an Indian express himself with such abandon about a troubling situation. Difficulties are so often ignored; I am told people could not survive if they gave their attention only to the problems besetting them. The sharp contrast between the happenings of the two days remains with me, but I can explain my troubled reactions to no one.

Some poets came to the house one evening to chant their works to Nehru. Several bowed to the ground and attempted to kiss his feet. He drew back, looked pained, made an involuntary movement with his hand to brush them aside.

Although willing to give his blessing to those whose work he respected, Nehru rebelled against all who played up to him. He flattered no one, nor did he countenance flattery and easy intimacies. I was sometimes baffled by his seeming indifference to actions and events that actually pleased him, until I realized it was due mainly to his shyness. If you didn't sense his appreciation, you would never know you had it.

From conversations with Nehru:
Nehru: "Gandhi is sometimes said to have wanted only yes-men around him. That is not true. He respected honest differences of opinion. In one

sense Gandhi and I complemented each other. He never tried to force me to adopt his personal habits. As for those who gave up their lives to be with him, to work directly with him all the time, he insisted that they follow his precepts. He never in any way held it against me that I did not.

"You see, I look upon discipline not from a puritanical point of view, but as the height of sophistication. I am not a puritan, nor could I ever have modeled my life on that of Gandhi. But I have my own, inner discipline."

Nehru: "People in India seem less frank today than they were formerly. Perhaps this is because of Gandhi's death. With him, I felt a need to confess. An essential dialogue always took place between us. That experience is missing for me now.

"Fundamentally Gandhi was right, whatever my inability to go along with him at a given moment. He seemed greatest to me during his last period. As the years have passed, the more right I think he was."

Nehru: "At the time of the 'Quit India' movement in 1942, when Gandhi called for the British to leave, I was opposed to civil disobedience. For once, Gandhi insisted I adopt his position. This created a certain bitterness in me for a short time, not because I was going to have to spend nearly three years in jail if I did what Gandhi proposed. Rather, there was a deep philosophical difference between us. Perhaps I was wrong to feel as I did, but then my bitterness vanished; there was, in fact, a fine harmony between Gandhi and myself."

Nehru: "The nonviolent approach in India was developed by Gandhi in protest against British rule. The collective use of nonviolent noncooperation ended with the termination of that rule. Yet nonviolence as a philosophy of life still exists in India; it cannot cease to do so. People go on believing in it and practice it in various degrees or phases. Gandhi was styled a pacifist but he was not passive in any way. You might say he sought to put into effect dynamic, peaceful methods.

"He concentrated on changing man. If this could be accomplished, the environment could be transformed; if people behaved correctly they would become integrated individuals. Some of his followers were interested in vegetarianism, some in cottage industries, others in nonviolence. To Gandhi each of these subjects was important, but none was his overriding preoccupation. He was so extraordinary, so exceptional, no one could ever live up to the ideals he represented."

I listened carefully to Nehru's considered remarks and incorporated them in an interview printed in the *Times of India*:

Nehru: "Virtually every great philosopher in every country, every era, every tradition, has spoken in favor of detachment. As does one of India's most important traditional documents—the *Bhagavad Gita*. But as was true of Gandhi, it did not favor inaction. I would not call India negative and the West positive. The *Gita* maintains that, even if it is necessary to kill in battle, one must remain apart from the act.

"Many different attitudes exist in India about how one should live. Indeed, there always has been great tolerance with respect to this matter, for no single person can know the whole of truth.

"We should not worry too much about whether beliefs held by others differ from our own. Others may have gotten hold of some part of the truth that has eluded us. Why not simply accept this possibility?

"People forget that Hinduism is neither a religion nor a dogma. Six so-called orthodox philosophies—each somewhat different from the others—have evolved in India under one general heading. No single approach can rightly be called Hinduism to the exclusion of the others. Each has evolved, flowered and faded in its time. One, for example, has been atheistic in character, another semi-atheistic. Buddhism, which might be called more or less atheistic, is itself an offshoot of Hinduism.

"In general the Hindu does not aim to proselytize, even though the Buddhists try to do just that. In some cases images have been worshipped in India, in others not. The important thing is that, under the general heading of Hinduism, people can do as they please. I admit that tolerance can have its bad as well as good aspects. But then, intolerance—a person thinking he alone is right—is worse.

"Mere passivity in any domain—intellectual, cultural or personal—cannot represent true vitality. Vitality can spring only from an acceptance of—a being open to—a multiplicity of forces."

Nehru: "The British set their ideals fairly low. They succeed pretty well in attaining them. The Indian sets his goals high, so he is much further from achieving them."

D.N.: "Listening to you, I think of how the West sees you—either as too revolutionary or too passive. Because you are nonaligned and seem unperturbed about Soviet Russia, it fears you favor her over the democracies."

Nehru: "I detest easy jumping at conclusions. People assume because they see some part of the truth—about nations or individuals—they see all of it. I oppose all absolutes and dogmas; I am alarmed when others become prey to them."

D.N.: "The popular notion is that Indians avoid conflict and are always seeking the 'still point.' "

Nehru: "I have little sympathy with the quiescent approach to anything. I want to get ahead as fast as possible with effecting necessary change in India, but refuse to be a dictator. I must bring the people along with me. I now recognize more fully what can and cannot be accomplished, but still aim for the maximum.

"In the international field I had hoped there could be regional, then larger federations, finally genuine internationalism. But this dream has faded, not because I have lost interest but because of the harsh realities of the world situation."

A guest asked Nehru why so much respect was shown to holy men in India: "It amazes me, since certainly many who claim to be saintly are not."

Nehru: "In other countries there is often a tendency to label such individuals as lunatics. In India we are more apt to give them the benefit of the doubt."

Another visitor: "How marvelous to think of the vast numbers of noble Indians who are preoccupied with 'becoming.'"

Nehru, impatient: "In my view, far too many Indians have been concerned with what they hope to *be*. It is high time we paid more attention to what we are going to *do*."

Nehru: "We won a victory in gaining Independence but we failed to achieve our other objectives: a unified India, a socialist state, a modern society."

At moments Nehru looks at me with the eyes of a child. Yet his intelligence is so vast in scope and he so overshadows those around him, I feel him trapped in a cage. Sometimes as he gazes about him, he bristles—with impatience. If too many burdens are on his mind, he seems far away. When he relaxes, is interested, looks as though nothing is troubling him, his charm is devastating. All—male and female alike—fall under his spell. With children he is full of laughter and joy; his love of animals is obvious; with both, he seems rejuvenated, momentarily without cares. Stupidity, inefficiency, lack of understanding, and the repetitive most confound him.

Only once did I hear him make a remark that could be interpreted as unkind. A full-grown man from Ceylon, a house guest, was childlike in his simplicity. He tended to forget things, was often late, and laughed heartily at the slightest provocation. He asked Nehru to guess his age. "Fifteen," Nehru replied, with almost frightening speed.

Nehru: "Yes, people can say my life has been wonderful. It has also been dangerous. I realize now the enormous restraint under which I have functioned for years. First my father dominated me; then Gandhi, to whom people constantly acceded. At times I doubted myself and surrendered to Gandhi's ideas, but I always have had a need to be independent. I am a natural protester. Much is to be said in favor of protest in itself. I had to react against my father and Gandhi, both privately and publicly. I conformed, of course, out of respect and a sense of discipline. Yet that did not keep me from protesting.

"Now there is no one against whom I feel any need to rebel. But since I have many conflicts within me, I often rebel against myself. In the Congress Party we were always asserting ourselves in favor of India's independence. But I was constantly declaring my own independence, too."

One evening only the family was at dinner. Nehru appeared in a hand-spun, hand-woven white woolen jacket, new and elegant. He looked shy and uncomfortable, like any schoolboy. The coat was admired; he replied with adolescent diffidence and self-consciousness: "I never did like pure white." He looked down at the jacket. "It fits very poorly. I must have it altered." He was correct, it needed adjustment. His jackets were so perfectly cut, anything ill-fitting was noticeable at once. But the white jacket, when fixed, would be the most beautiful of all.

Nehru wears his clothes with easy grace and unconcern. His daytime jackets are natural beige or brown; never overtailored. The rest of his dress is invariably the same—hand-spun, hand-woven white cotton jodhpurs and shirt, and a white Gandhi cap set jauntily on his head. In the evening during the winter months, the jacket is often dark blue, the wool incredibly soft. He is always meticulously groomed.

Someone speaks of buying an old Kashmir shawl (no first-rate ones are now made, few from the past are for sale). Nehru: "I would dislike putting on an old piece of material worn by someone else."

Nehru always wears a fresh rosebud, usually red, in a buttonhole; the supply seems inexhaustible, as are those who are eager to give him his favored flower. Each evening a woman appears toward the end of dinner. She hands Nehru a marvelous rose, fuller and larger than any he habitually wears. They exchange no words. She goes quietly to the other end of the table, sits down, and remains silent, until we rise. She then departs as unobtrusively as she came.

One day Nehru's rose must have dropped, unnoticed. A woman standing nearby becomes aware of it and rushes, almost in a panic, to get another flower at once. The absence of the rose seems to represent an evil omen to her; Nehru has been somehow stripped of a secret power that depends on the presence of the accustomed rose, much as Samson was weakened when shorn of his locks.

14

A cartoon appears in a New Delhi newspaper depicting the United States Ambassador sitting on an enormous bag of wheat; in the corner a small, thin Indian cowers, a symbol of destitution, neglect, hunger. I ask our Ambassador, Loy Henderson, why we don't send wheat to India, in view of her mounting food shortages. He shows me a confidential report he has just transmitted to Washington, requesting that precisely such assistance be given. He explains that Congress cannot take action, however, unless India makes a formal application.

I question Indian officials about their failure to ask for aid. Their attitude is much the same as was Nehru's in the United States: India, hurt by the heritage of imperialism, fears being placed in a dependent position ever again; it feels too proud to be indebted for anything at the moment. Nehru's quip about receiving a loan without having to ask for it becomes ever more comprehensible the longer I remain in India. As does India's fear that the United States will tie strings to whatever assistance might be given.

That our effort to eliminate discrimination in the distribution of foreign aid with respect to race, creed, or color should be looked upon as a "string" seems odd to an American. We are unable to convince India that we must have strict accountings rendered about supplies received and meted out. The

United Nations Relief and Rehabilitation Administration experience in Europe has taught us that all too often supplies are distributed unjustly to the favored.

Nothing was said in Washington about India's having to follow U.S. foreign policy in return for aid, which Nehru admitted to me in New York. Yet convincing a single Indian leader that the United States will not attach "strings" to assistance is impossible.

The claim that India is spiritual, as opposed to the materialistic United States, is repeated again and again. An Indian has just so asserted; an American smiles and replies, "Think of the great machines and small needed to create the civilization that produced even such tiny items as Gandhi's simple dollar watch and his eyeglasses." The Indian: "Gandhi would have been quite content without them."

I frequently met a young Indian fellow traveler whose forehead was broad, his face square, his lips soft. I thought of him as following some invisible Prussian discipline he identified with that of the Congress Party. He masked his fantasies behind a tensely nonchalant manner; talked revolution and secretly admired Russia; seemed cruel, cold, and self-righteous. He told me proudly that Stalin, with whom he personally identified, went about unaccompanied, unguarded in Russia, as though this fact reflected glory on himself. His statements were untrue. He boasted that China was unified for the first time, as though he were Chinese and therefore had every right to take credit for the event.

He regarded me with suspicion, addressing me as though I, being an American, were in league with the devil. "You write for a newspaper, I hear," he said with ill-disguised disbelief. "Yes," I replied. "But of course you can't mention your Negro problem." His voice was cutting. "My column"—my words were coldly polite—"concentrates on race relations, civil liberties, social welfare, politics." I couldn't resist: "You may be interested to know I recently received a prize for my writing against discrimination." He glared at me in silence.

Edwina Mountbatten is a new family guest. She is a historical figure to me, the handsome wife of the handsome Lord Louis Mountbatten, Earl Mountbatten of Burma. Together they have established an enviable reputation in India as Britain's last Viceroy and Vicereine.

Mountbatten swiftly succeeded in transferring power to a free India and a free Pakistan after years of tense and frustrating maneuvers by others. Indians are now trying to forget the tragic slaughter of Hindus and Moslems at the time of partition, the unfortunate division of the subcontinent, and Gandhi's assassination.

Lady Mountbatten, who is extremely intelligent, worked imaginatively, with compassion, and tirelessly through a grueling period in India; she is a heroine to all I meet. She calls everyone by first name, is gracious, outgoing, warm. She and Nehru obviously adore each other.

Edwina takes pains with her clothes, dresses in the style of upper-class Englishwomen; everyone comments on the great trouble she takes with "dressing up" and how beautiful she looks. (I am constantly reminded of Louis Fischer's advice to me.) Her face is curiously lined for one so young, but I soon forget this as she speaks with sparkle and animation. It seems odd that one of England's richest women, close to the royal family, living lavishly, should consider herself a Socialist, but she never labors the point. Gradually I learn how selflessly Edwina has acted in behalf of the poor and needy in India, and throughout South Asia. Earlier she was extremely active as an anti-Fascist and anti-Nazi. The British left-wing intellectual Harold Laski dies while we are at the Nehru house; she and the family sincerely mourn the loss.

The only time I see Edwina behave in spoiled fashion is when a servant fails to find her glasses. She flares up violently, but then quickly regains control of herself.

During one of our conversations she is almost diabolically convincing as she half-fondly reminisces about Empire. "It must have been like innocently gathering shells and then suddenly, to your surprise, you found you had a lot of them."

Madras: Mr. X., an engineer, born in Russia, has worked in the United States and the Soviet Union, but is most sympathetic to the latter. He and his wife, whom I have met in Delhi, come up to me at a concert and greet me effusively. On hearing I plan to drive to French-held Pondicherry, they ask whether they may accompany me. My host, the Governor of Madras, has offered me—as a guest of Nehru—a government car and chauffeur for the journey. Throughout my trip I have accepted the warm hospitality and transportation proffered by officials who are my hosts, with gratitude.

I have been invited to visit the Aurobindo Ashram, stay at the guest house, and have an interview with the Mother—Aurobindo's most devoted disciple and spokesman. The prospect of appearing at the Ashram with a dialectical materialist scarcely fills me with joy. How can I ask questions freely and learn anything, or expect to have a relaxed relationship with anyone, if my dogmatic acquaintance expounds his own theories at every turn? It seems selfish to refuse Mr. X.'s request, but I don't know if I can allow others to ride in the government car. I find out I may do as I wish, and take the X.'s with me to Pondicherry.

In the automobile Mr. X. expresses his intense dislike of Bach, Beethoven, Brahms, Mozart, Haydn, Wagner—the entire sweep of pre–Russian Revolution European music. I ask which music he does like; his voice rises high, his right index finger is shaken, but he fails to mention a single composer of whom he approves. His wife explains how much she loves Bach, Beethoven, and the rest. But Mr. X. continues to shake his finger, squeak, look superior and wise.

"On a visit such as this one," I venture, "I try to speak to people unaccompanied. If I'm not alone, I learn nothing. I never express my own opinions; it inhibits those interviewed. After we arrive, we must go our separate ways. I don't know where you're planning to stay and I have no way to help you find rooms. I'm sorry, I don't mean to be rude, but it's necessary to be honest, otherwise no one can be free."

At the Ashram, Mr. and Mrs. X. follow me as I am ushered into an anteroom; a disciple greets me before I am taken to my room. The X.'s do not go their own way, but remain standing next to me. I have no choice but to introduce them. As Mr. X. shakes hands with the disciple, he says vehemently, "I just want to make my position perfectly clear. I am a Marxist, a dialectical materialist, and do not believe in mysticism. It's absolute nonsense. I just want you to know how I feel."

I interpose quickly to the X.'s: "I'm so glad to have seen you," and shake hands. "I shall be happy to take you back to Madras"—my voice is cold and flat—"and now I am sure you want to see the Ashram and Pondicherry on your own." At which point they sit down beside me, ready to take part in the ensuing conversation, as though I had not spoken. Mr. X. looks delighted—a conspiratorial warrior poised for the dialectical kill.

The Aurobindo disciple sits before us. Without waiting for him to speak, Mr. X. begins happily, "I warn you, you are engaged here in an imperialistic parlor movement and inevitably there will be a parlor reaction as part of a dialectical process. I feel the Congress Party in your country is just as misguided as you are. Fascism will follow your high-minded government and then Communism. How will you work here when that occurs?"

The disciple looks as miserable as I feel. In a voice that trembles, he replies: "Your fears are not likely to be fulfilled. Neither Fascism nor Communism will come; here at the Ashram we shall achieve what we have set out to do." He turns to me: "Our wish, even though we seem to have cut ourselves off, is to remain part of the world. We want those who come to us to experience a feeling of devotion, to acquire knowledge and integrate such qualities into their lives. The atmosphere here is the best one in which to practice ancient yoga. Through it and through being part of the Ashram, divine realization can be attained.

"All our work is performed in the service of the Mother. We are all her children. She looks after us, so whatever we do for her can never be too much. She represents, as you know, Sri Aurobindo. He speaks through her. She is in constant touch with him. Ultimately, the Mother works for the Master and the divine. We identify her with the divine."

Mr. X. can suppress himself no longer. "Man's psyche will change only with economic readjustment. Social and economic life must be transformed first. Otherwise there can be no moral values. No idealism."

The disciple continues as though Mr. X. had not spoken: "This Ashram was founded so that man could have the experience of cosmic consciousness. When we break away from the ego, we are released to the divine. The divine can affect things everywhere."

Mr. X., unheeding: "You are an island. You influence nothing. Lenin was fighting not for an elite, but for a revolution that would affect everyone."

The disciple, quietly: "If the psyche of man can change, if even a small number of men can achieve a higher, supramental reality, they will influence others—that is, if they live inwardly out, not outwardly in. We must create an elite through yoga that will be fully trained, that will have found the only valid means for the search for truth—for the solution of man's problems. Our achievement at the Ashram is beyond everything that has been accomplished before. Aurobindo and the Mother show us the true way."

The disciple rises and politely but firmly ushers me to the door and to my room, leaving the X.'s to their own devices.

The guest house in which I stay is modern, in excellent taste. It was designed by a Czech architect named Raymond, who lives in America, and by a Japanese who helped with the décor. The Mother has been responsible for the furnishings. The Ashram itself is composed of beautiful old buildings.

Pondicherry, developed by the French, differs in many details from British India. The French have walled in their splendid houses, which the English never did. They also have placed statues of their political heroes and statesmen on beautifully carved, ancient Hindu pediments that dot the landscape, and on which at one time stood sculpture dedicated to the gods.

Aurobindo, I discover, had once taken part in the Indian fight for freedom. He was twice arrested and acquitted—in 1907 and 1908—then left Calcutta and came to the French enclave of Pondicherry in 1910. Here he gave up all political activities, wrote only about mystical subjects, and in 1926 founded his Ashram.

The Mother is French—some say Algerian. She was a dancer, a great friend of author and Nobel Prize winner Romain Rolland. One day she felt she had a mission to perform and set sail for India. Arriving in Pondicherry in 1914, she found Aurobindo, who moved her greatly. She went on to the Theosophical Center in Madras, but returned to Aurobindo and became both a disciple and the person closest to him. She has run the Ashram for years.

Mainly Indians lived at the Ashram, well-dressed and upper middle-class. One of the first I met was a history professor from Benares. He explained: "I was troubled. I wanted to withdraw from the world. First I went to another swami, but I know now I belong here. This place is more modern." He smiled. "I have lost a pound of flesh. It must be proof of something. I stopped smoking. Smoking interferes with attaining higher consciousness. I have found peace." He dropped his voice. "I didn't like multi-millionaires. I didn't feel right among them. That is why I am here."

A young engineer: "I don't have the courage to become a permanent member of the Ashram, but I come whenever I can." D.N.: "Why does it take courage?" "Because you have to give up everything else. The Mother makes all decisions for you. I would gladly have her tell me what to do and follow her instructions. Yet so far, I don't have the courage." "Is it really a lack of courage?" The engineer assured me: "Yes, definitely. You have no conception of the power of the Mother and Aurobindo."

As I was about to photograph an early portrait of Aurobindo, a young member of the Ashram carrying a camera came over to me and said sternly, "You are not allowed to take pictures of anything." I apologized, saying I hadn't known. "I am the photographer here," he replied proudly. I asked him about himself. The photographer: "My family has been here for many years. At first I refused to come with them. All this seemed absurd. Then one day I came to visit and was taken to see the Mother. This, you realize, is a great privilege. She looked at me and I fell into a dead faint. When I came to, she was telling me I must stay and become the photographer for the Ashram. Of course I obeyed her and have been here ever since. My entire life has changed."

I am permitted to observe those who meditate in the lovely courtyard; am taken to the Ashram's carpentry and shoe repair shops, bakery and book bindery. Everyone who stays must participate in the work, according to the Mother's dictates. Some help with the cooking and household tasks or work on the land. Others assist in the shops and with the printing of Aurobindo's books and the Mother's sayings.

Devotees tell me they first came to the Ashram to be in the presence of Aurobindo on one of his Darshan days, during which he appears in fine robes; visitors or pilgrims bring elegant saris and much gold, which they lay at the feet of the Mother. Only at these quarterly intervals can the public see Aurobindo. Otherwise he remains in seclusion on the second floor, available only to the Mother and a few chosen disciples. His poetic and metaphysical books were written years ago; now he publishes only occasional articles on current political happenings.

Those who remain in residence are so deeply affected by Aurobindo and the Mother, they give over their lives to the Ashram. Many bring their families and present all their worldly possessions to the Mother. Their children attend the Ashram's school. All serve the Mother gladly, for she is the divine. It strikes me, as I walk about, that outside professionals do most of the difficult or tedious chores, even though I am told the reverse.

Late in the afternoon members of the Ashram—some are European or American—and visitors gather out of doors. A few Indians perform advanced feats of yoga; to me, their complex acrobatics suggest overly proficient performers rather than authentic residents. Young women in white shorts, sneakers, and headbands, and young men also neatly dressed, do Swedish exercises with extraordinary precision and grace. Their daily practice has made them fit and expert. There is no sound.

Suddenly I am aware the Mother is standing nearby at attention, watching. The well-trained participants finish and remain perfectly still. Everyone observes a "moment of silence" that seems to last an eternity. I sense a strange tension in the atmosphere, as though a spring has been wound too tight and refuses to uncoil. It is said that often at this time, as youngsters pass by, the Mother hands them chocolates and other tidbits. Today she does not.

A fine-looking young Indian woman in shorts, tennis shoes, and white net headband—exactly what I wear for tennis—talks with me. (At certain moments I feel as though I were at a country club.)

"What do you do if you need a new pair of sneakers, or some other object of clothing?" Young woman: "There is a shop upstairs—we call it the Prosperity Shop. If we need something, we hand a chit to the Mother. If she thinks we should have it, we receive it. If she doesn't, that of course settles the question."

The people of Pondicherry look desperately poor. I ask a young man whether the Ashram ever helps them in any way. Young Man: "The Mother is not political. We act exactly as she tells us to. She has never suggested giving to anyone in Pondicherry. After all, we are serving the Mother. Thus we serve the divine. We wouldn't think of doing anything she didn't tell us to."

Very early in the morning the Mother appears on a balcony. Every member of the Ashram and all who have come to visit throng the area below where she stands. (No one is allowed to photograph, but I surreptitiously click my camera.) Her long, dyed, harsh carrot-color hair hangs down. She gazes at us as though her eyes were looking not at a crowd, but at each individual separately. She moves an arm ever so slightly, majestically, back and forth, much as does the Queen of England.

Interview with the Mother: she wears a white shiny satin tunic, pajama trousers, a white bandeau wrapped around her head. She is about seventy years old, has recently taken up tennis. Her cheeks are heavily rouged, her lips painted bright red-orange. Her eyes are milky gray, enormous.

I am seated opposite her; she stares intently into my eyes, as though to hypnotize me, to seduce me into joining the Ashram, into giving over my life to her. Horrified, I find myself resisting.

I ask whether demanding chastity of those who remain at the Ashram will not eradicate the elite. She says it will not and changes the subject, speaking vaguely about the aims of the Ashram, of Aurobindo's ideas, of the supra-rational. Those eyes. Those alarming eyes.

I come away unmoved. I have learned more about the Ashram and the Master from the first disciple.

Luncheon next day at the Indian Legation in Pondicherry: my Indian host welcomes me profusely. I tell him I have come especially to visit the Ashram; he is delighted. I ask if he is interested in it. He looks at me in amazement. "Interested?" He points to a large map of India on the dining-room wall. "The Mother is the divine. The Mother is India. In serving the Mother, one serves India, one serves the divine. Most of my waking thoughts are spent in contemplating the Mother. You see this map? Mother India. The Mother is India."

Conversation with the official in charge of the French Legation: Is he interested in the Ashram? He replies with enthusiasm, "Interested? It has the best tennis courts, its beach is beautiful and clean. I always play tennis, exercise, and swim there. It is most useful."

The Mother, I am told, has been against the Indian freedom movement; she does not want Pondicherry to become part of Free India. Some say she feels she can have more scope to function in an enclave of France than under Indian rule. Some believe she has been an agent of France and still works to help it retain a foothold on the subcontinent. The facts are never made entirely clear to me.

I returned to New Delhi, to Nehru's house. He asked what I had seen on my trip to the south. When I mentioned Pondicherry, he was amused. "Once, not too long ago, when I went to south India, I wanted to see Aurobindo and the Ashram. The Mother refused my request." We exchanged wry smiles. (He did pay other visits.)

Back in New York, some months later, the phone rang. "This is Upadahya, Indian philosopher. I want to interview you about your philosophy of life. I already have spoken with Aldous Huxley and other prominent Western philosophers. When may I come to see you?" "But I am not a prominent Western philosopher." "That makes no difference; you are on my list. I have been told I must interview you." Amused, I receive Upadahya.

After we discuss our "philosophies of life," he says, "I understand you went to see the Mother at the Aurobindo Ashram when you were in India. Would you like to meet her husband?" This is the first time anyone has ever mentioned him. "I would very much enjoy meeting the husband of the Mother." "I shall arrange it. Monsieur Richard lives near New York, at the Nyack Country Club." With difficulty I manage not to smile, recalling how the Ashram had reminded me of nothing so much as a country club.

Monsieur Richard, whom Upadahya brings for tea, is tall and has a meticulously trimmed beard and the look of a scholar, but something about the man, the more I regard him and the more we talk, suggests a "professional" philosopher rather than a genuine one. He is writing a book about his philosophy of life which describes the seven phases of man. He asks me my philosophy; I reply mine would be of little interest to him. And then, without a pause, he says, "I hear you met the Mother. What did you think of her?" There is a sarcastic edge to the question. "Most interesting." "Do you know the story about our going to India?" "Only vaguely, but I should love to hear it." He proceeds eagerly.

"The Mother—my wife, Madame Richard—and I set sail for Pondicherry years ago. She had a strong desire that we should stay at the Theosophical Center in Madras—Kalakchetra. We both had a profound interest in Indian thought. At Pondicherry we met Sri Aurobindo. The Mother was much taken with him and his view of life. But we proceeded as planned to Madras. We had been at the center for some time, when one night a terrific thunderstorm blew the roof off the building in which we were staying. The Mother arose, pointed a finger, and said, 'Ah, that is a sign.' The next day she left for Pondicherry and we have never seen each other again. She has given the rest of her life to Sri Aurobindo and the Ashram."

Monsieur Richard promises to send me his forthcoming book on the seven stages of man, which he does. I try to thank him but he is no longer at the country club and has left no forwarding address.

Jayaprakash Narayan, the young Indian Socialist leader whom I first meet in sprawling Calcutta, strikes me as outstanding, a natural leader. I can well imagine him as India's future Prime Minister. He is fine-looking, calm, serious, disciplined, highly intelligent, and possessed of natural dignity. Educated in America, he was once a Communist but soon rebelled.

He invites me to a meeting in the apartment of a Socialist friend where he is staying in Howrah—a poor, heavily populated district on the other side of the river. Nearby there have been communal riots; Moslems and Hindus have been burning down each others' settlements.

Narayan and his colleagues have called their meeting for 8:30 A.M. to discuss what can be done to calm tensions. The room is sparsely furnished, its floor covered with immaculate white sheets. We remove our shoes at the entrance and sit cross-legged on the spotless floor.

Jayaprakash commands the attention of those who have gathered with his quiet, firm, determined voice. Plans are under discussion when the telephone rings. Jayaprakash answers, listens, puts down the receiver. In a controlled tone he tells us that a *hartal*—general strike—has been called in Calcutta, mainly to protest against Hindu-Moslem violence. Public conveyances have stopped running; more and more shops are closing; vehicles in the streets and those trying to cross the bridge are being stopped, overturned. Jayaprakesh advises me to leave at once for my own safety.

I have come in a Government House limousine. In spite of the excitement in the room and the brisk allotting of tasks to be done, someone courteously escorts me to the official automobile, with its gay national flags. The imposing car strikes me as preposterous standing before the modest doorway.

I am driven back over the bridge, on which there are numerous trucks filled with strikers intent upon molesting anything in reach. Many vehicles lie on their sides. What will happen to the elegant, beflagged official car in which I ride?

As though we are protected by fate, no one seems to notice us either on the bridge or during our drive back through the city. I arrive at Government House with vast relief. The damage in the city is fairly great, but the following day everything seems to have returned to normal.

My new Socialist acquaintances take me about to see the worst conditions imaginable and are eager for me to receive and read their literature. They explain their program and their dreams.

As I move throughout India, I find those allied with Narayan outspoken against all social ills, and sincerely eager to arouse others about the most troubling situations, yet they are always as restrained and disciplined as they seem dedicated. Nehru is criticized for not having Jayaprakash in his cabinet. Nehru explains to me he has invited him, but cannot agree to fulfill the demands he has made. "I am not a dictator," Nehru protests. "How can I be expected to make promises in advance, as he wants me to do, when I have no idea which of them will be approved by Parliament?"

Traveling about the countryside, I am filled with compassion and distress. Misery is reflected in the face of almost every villager. Bodies are shrunken, painfully thin. A numbed worshipfulness stares out of often faraway eyes. Is it,

I wonder, really worshipfulness? Then a rare and sudden warm smile of trust and welcome—like a beam of sunlight—illuminates otherwise impenetrable darkness.

I am taken by a Socialist to a small settlement near Calcutta with open latrines, open sewers filled with filthy water in which debris floats. The ground is strewn with bits of decaying garbage. There is a horrifying stench of defecation, of rotting substances disintegrating still further in the blazing sun. I am ashamed as I gag, choke, weep. I feel apologetic, but cannot speak. I find it impossible to say anything to those who shepherd me about. The Socialists do not need to tell me how horrifying the scene is, yet with minor exceptions only the Socialists I meet admit freely what is wrong.

Stella Kramrisch, one of the leading interpreters of Indian art and myth—perhaps the greatest since Coomaraswamy—lives in Calcutta. She is the author of a mammoth two-volume work, *The Hindu Temple*. Various scholars in America have urged me to visit her, which I am eager to do. No one at Government House has ever heard her name, but finally we locate her address. The junglelike landscape that we traverse is tropical, brooding, mysterious, but suddenly a two-story house with orchids clustered around it is revealed.

Dr. Kramrisch—small, European, shy—appears on the second floor. I had not realized she is Viennese. In spite of oppressive heat, the stone structure is delightfully cool. She leads me through one of the most beautiful rooms I have seen in India. Small Hindu sculptures are perfectly displayed. The cloth on a table is simple, yet elegantly embroidered by village craftsmen. The furniture, Sheraton in style, was made in India in Sheraton's own time, she tells me. Dr. Kramrisch, I note with pleasure, is wearing a gown made of Indian material; it reflects her sensitivity to lovely peasant fabrics, largely ignored by the "sophisticated" Indian.

I am full of questions about the Hindu temples I have seen, as well as about every object in the room. The apartment's originality and beauty are dazzling. I cannot see why others do not have similar quarters, instead of tepid imitations of British nineteenth-century households, nor why the country's magnificent crafts are so largely ignored by the wealthy. As Dr. Kramrisch speaks, I sense how profoundly she understands the meaning of every aspect of

Indian art. Realizing I am in the presence of a superb teacher, I ask whether I may take notes. Later I write about her in *Marg*, an Indian magazine of the arts:

"Indian art has gone through various cycles of development, just as do all art and all organic life. It has produced, again and again, the contained form of the primitive, the full manifestation of the classical, the exuberance of the baroque. . . .

"The cycles through which Indian art has passed have reached different levels of realization. Yet all the cycles have been promulgated with a single aim. There has not been uniformity. But there has been coherence. The level of the art depends upon the spiritual and material, living personality of the particular artists who have functioned. The art's quality depends on the type of emotion conditioning the life around the artists. . . .

"The particular quality of form in an Indian work of art is supported by the tension of the pairs of opposites represented. The seeming immobility of a seated Buddha image, or of a Vishnu image standing as straight as is the World Pillar, carries compelling power in its calmness because of the balanced tension of line, mass and weight.

"Indian art is said to be anonymous. There are in fact but a few names inscribed on it. It was not the intention of the artist to be known for the individuality or uniqueness of his work but for its excellence, showing that he had done his best, challenging others to surpass him— and being himself wonder struck when seeing his completed work. One master, on seeing his stupendous creation—the great temple at Ellora— exclaimed, 'How was it that I made it?' He was overcome by awe for the genius that had worked through him. The artist's name is not known.

"What seems permanent throughout the long creative life of Indian art is a fluidity of line and modelling, as though its figures were breathing, as though their shapes were full of sap, like ripe fruits. Their form is due more to empathy than observation; their 'naturalism' amounts to a creative re-production of life that animates and shapes all that is observed. The artist sees not the shape of a plant as a given form but in the process of acquiring that form; he is a master in showing the opening of a bud, the energy by which a petal leaves the close company of the others and presages the full blown flower. Into this basic creative disposition of his, the artist lets sink those conceptions that define the imperceptible gods. They rise from his work imbued with the life he knows how to infuse into them. Their other-worldly dimension rises from the work, replete with the warmth and rhythms of life. The fusion of, and the tension between, the religious or metaphysical theme and the lived naturalism of the artist make for the permanent recognizability of a work of art as Indian."

As I listen to Dr. Kramrisch, I am electrified by the way in which the slim, tiny figure becomes transformed as she talks. The glow in her eyes, an inner rhythm, the way in which she presents her ideas, turn her into a dancer. I have never before seen this happen to anyone sitting quite still, making no dramatic gestures. The more involved and enthralled she is with her subject and her identification with it, the more powerful is her ability to communicate.

As I leave, I say, "This has been extraordinary. While you were speaking, you became a dancer; you performed what your words were saying, they were so much a part of you." She smiles shyly. "I was a dancer. After I had given a lecture on Indian temples in Oxford and danced for Rabindranath Tagore in London, he invited me to come to India and teach at his university, Shantiniketan."

My visit to India ends in the spring of 1950. I leave the Nehru household at 5:00 A.M.; its members come to the door to say goodbye; several accompany me to the airport. Everyone has been so kind, warm, thoughtful, courteous—I realize how attached I have grown. In New Delhi the Prime Minister's house has been home to me. My three and a half months' stay in India has been most auspicious.

After affectionate farewells, I sink into my airplane seat overwhelmed by a thousand warring emotions. I become aware of the stifling pools of silence that have engulfed me at times against my will, beyond my control—questions I could not ask, pent-up reactions I could not confess, vast sympathy I could not express. Joy is the only emotion I have been able to share.

The unforgettable face of Nehru haunts me most of all—its every feature and nuance. And the art, the great temples, the strange beauties of landscape, the handicrafts, the flowers, the touching moments with so many diverse individuals. But always the needs, the sufferings, the specter of starvation. Tears well up and cannot be stemmed. The moment I return home, I must go to Washington to plead that we send India wheat—help of all kinds —without delay. I must.

Looking down from the plane about to land in familiar New York, I realized I was a changed person. Edward was at the airport to meet me; I was overjoyed to see him. But I was looking into the face of a stranger, and he was, too. He took me in his arms and kissed me; I felt the same love for him in the same sweet way I did during our first meetings so many years ago.

"Kiss me. Hold me," I whisper. I know that our feelings are identical. We mean deeply every syllable we utter and clasp hands like two enraptured children, while recognizing all too well the knife of reality that divides us.

I am profoundly happy to be back; I belong here. For all the wonder of India, I know that Edward, the children, and New York are my reality. As we drove from the airport to our handsome house on a quiet street, my hand was held lovingly and firmly by the man I fought to marry. I struggled to keep back my tears. Why was I not simply glad to be home? Despite the difficulties, I still yearned for our marriage to work.

Behind New York's obvious beauty—towering buildings, bridges, electrifying vistas—the city's poverty and ugliness seemed appalling. Then, with a sudden jolt, I thought of India, and any sense of destitution in America paled. All the committees on which I had served for so many years, trying to help the underprivileged, seemed suddenly unreal. Poor health services, neglect of civil rights, child abuse, faulty education, a thousand ills—all must be taken care of. But our tragedies are petty in comparison with those of India.

Riding up Park Avenue, I feel a certain hostility toward the surface of well-being around us. The problems abroad I have been reflecting upon are too large even to think about, much less resolve. But I must do something at least modestly meaningful for India.

Once in the house words of love, of gladness at coming home, poured from me, but everything I tried to tell about the trip sounded banal, stereo-typed. "India was marvelous—and terrifying; thank you for letting me go," I blurt out. "So much beauty exists there, and so much poverty! I want to try to do something about it." My words sound childish. Everywhere in the world voices are crying for help. All each of us can do seems so finite, so slight.

I needed a moment's time in which to regain equilibrium. There before me was Edward, filled with his own problems, anxieties, his own deep desire to do good. He had missed me as I had missed him, but each had had his own world. What was he feeling? I couldn't read him. There was tension in him. The stability of our marriage seemed to have been shattered long ago. Let us just be quiet together and find each other again.

After talking with Indians, foreign diplomats, and American officials about aid for India, I cannot rest until I go to Washington to see what can be accomplished. Heretofore, I have pleaded for legislation at the city and state levels, but never directly for the passage of federal laws—a wholly new experience.

I make an appointment with members of the India desk at the State Department, some of whom I already know. The new building is clean, trim, impressive. The room in which we meet is ludicrously well-appointed, compared with its Delhi equivalent. Everyone is eager to achieve the same goal—to help India. But the obstacles described to me by Ambassador Henderson are omnipresent. Until India requests aid, Congress can do nothing. The State Department is not permitted to become involved in legislative matters; it is strictly part of the Executive.

I beg Indians at their embassy to request assistance. The United States, I say, is enormously sympathetic to the plight of the Indian people. Nehru's visit undoubtedly has had a good effect. They can do nothing.

In New York, I talk with Sir Benegal Rau, India's representative at the United Nations—a highly intelligent man, largely responsible for the writing of India's democratic constitution. He, too, is eager for India to receive aid.

Talks, talks, but nothing happens. Then one day the telephone rings: the India desk at the State Department. "Dorothy, you said you wanted to do something helpful about wheat for India. A cable has just arrived from Delhi requesting two million tons of grain. Now is your chance to do that something." I express relief that the cable has materialized, but what specifically can I do? How should I—a private citizen—proceed?

"Just go ahead," says the voice, "you'll know what to do." Within a few minutes the telephone again: Sir Benegal Rau, who tells me in strictest confidence that a cable has just come from Nehru. Technically, it has to be delivered to the embassy first, but he is notifying me out of turn because of our talks and my interest. He knows I won't betray his confidence. "Go ahead and do whatever you can," he says in his kindly fashion.

In a short while, the Indian Embassy in Washington informs me about Nehru's cable. Fascinating to receive the same piece of secret news in so little time from three different sources, all of whom suggest I get to work, though none offers any advice about how to proceed. But experience in preparing releases about political issues has taught me one thing: the need for haste. Important support for any issue must be announced immediately after the initial news statement is made. Nehru's cable undoubtedly will be published in the morning press.

I call a press conference at our house for the next day, with nothing really to announce except that, in view of India's formal request for aid, action must be taken at once. I create a committee—in my mind—to pressure Congress to pass the necessary legislation with great dispatch.

Quickly I invite a few concerned friends on whom I can rely, and urge every church and labor organization I can think of to join the "committee" and attend the news conference. As rapidly as possible I compose a release for the press. Needing certain data to back up my case, I phone the Indian Embassy for facts, which are not readily available. I call the State Department; the needed information is dictated at once, to my relief. The rest of my time, up to the moment of the conference, is spent expanding and polishing the release, and asking every social welfare organization I can think of to send a representative and join the effort.

I greet members of the press as they arrive promptly and in great numbers. Friends and others cooperate, so that we appear to be a committee; I receive permission from numerous church, labor, and foreign-policy groups to use their names. Dignitaries from the Indian Embassy in Washington attend the conference and are helpful. News coverage the following day is excellent; the committee suddenly exists and starts to function.

Now begins the hard work of following up the initial move. I compose a letter, to be circulated by committee members, intended to arouse people to write, wire, or visit Congressmen. Thousands respond to our suggestion; letters pour in to Congressional offices. Then more difficult questions arise: What kind of a bill should be written? Who should introduce it? Should the two million tons of grain be a gift or a loan?

In Washington again, I hear that Senator Herbert Lehman is planning to introduce a bill proposing wheat for India. Experience plus common sense tell me that such a bill must have bipartisan support. I rush to Lehman's office, explain matters to his assistant, and am delighted that the Senator agrees to wait until there is backing from both parties. What a superb man Lehman is, how fair and considerate!

To testify before a Congressional committee seems terrifying. I know few people in the hearing room. Senator Jacob Javits, with whom I have often worked, greets me warmly and pats me on the shoulder. My turn comes and I am questioned. Fortunately, I can answer the technical inquiries with some authority. Then Senator Javits asks, "Would you say, Mrs. Norman, that Prime Minister Nehru has ever been a Communist?" This is the kind of query I had expected an opponent to make, not my friend Javits. I realize later he may have been trying to prove Nehru was not a Communist by way of my answer. I am staggered that it should be considered helpful to bring up the matter at all. I state firmly that Nehru is not and never has been a Communist. In particular, he detests the Indian Communist Party. The hearings are difficult but backing for aid increases.

One problem remains: Should food be a gift or a loan? On inquiry, I am told repeatedly no one can advise me; I must make up my own mind on the subject. I feel intuitively the wheat should be a gift; only problems will lie ahead if it is a loan. I ask the Indian Embassy to contact Nehru at once and am assured that India will gladly accept the gift.

But then, after a complex bill is worked out, word comes that India prefers a loan. The entire process must be repeated to gain support for different legislation. Why the whole project doesn't simply fall to pieces I never understand. After tedious weeks of work, the two million tons of wheat are offered to India as a loan.

Despite passage of the aid legislation, tensions between India and the United States persist. As chairman of a series of Citizens' Committees for Aid to the Third World, I am eager to discover directly from Nehru the reasons for continuing dissensions; I finally ask him to explain India's position. He replies:

As usual, you have taken up this good work with all energy and enthusiasm. . . . I need not tell you how grateful we all are for your deep interest and work for India.

We have welcomed U.S. aid . . . but, to be quite frank, I have sometimes wondered how far it was a good thing for us to have these controversies on this subject. . . . Naturally we have stood in need of help and any help that came would push our development programme. But I was not at all happy at this controversy in the U.S., which naturally found its reactions in India.

As you know, some of your Senators taunted us for accepting aid when we had criticised American military aid to Pakistan. This comparison . . . was not justified because there was a great deal of difference between military aid and normal aid for civil purposes and especially development programmes. Nevertheless, there was an atom of truth in the criticism and we were hurt by it and felt some doubts in our minds about accepting aid in present circumstances. Also, while aid was welcome, it may well be that large scale aid might produce a sensation of dependence on others and not self-reliance. That is, I considered, bad, because I am convinced that a nation progresses ultimately not by money but by the spirit of the people.

Both these reasons, therefore, made me rather reluctant to accept aid. . . . Our relations with the U.S. . . . were none too happy and I was exceedingly reluctant to say or do anything which might worsen them. For us to indicate that we did not want this aid would undoubtedly hurt people in the U.S. and estrange our two countries still further. . . . Because of this consideration I preferred to remain silent. . . .

I know it would be grossly unfair for me or for any of us to judge of the United States by the speeches of some Senators. I do not think we make that mistake. But inevitably there are reactions in India to speeches and writings in the Press, just as there are reactions in the U.S. to speeches and writings in India. I do not think that there is any basic antagonism to the U.S. in India, but it is true that in regard to certain policies which the U.S. has followed, there is a strong difference of opinion here. I refer more particularly to policies pursued in Asia.

Nehru is often criticized in the United States for failure to condemn China for its actions involving Tibet, and for not exchanging ambassadors with Israel. I understand that India, a weak nation, can do little about China; her stand on Israel stems from consideration for Moslems and need for trade with Arab countries. The third issue—the appointment of Krishna Menon as High Commissioner in London and Ambassador to the United Nations—is disturbing.

I first met Krishna Menon at an India League meeting in New York, just after he arrived from England in 1946. Thin, sinister, with a forbidding hooked nose, hostile eyes, and tousled hair, he was the only person in the Indian Freedom movement who had something diabolical about him.

I saw him often in the following years; each time he gave me the same uncomfortable feeling. In spite of his expensive Savile Row tailored suits, he always looked disheveled. He claims he drinks tea, eats nothing. In New York friends attest to his visiting a delicatessen late at night to buy food that is not tea.

Menon's political statements strike me as distorted, inaccurate, mischievous. I cannot understand why Nehru so consistently favors him. The assessment that his cleverness and hard work in pre-Independence London made him invaluable to Nehru and the Indian Government fails to impress me. It is said he was responsible for getting Nehru's first book published in London. But other Indians were active in the Independence movement and helpful, too, and they are not so honored.

At various times I cannot refrain from telling both Nehru and Indira Gandhi that I think Menon does India more harm than good each time he makes a public or private utterance; that he is destructive not only to India, but also to the entire free world and everything in which we believe. My efforts are of no avail.

15

In Washington for talks with the State Department about aid for India in 1950, I encounter the French poet Alexis Saint-Léger Léger—Saint-John Perse—who lives there. While I worked with the Free French in New York, Henri Bernstein, my good friend Pertinax, and many others spoke to me with admiration about Perse and were eager to bring us together. Long before that, Paul Rosenfeld extolled him to me for *Twice A Year*. But no matter who wanted us to meet, something always intervened; we seemed doomed to be kept apart. Now he comes to see me.

Perse is startling, his eyes so intense I barely see the rest of his face. He gazes at me with an unsettling fierceness. We sit silent for a moment, without breaking the incredible, deepening contact of eyes. And then, without introductory warning, he asks in a voice at once pleading and commanding, "When did you last cry?"

Nothing this man does or says surprises me. I feel only some hypnotic power overwhelming me.

"I don't mean cry for yourself, but for something beyond you." "On the plane, leaving India." "Go on." "I wept not for myself but about the poverty and misery I had seen. I couldn't talk freely about my reactions to anyone—not even those to whom I felt closest. I dared not ask questions; I couldn't confess my anguish. My experience of India was also rich and rewarding, but the often terrifying moments paralyzed me. I didn't realize how pent-up my emotions were until I was leaving. I felt absurd, weeping, weeping, as though all the tears of the world were flowing into and out of my eyes."

Each time I looked at Alexis, his face changed, but never the eyes. A thunderstorm was brewing as I photographed him in his apartment. We had to move nearer and nearer the window so I could focus properly; the light was fading. Concentrating on his eyes, I noticed a map of an island behind his head. Startled, I stopped clicking and looked around at the walls lined with maps of islands. I had seen them before but they hadn't registered. Alexis had been born on a small island off Guadaloupe. He had been a solitary person—an island—all his life. The image in my lens became a metaphor, a symbol of the man.

I moved my camera and continued to photograph. But the pictures I took now had nothing in the background. It was Alexis's head that became an island in a pool of surrounding darkness—a ray of intense light emerging from mysterious depths.

I sent him prints; he said to me about one profile that whatever I decided as the photographer, he considered this his definitive, unique portrait. He would be happy to use it forever, not only for his private needs and those of his publishers but for any publicity purposes.

He told me the profile shot was by far his favorite, that it seemed best to do honor to my art as a photographer. He also found it the most psychologically pleasing, both understated and natural.

Alexis Léger is already a legendary figure. I learn how he jeopardized his career in the French diplomatic service by his early defiance not only of Nazism but of Pétain. Yet as he sits before me, I don't see the skilled diplomat, only the poet—sensitive, uncompromising.

He speaks of his escape to England shortly before the fall of France in 1940. I ask about the devastating experience of having his unpublished manuscripts destroyed by the Gestapo. He replies philosophically, without self-pity, "Most of my poetry, known today, was written in America. Your country has inspired me; the influence of American themes in my work is no mere accident of history."

Deprived of his French nationality by the Vichy government, Perse was fully reinstated in all his "rights and privileges" after the liberation of France, but he did not return.

"I chose to remain here after the war and declined all ambassadorial missions. I am nobody here. Which is good. I can write. To go to a foreign country in that sense is to reach the greatest height." A smile flickers. "I am anonymous here. What is one, after all? To whom does one belong? Once I suppressed a poem because it revealed too much of myself."

I have been told a lovely story: although Perse had lived in America for some time, he refused to speak English because of his great love of French. Edgard Varèse, meeting him one day, boasted how much his own English had improved. Perse looked at him with mock disdain and said, "You have not sufficiently resisted."

Perse asks me how I first became interested in India. "Through reading Coomaraswamy's *Dance of Shiva*," I reply. "Shortly after that I met him and we had long, strange talks. He aroused my interest in India's art, philosophy, and her struggle for freedom. The concept of Shiva made a specially profound impression on me."

Perse, with a mischievous smile: "Amazing. Shiva has played a great role in my life, too. When I was small, in Guadaloupe, my Hindu nurse was a so-called priestess of Shiva—in secret. One day, while my parents were away, she painted me black and took me to a Shiva temple. I was placed in a niche above those who came to worship and was approached as a little Shiva. My nurse carried me to the home of plantation workers and had me touch the foreheads of those who were ill. It was an extraordinary experience. I always have had a great interest in Shiva."

D.N.: "You know, of course, what a black Shiva signifies?" "Tell me." "Black alludes to total darkness in which all distinctions vanish and out of which everything originates. From absolute darkness the God Brahma, the creator, emerges. All of us must pass through the same 'black' if we mistakenly cling to ego and illusion. But a white Shiva is covered with the ashes of the burning ground. That is where our egos and illusions are cremated."

Alexis's face is transformed; it becomes even more intense and alive than before.

Alexis: "I greatly admire the poetry of Rabindranath Tagore, whom I met in London in 1912. He asked who would be a good translator of his *Gitanjali* and I suggested André Gide—not yet well known. After Tagore won the Nobel Prize in 1913, I felt perhaps I had made a mistake; I should have suggested someone more famous and called this to Tagore's attention. He replied, 'If you thought Gide the best man, just leave it at that.' This only added to my respect for him."

One day I tell Perse that for me his poem *Anabase* transcends past and present, East and West. Perse: "That is true; it's not really about any place." He remains briefly lost in thought. "Let me tell you of an incident in the Gobi Desert. Water was running out. I was with the most civilized individuals I had ever known. The question arose: should the dwindling supply be saved entirely for human consumption or should a fair amount be given to the flowers that were dying, and to the goldfish—the beautiful goldfish—that also would perish if deprived of water? The final decision was made without hesitation. The last water was given to the flowers and the fish. That is civilization at its highest point."

Perse looks at me as though to test me. If anyone else had told me such a tale, I would debate it. With Alexis, I accept his words. I am listening to the poet's split-second pleasure, not a moralist's judgment.

Alexis: "There is an Arab saying: when you meet for the first time in the desert at an oasis, there is the right to ask all and give all. At a second meeting, each may well pass the other as a stranger, not even nodding. The third time, if the relativity of lives creates a relationship—well and good."

Again, about the desert: "The wish of the East, 'May water never fail you on your journey!' The wish of the West, 'May thirst never fail you on your journey!'"

Perse's eloquence and depth of perception, his inexhaustibly rich vocabulary, defy imitation or duplication. He sings of the elements; of birds and winds, of snows and rains; of the sea. His rapturous poems of woman epitomize the myriad mysteries and vagaries of love.

Alexis's speech is not poetic in a conventional or strained manner. Yet to listen to him is always to hear the poet: "We must have a sense of laws—to be broken. To break the law of reverence means there must be more reverence. Bad laws stem from fear. Good ones from reverence."

"How I dislike all pretense of good. If someone says, 'You're an angel,' that's an insult."

"I find it a benediction to be oneself. Not like others. With thoughtfulness, with the capacity for love, but without using the word or making any claim."

"Tenderness is a greater poison than passion."

"That which I seek is denied me. To have it granted would make me a failure."

After one of our meetings, I leave behind a pair of gloves. Alexis says that their presence was "not like a farewell, but plumage shed in full flight."

After my return from India, I observe a new quiet in Edward—more in the nature of having gone dead to things than being at peace. Unhappily, calm periods alternate with the customary irrational furies that grow ever more terrifying.

Whenever Edward has complained about my not living a frivolous, fun-loving existence, I have suggested he find a woman who will satisfy him, who can enjoy the kind of life he now prefers and which he has known from the beginning I couldn't share. Then he should marry her. I don't want our family to break up, but the children are grown and Edward's excessive violence, alternating with abjectness and exaggerated love, make me increasingly frightened. I feel deeply compassionate toward him, but that doesn't help.

One afternoon, at a party in New York, Edward introduces me to Mrs. J. R., with whom he has become acquainted. They speak to each other animatedly, but not at all in the elevator, when we leave at the same time. Neither does he mention her in the cab driving home. I have a curious intuition they know each other very well.

During the summer Edward asks me to invite J.'s young daughter to stay with us for a while at Woods Hole. I make a sincere effort to have the visit go well, but it is not highly successful. One evening Edward and I are sitting on our porch; he mentions casually that J. is going to Europe. Out of the blue I say, "Bunny dear, I love you and always will. But maybe J.'s the woman you need now. You're not living in a way that satisfies you. Why not join her in Europe? Try it out. I have a feeling you're in love with her. Marry her, if that will make you happy." My words have poured out without my having had any idea I was about to utter them.

As though we were discussing the weather, Edward replies, "That's a good idea. I'll do just that."

That's all we say and the matter is settled. Incredible. The evening Edward is to leave, he becomes forgetful and even more expressionless as he mutters a few unemotional, trancelike words. The children are away. His bags are packed, standing at the door. As always, he is ready early; we sit on the porch motionless, silent. Edward looks numbed and gazes into space, as though barely conscious. I don't know what to say; it's too late to say anything. I feel unutterably sad, but hope this is the right solution for us both.

Time passes; we should leave for the station. I can't say this to Edward for fear he'll think I'm trying to be rid of him. Vaguely, I ask if he has any idea what time it is. He jumps up. "I'm going to miss the train!" he blurts out angrily, as though some dreadful plot had been devised against him. "Hurry, hurry!" We rush to the automobile. "Get in. Get in!" He drives like a madman, paying no attention to sharp corners. It is Sunday evening; weekenders are trooping back from Martha's Vineyard and Nantucket to pick up their cars along the route to the station. They pull out in front of us and behind us, but Edward pays no attention, spurting ahead at top speed. Terrified, I gasp, "Oh, Bunny!" "I'm not going fast," he snarls. I am silent, but my terror does not diminish. We arrive at the station just as the train is about to leave. He climbs aboard. I barely have time to say goodbye.

Many friends stand nearby, but I rush back to the car. My eyes are filled with tears and I tremble, driving slowly to keep control of the car and myself. Dazed, I reach home.

What have we done? I could never have sought a divorce myself. I couldn't have left Edward unless he had found someone else. Now everything is a question mark.

Edward returns in a month; the trip was a great success. Just before we leave for the city to make plans for a divorce, the phone rings. The State Department asks if I can go to India on a grant, to lecture about Indo-American cultural relations, all expenses paid. It strikes me that nothing could be better than for Edward and me to be apart during this trying period. I am relieved to accept the invitation.

Back in New York, sadly I get ready for the trip. It is strange, even beautiful, to realize I still love Edward, though the conviction grows that we mustn't remain together. I am frightened for him. All suggestions that he see a psychiatrist upset him.

This time—only two years after my first visit—I go to India with a heavy heart. Yet seeing people on the way in London, Paris, Rome, and Greece lifts my spirits. I feel I can be myself with those who have the same dreams, are in harmony with the kind of world I cherish and want to help build. I will not give in; I will not feel sorry for myself; I will not desert the values in which I have always believed.

On my return Edward tells me he has decided not to marry J.; she "hasn't measured up." Pitifully, he pleads with me not to go ahead with the divorce. But both my lawyer and a psychiatrist have warned me of the real danger of staying married to Edward, because of his instability and violence. I am stricken by the need to follow their advice, but I know it is sound.

1953: Reno, Nevada. Sinking feeling. Divorce. Can't believe I'm here. All the years of love and effort to rescue a relationship that couldn't be saved. We were so young, so blind and sure, so full of love. I weep for our dreams.

After registering at the main hotel, I have a *pro forma* meeting with the lawyer handling my case. Everything has been decided in New York. The only rule I must obey is to stay in Nevada every day for six weeks.

I walk down the street near the hotel to get a feel of the place. Slot machines, slot machines, slot machines. You can't move without them glaring at you. I see a sign on a small French restaurant, the Moulin Rouge: "Famous Onion Soup," and next to it, "No Slot Machines." That's where I'll dine this evening.

A quiet little inn in a nearby valley is recommended. Mrs. W., an ex-

Boston debutante who has been divorced and settled down with a new husband, does a good job of managing a comfortable, simple house with a few separate one-room cottages. She is handsome, but her face looks tired, expressionless. Greeting me warmly, she shows me the first floor; a slot machine stands in a corner of the bar–living room. I blanch but look away.

We exchange a few words about ourselves. She went to Falmouth, near Woods Hole, in the summer during her youth. "I married a tennis champion," she confesses tonelessly. "If there's any game I hate, it's tennis. It was unbearable. I came out here to get a divorce. And what did I do? Married a Danish prince who was a tennis champion." There is no mirth in her eyes, nor in mine.

My luggage is taken to a cottage. I want to sit down and cry. I mustn't. I have brought my Stieglitz manuscript to work on and several empty notebooks, but I cannot concentrate. I walk outside; the air is clear and caressing. The Prince asks me to play tennis on a nearby court. I have been warned about overexertion in the high altitude, but nothing pleases me more than to rid my body of pent-up energy by swinging my racquet hard at a tennis ball. At the moment my love of the game serves me well.

I call my Reno lawyer to let him know where I'm staying. The lawyer: "I told my wife about your political activities. She's eager for you to talk to a League of Women Voters meeting. Would you be willing?" I say yes.

Mrs. W. wants me to meet a friend, a wonderful woman who lives in a beautiful Mormon house. Again I agree; it's best to be in touch with people. I'm not yet ready to write.

The white Mormon house of Mrs. Y. is indeed outstanding, surrounded by great trees and a lovely landscape. I feel myself back in New England. Inside, the furnishings reveal the owner's impeccable taste. Mrs. Y., large, imposing, not handsome but with a fine face, lives alone in her beautiful house, but has a full inner life. "Tell me about yourself," I ask impulsively.

"I was born in New Mexico. I've spent a great deal of time collecting songs of various Indian tribes there and in Mexico. I have many other interests." She speaks rapidly. "About eight women out here in the valley are studying history from the point of view of the repercussion of events in one country on places far away. We have formed a little club; each of us reads about a particular nation. We pin markers on a large map to show that a period of unemployment in New England resulted in great hardship for China.

Products previously exported to America were no longer in demand. The economic disaster in China affected countries with which she had traded. Such interaction led to war. Our studies have helped us establish similar patterns on a worldwide scale."

Mrs. Y. fills me with wonder. I feel close to her and grateful. Here in her isolated house, in a peaceful but lonely valley, my sense of horror lessens for the moment. She begs me to come again, and I do.

As I wander around Reno in the short intervals I am there, I seem never quite to get my bearings. I find the people who work in shops and at the hotel —like those at my small haven of an inn—lovely; they have no interest in the slot machines surrounding them nor do they ever discuss gambling.

Only tourists—pitiful tourists—walk in and out of vulgar buildings, wandering aimlessly, preoccupied with nothing save slot machines. These mechanisms and the honky-tonk environment are barbarous and intimidating.

I was invited to a party in Silver City, the former capital of silver mining. I had always disliked costume parties, but since everyone at the inn was planning to attend, I had no choice but to join the group. I refused to dress up.

Masses of people, all drinking, gathered around gaming tables in a large building. The costumes were makeshift, tawdry, pathetic; some of the women were heavily made-up. Surrounded by a large group, a Russian prince, said to be very wealthy, was gambling obsessively. His hair was silver-gray, as was his suit. In one hand he held a crystal glass filled with what looked like water but was pure gin. With his other hand he made his bets with the stacks of silver dollars before him. The spectacle of this silver drama occurring in Silver City was one more astonishment.

No matter where the Prince placed his coins, he won. More people crowded around the table, as his stacks of silver dollars grew higher and higher; they became so enormously tall they toppled. Coins crashed to the floor, rolled in all directions. No one moved to help the Prince recover them. On the contrary, each person standing near the table slyly put a foot over the nearest coins. No one shifted an inch; each face remained expressionless. The Prince stood, shocked into utter immobility. The tension mounted.

The croupier had difficulty starting the betting again. Finally the unbearable atmosphere caused the Prince to gather up his remaining coins and leave. I watched as shoes were moved aside surreptitiously and hands were stealthily lowered to pick up and stow away in pockets and purses the concealed coins. Then the group closed in around the table again and gambling resumed. I moved away, revolted.

A young man and a girl, each of whom has just received a divorce, come to our inn. They plan to marry at once. Knowing no one in the vicinity and needing a "best man" and someone "to give the bride away," they ask a woman in the next cottage and me to serve. The experience is so ludicrous and sad that, as so often in Nevada, I'm on the verge of tears.

We, who have never seen the two young people before, accompany them to the courthouse and act in the capacity of the father of the bride and the best man. The judge calls the couple by their first names and wishes them well. They disappear from our lives as abruptly as they entered them. But they are properly married. Good luck to them!

Six weeks are up. Edward has found someone he plans to marry. I am glad and relieved for him. I go alone to the court; my nice lawyer meets me there. Papers are signed and I am divorced. In spite of all that has torn us apart, I know that Edward is secretly as heartsick as I am. Not for a moment do I feel unmarried to him.

After Edward and I agreed to have a divorce, I knew I must go to Philadelphia to tell my mother. I dreaded facing her with my troubles, in view of the many she herself had borne. I feared she might break down. She listened quietly, without visible emotion. Looking into my eyes, she said calmly, "My dear, I have seen your face all these years." The conversation was at an end.

I began by believing all problems could be solved, love could melt away every suffering; larger wars, like personal ones, could be avoided. I realize clearly I am still the child who was under the power of every beautiful illusion, even while inexorably knowing that tragedy is inherent in life, that small wars and large ones face us on every side; even in our enlightened age they have not been eliminated.

"Get on with life," shrieks up at me as I try to hide the tears of the still all-believing yet somehow-knowing adult. And then a wave of what—faith?—curious and unexpected, rises in me as I walk back into life.

It is late spring. I do not return to Woods Hole for the summer months. To go to the Cape again would be a torment. I make a clean break and choose East Hampton, Long Island, as the place in which to settle. It is an auspicious area —another piece of New England, but nearer New York; the season is longer; I have friends there with whom I feel at home.

Driving along the highway, I spot a simple white Federalist structure under a group of tall trees—a traditional meeting house. I have photographed its counterparts near Woods Hole for years. The form of the building is Greek, classic, pure. Because there is no spire, I feel I could live in it without seeming pretentious. Although not available at the moment, within a year—as by a miracle—it is.

I have it moved to a former potato farm near the ocean. Standing in the unplowed field without a tree or bush in sight, the little meeting house, un-painted, is one of the bleakest sights I have ever beheld. Traces of bulldozing gash the land. But then, freshly painted white, the structure looks beautifully austere and three times as large as before. The trees with which I surround it grow quickly. The flowers that spring out of the rich soil are also subjects I have portrayed with love on the Cape. But, to my horror, I have so strained my eyes I can no longer photograph and print. The period is a painful one, but making a habitable home is challenging, the choice of house and location com-forting. Now I can concentrate on writing and unwind.

Living alone is a shock to which I become accustomed only with difficulty. I am in need of giving and receiving love. Fortunately, for a few summers Nancy and Andrew live nearby. Then, with husband, wife, and beautiful offspring—who give me unutterable joy—they sensibly return to Woods Hole, a much better place in which to raise children. Happy memories of their childhood make them feel rooted on the Cape. But at least we all live in New York in the winters.

On a visit to East Hampton before our divorce, Edward and I were taken to see the artist Alfonso Ossorio in his splendid, recently acquired nineteenth-century house. There, on the edge of magnificent Georgica Pond, with dunes and the Atlantic Ocean in the distance, we were shown a vast assortment of his huge paintings—still being hung—many of them powerful and colorful, some disturbing. Ossorio talked of his complex reactions to Catholicism, and to the Philippines, where he was born.

A group of pictures by the French artist Jean Dubuffet seemed equally strange and provocative, as was a collection of *L'Art brut*—savage or raw art— chosen primarily by Dubuffet, some by Ossorio. The walls were crowded with works by Jackson Pollock, Lee Krasner, Clyfford Still, Willem de Kooning, Fautrier, Wols, and others coming into prominence since World War II.

L'Art brut at first repelled, then fascinated me. Dubuffet wrote of its having been "done by people uncontaminated by artistic culture. . . . The makers draw all from their own beings and not from hangovers of fashionable or classical art." *L'Art brut* is at times called the art of the insane, but its adherents firmly refuse to accept such an attribution.

Although Ossorio and I are of such different temperaments, we become fast friends. His intelligence reflects a profound awareness of experience with which I am largely unfamiliar. I tell him that, in his paintings relating to Catholicism, he often appears to reverse the usual glorification of Christ in traditional iconography. His reply: "I don't show the reverse, but, rather, how enormous the scope of the subject is." I am reminded of the Book of Revelation, and of the Book of Job's "Behold now Behemoth, which I made with thee. . . . He is the chief of the ways of God."

We have lived through a period of depression, war, social upheaval and turmoil. Inner and outer worlds have exploded. Giant disorientation has been fearlessly reflected in the art of Europe and the United States. Nightmare, tortured visions, distorted forms have taken over, even while the ordered abstractions of such an artist as Piet Mondrian have evolved. Myth and primordial forms are pervasive influences. Abstract expressionism is gaining the ascendency, first in the New York area, then in the world at large.

Action, reaction, and again reaction follow one another in classic succession. Ecstasy before the beauty of nature, romanticism, are not artists' preoccupations now. The Americans who have succeeded the European innovators of the late nineteenth and early twentieth century have temporarily fallen into the background.

Before moving to East Hampton, I had met some of the artists of the current period. Arshile Gorky, whose early work I admired, often came to An American Place carrying a huge portfolio that he never opened. His eyes were large and sad, his manner shy, hesitant.

I was escorted to Franz Kline's studio by a young Japanese artist, Sabro Hasagawa. Although Kline was said to be affected by Japanese calligraphy, Hasagawa admitted to being influenced by Kline.

In New York, I have talked with Willem de Kooning—a resident of Springs, part of East Hampton—witty, endearing, handsome. Many women must be in love with him, I imagine—and they are. His sensitive early work was in the Dutch tradition. His later paintings are harsh; I remember his remark that he didn't mean them to be monstrous and grotesque, but they always became so. (The sculptor Isamu Noguchi said to me, "I wonder whether he really hates women; perhaps he loves them too much.") At times de Kooning speaks of his paintings of women as comic, not savage, and about his art as "unexpected." He claims to watch the landscape as he speeds by in a car and to depict the slashes he observes.

I discover still other artists I know who live in East Hampton during the summer: Saul Steinberg and his wife, Hedda Sterne. The critic Harold Rosenberg and I, who disagree about most painters, conclude amicably that Saul is a genius. The originality and witty depth of his vision are unique; equally individual is the feminine delicacy of Hedda's art.

Painter-sculptor Constantino Nivola creates terra-cotta beds, primitive figurines, and line drawings. He is one of the few artists to have come through to a humanistic period after sculpting mostly abstractions, influenced primarily by Le Corbusier.

In 1950 Marin, the first artist invited to exhibit in the American Pavilion at the Venice Biennale, had been given a reception by the Museum of Modern Art. With his usual grimace, accompanied by a smile, when any special attention was paid to him, he first said, "I won't go," then added, "Unless you go with me." "I'll hold your hand." I smiled at Marin and we went.

At the reception I felt much like Rip Van Winkle. After having been involved with so many artists over a long period of years, I knew almost no one present. Marin and I clung together, strangers in the unfamiliar assembly. Jackson Pollock and Lee Krasner, his wife, were introduced to me; in turn, I presented them to Marin. As they walked away, Marin whispered, "Who's that Johnny?" A new period had indeed been born.

The first time I saw Pollock's work was in the entrance to Peggy Guggenheim's apartment, when Edward and I dined there in the forties. In the dimly lit hallway hung one of Pollock's large oblong paintings—a portable mural—its primarily beige pigmentation heavy. The picture was abstract, with swirling curves. I had no special reaction to it.

I often meet Jackson and Lee in East Hampton. His intensity and honesty constitute a blazing challenge. Lee, an excellent artist, has stood by Jackson and believed in him during many difficult years; I respect her for it. The first time they came to my house, Jackson walked about picking up shells and examining them. He took up every object as though to test it. What was he doubting? After each scrutiny, he said, "That's real." Was he confirming my integrity?

He took me out of the living room and said at once, "You were Marin's girl friend." I was astounded. "No, I wasn't." "But you were." The conversation stopped, then Pollock added, "You know, I admired Marin greatly and for a while was even influenced by him."

Someone asks Jackson why he doesn't paint nature. He replies, pounding his solar plexus: "This is nature, isn't it?" I feel a great wave of compassion as I become aware of the problems that beset him and that clearly he cannot resolve.

One day he looks at me with tears in his eyes, "I am like a clam without a shell." By coincidence I am rereading letters I wrote to Stieglitz in the late twenties. One page, I note, included the lines: "A shell that protects something inside so soft it can't live without a shell. Damn the shell. Thank God for the shell. This is from inside—the shell itself is strong, unbroken!"

I relate Jackson's words to Isamu Noguchi, who replies, "Every artist feels that way."

Lee goes to Europe for a short time. At Jackson's studio one afternoon, he shows me everything in it. I am amazed by the beauty and delicacy of much of his work at close range. (Jimmy Ernst had told me that, during Jackson's first show at Peggy Guggenheim's gallery, she took Mondrian over to Pollock's paintings and exclaimed, "Aren't they awful?" Mondrian replied emphatically, "I find them extraordinary. They are saying something absolutely new. If I were you, I would buy some of them." She did.)

During the following days I saw Jackson several times; he was thinner and looked ill. I invited him to lunch with others, and paid special attention to him so that he would eat. Friends soon took him home because he became faint. Later, he in turn invited me to lunch; I was to photograph him. At the last minute he phoned to say I had better not come; he was in bad shape.

That same evening—the weather was fine but strangely ominous—I was invited to a formal dinner. The splendid, overbrilliant sunset lingered. The guests, one by one, couple by couple, arrived late, curiously disturbed by unrelated events that had made them tardy. The hostess, whose delicious dinner had been spoiled, was politely perturbed.

I drove home. The phone. "Jackson has been killed in an automobile accident."

As though we had lived in East Hampton all our lives, those of us who had known Jackson and Lee felt closely related. We called each other frantically to see what we could do for Lee, who returned from Europe at once. Deeply religious, Jackson had wanted to be buried in nearby Green River Cemetery.

We filed into the small white church in Springs like one great family—painters, writers, local fishermen, tradesmen, and farmers who had known Jackson well, loved and protected him. Critics who had warred over his paintings walked into the church side by side, their arguments temporarily forgotten. The traditional service was recited, the traditional music played. An atmosphere of healing pervaded the unpretentious building. We walked out shocked, awed, speechless, but comforted.

Jackson had moved stones of the area to the back of his house. Lee selected a large boulder to stand as a marker over his grave.

After seeing a Jackson Pollock retrospective, Lewis Mumford later wrote to me:

> Our friendship, dear Dorothy, is a succession of beautiful and incredible coincidences. Before your letter came I was on the point of writing you. . . . I managed to steal a half hour to see the Jackson Pollock show and I wanted to tell you, you above all other people, how deeply I was impressed by it. I had only seen a few of his pictures, the least convincing ones: and I never appreciated either his range or the masterly quality of his design. You are right: he is one of the great ones of our age. His method of laying on paint was irrelevant to the final effect—which he is capable of achieving with a brush or even in water color. The painting that moved me most is a pure abstraction, which resembled one of the great Chinese masters doing a waterfall. . . . That painting, though muted in color, on a white background, is most in his "usual style": but it contains everything else and transcends it. And . . . when I saw the show . . . I said to myself: I must tell Dorothy my response to it! And now you are told.

The eminent Protestant theologian Paul Tillich and his wife, Hannah, spend part of the year in East Hampton. I have long admired his independent spirit, his early rebellion against and flight from Hitler. He invites me to the beach for a talk. I recall that he built sand mounds as a boy, rather than castles. He made the mounds as tall as he could, stood on them and gazed at the farthest horizons.

On my way to Tillich I meet a woman whose jealousy and pettiness irritate me. I try to greet her politely with little success. Because Tillich is a man of the church, I ask him what he does when he must be courteous and spend time with those who are offensive to him. "I do only what contributes to my essential work. I cannot spend time on those who happen to come to me or whom I come upon when nothing of value will result. I must concentrate on my work and on those who are closest to me—who contribute to me and to whom I can contribute. That is what the Bible says to do."

"Doesn't such instruction bother you?" "Oh, yes." He smiles with terror in his eyes, then laughs, trying to mask an enormous sorrow too great to bear. "What is it that always makes you look in pain?" I ask. "God," he whispers. "How?" "I have a private war with God. I cannot forgive Him His injustices." "Can God be unjust?" "That is precisely the trouble." An anguished pause. "We simply do not know." "You always look as though something else were troubling you." "Something is troubling me." "What?" "I feel guilty about everything; I cannot forgive God for making me feel guilty." "But you said you feel guilty about everything?" "Yes." "Everything?" "Everything." Tillich looks hard into space. The blue sky shines. The blue water sparkles to the farthest horizon. The blue eyes—beautiful. All one blue.

New York: Edward Steichen talks to me excitedly about a photographic exhibition, *The Family of Man*, that he hopes to present at the Museum of Modern Art in 1955. Prints from various parts of the world will stress the oneness of man's preoccupations, aspirations, hopes, fears. Ready to hang the show, he phones to say it is lifeless. Words are needed to pull it together; he wants me to chooose them. Having other commitments, I hesitate. He pleads: "We need short, evocative, poetic statements from the literatures of the world, of all time. The selections must emphasize the important themes of the show. You are the right person—the only one—who can do it." I give in.

At the museum I am shown small copy prints while Steichen describes the ideas he wants to stress: man's quest for light, love, harmony, unity. The first picture I see is a reflection of sun or moon on earth and water. I say, "Only one quotation will do: 'And God said, Let there be light.'" Steichen agrees.

Next, an image of lovers in intimate embrace. Again I suggest that only one passage is appropriate—the end of Joyce's *Ulysses*: "And then I asked him with my eyes to ask again yes and then he asked me would I yes . . . and first I put my arms around him yes and drew him down to me so he could feel my breasts all perfume yes and his heart was going like mad and yes I said yes I will Yes."

Steichen looks at me aghast. "You can't possibly use that." I stiffen. "Nothing equals it—it has to be used." I want to say, "If you think it isn't right, you had better get someone else." Instead, I argue; Steichen gives in and we examine the rest of the photographs.

If a phrase doesn't spring directly to mind, I pore over my books. I am amazed at how many lines I cull from the Bible, Greek tragedy, Saint-John Perse, the Bhagavad Gita, sayings of American Indians—particularly the Sioux. I stress the poetic throughout, and end with Perse's "A world to be born under your footsteps."

The exhibition opens; the words I hear most often repeated as I walk through the galleries are Joyce's "yes I said yes I will Yes."

The Family of Man is a worldwide success, but I have misgivings about certain of its aspects: blowups of fine photographs are often grainy and dilute the quality of the originals; some purely journalistic images offend. I recognize both the difficulty of creating such an enormous exhibition and the genuinely healthy impact it has at numerous levels.

The legacy of Stieglitz affects me strongly, even though no tradition can remain static. A letter from Lewis Mumford, after he attends the exhibition, corroborates my general attitude:

10 February 1955

I was in New York just long enough the other week, dear Dorothy, to see the Steichen show; and ever since . . . I have been wanting . . . to congratulate you on your part, for your incredibly good captions seemed to me to carry it over the soft and thin places, where the sentiment—which was always right—was not supported by an idea. Steichen brought together the richest sort of visual fare and the first impression of it was overwhelmingly good; but my second thoughts were not quite so keen in appreciation because I felt that, with the whole world of man's experience to draw upon, he had erred on the side of simplemindedness and folksiness, and hadn't quite risen to the heights of human expression: this was the People, Yes, but not The Place where the great City

Stands. Whatever the intention of it—and of course I can understand the intention—the color photo of the atom bomb explosion was inanely bathetic: I have seen infinitely better black-and-whites that gave one a sense of lonely terror, and not of a bad Victorian chromo. But the fact that so much nevertheless came through is a great triumph for Steichen; I can imagine what Stieglitz would have said about it, and I shall have to let you imagine most of my own reactions. Fortunately, at a critical moment, the pictures would pull me back to your quotations, or the quotations would lift me back into the pictures.

The photographer Minor White, editor and publisher of *Aperture*, invited me to write about Stieglitz for an expanded 1960 issue of his magazine, which is devoted to photography. I called the monograph, "Alfred Stieglitz —Introduction to an American Seer."

With Minor White, whom I greatly admired, I had an extraordinarily harmonious relationship. He had become interested in Zen and, as the publication was composed—an exacting task—we drank tea constantly. Minor and I first agreed on the photographs that would give a fair cross-section of Stieglitz's work within the scope of sixty-four pages, which were to include my text. I had to write to space, while covering Stieglitz's entire life.

Minor let me oversee the printing of the photographs and layout when the special number was published in Rochester—the first publication about Stieglitz, except for the *Memorial Portfolio*, to appear after his death. The publishers Duell, Sloan and Pearce asked to issue the little volume in book form. Between hard covers it took on a permanent aspect. As the title foretold, it became the seed of the larger life of Stieglitz I had always intended to write and which now, gradually, took form.

Again from Lewis Mumford:

21 July 1959

Bravo for your success in finishing the [*Aperture*] Stieglitz: I can well imagine all the private storms you encountered before you brought that venerable ship, with its proud topsails and its barnacled hull, to port. I have something of the same feeling about my old master [Patrick] Geddes . . . that you must have had in dealing with Stieglitz. We know the best about these men, and understood their magnificent qualities before many others did: but we also know the worst, as more superficial admirers do not; and though we ourselves can stand the whole truth, or at least have learned to take it, and can . . . recapture much of our original feeling about them, to unfold everything before their ordinary admirers seems almost an act of desecration, even a betrayal.

Mumford puts into words the experience I have in writing my more extensive book, *Alfred Stieglitz: An American Seer*. Over the years I learned to know his weaknesses but his greatness so overshadowed the dark spots on white that at the end of his life I had the same feeling that moved me from the very first.

For a long period I have had the privilege of living with Stieglitz's magnificent photographs. He gave me almost all of them, forbidding me to buy but a few. "I do not want money to enter into our relationship," he said. "In the end it always spoils things."

I look at the prints as they surround me in New York. I must decide about their future. I refuse to sell them and cannot bear the thought of their being scattered after my death. The only solution is to found a Stieglitz Center at a well-established museum, and give some of his work to Nancy and Andrew.

In the city, the Metropolitan Museum has some Stieglitz photographs but does little about showing them. The Museum of Modern Art does not strike me as the right place to which to give his prints.

Because Philadelphia's great Museum of Art—through the good offices of Carl Zigrosser, a most sensitive curator—held an outstanding, imaginative, and well-documented Stieglitz exhibition in 1944, while he was still alive, I speak with the Museum's new Director, Dr. Evan Turner.

Philadelphia already possesses not only work by Stieglitz, but also much significant modern art, including its Walter Arensberg and Albert Gallatin Collections. It also is to receive additional work by Marcel Duchamp, and there is the "logic" of my having been born in Philadelphia.

Turner is enthusiastic about creating the Center, to which I plan to give not only my Stieglitz prints, but those I possess by Paul Strand, Edward Weston, Henri Cartier-Bresson, Eugene Smith, Minor White, and others. And so the Stieglitz Center is established.

I continue to talk with Natacha Rambova about myths of the hero; to read about them voraciously; to search for evocative images in museums, libraries, and wherever I travel. I collect everything from excellent postcards and photographs at galleries to rare prints and tomes I ferret out in small, obscure antiquarian shops. I seek out experts in various traditions and question them endlessly. Patterns of meaning emerge with blazing clarity; they coalesce into a poetic concept I name "The Heroic Encounter."

I conceive of presenting an exhibition based on verbal and pictorial material that will orchestrate the underlying theme. Throughout the ages symbols of the heroic quest have evolved with astonishing universality. Poets and artists have portrayed the opposing and complementary forces in the world as the two great luminaries sun and moon, or as lion and bull.

I recognize ever more fully that our eternal conflict involves a struggle between light and darkness, the spiritual and the material. The great challenge for the hero—for man—is to raise the destructive forces within himself to a creative level. The seers have shown that transformation occurs at moments of crisis: our hearts are pierced, awakened; we are struck as by a thunderbolt. Each evocation illustrates the necessary journey of the hero into the depths of his unconscious—the cave, the pit, the tomb, the labyrinth, the netherworld of himself. He must bring the unconscious over into consciousness, into the light. Yet he never dares deny the shadow within, or through pride consider himself the hero, or he is already the dragon, the tyrant.

It happens again and again. After working at full speed on the exhibition, I stop; my eyes are tired. Out in the garden at East Hampton, my hands go deep into the soil to pull up weeds or transplant zinnias, cosmos, lilies of the valley. I leave behind the pages I have been concentrating on and enter another world.

The events of my life take shape before me; I have been dedicated, without having been aware of it, to the "myth of the hero" at the human level. What is the fight for civil liberties, after all, but a risk-laden battle for freedom? A writer's avant-garde book is censored, a meeting of courageous workers takes place because they want a better life—all the forces of reaction are against them.

I have aided heroic opponents of Mussolini and Franco, anti-Nazis, anti-imperialists. What have these fighters signified, but resistance to the despot? I stand transfixed. I see just how the great mythical figures of the past have played their roles. My eyes feel rested. I go back into the house a new person. Heracles, Gilgamesh, Horus are singing a chorus for me, like the writers in *Twice A Year*.

Joseph Campbell, author of *The Hero with a Thousand Faces*, and Edith Porada, at the Morgan Library—famous for her work on ancient cylinder seals —are extremely generous and cooperative in giving their time to talk with me. Samuel Noah Kramer, the great Sumerian authority at the University of Pennsylvania Museum, is skeptical about interpreting symbols and tells me with humor he is only a "data man." This from the scholar who has done more perhaps than anyone to decipher heretofore perplexing Mesopotamian script! I examine the extensive early Christian archives at Princeton, and confer with Stella Kramrisch about Indian myth and art. At the Bollingen Foundation in New York Jessie Fraser, in charge of its vast collection of pictorial symbolical material, brings to light fascinating medieval alchemical drawings.

To clarify my insights further, I attend the 1954 Jungian-based Ascona-Eranos Conference, held on the shore of Lake Maggiore each August. Authorities on ancient traditions gather to discuss myths and symbols of various cultures. (My only complaint is that church bells ring every fifteen minutes, which scarcely helps my perpetual insomnia.)

Suzuki interprets the ox-herding series of Chinese and Japanese tradition: a youthful ox herder, alone in the wilderness, has lost his way and his ox. He finds and follows the traces of the animal, who is wild, unruly, difficult to tame. He mounts it triumphantly and plays his little flute, only to discover it was not the ox he had lost but himself. The next picture is a great circle from which both ox and herder have disappeared; all distinctions are wiped out. And finally a representation of the blossoming of the universe: the ego of the herder is obliterated; the nondualism of all living things is affirmed. Only after achieving such integration and serenity can the ox herder properly give to others, "entering the city with bliss-bestowing hands."

Back in New York, I talked with Marian Willard of the Willard Gallery about my ideas. I explained the theme of the show and how I visualized its being presented in word and picture on heavy plaques of gold, terra-cotta, gray and black. The most telling images I had garnered should be displayed in enlarged reproductions, on beautifully proportioned circular, rectangular, or square forms. Color transparencies in specially lighted cases were to be seen from above. Texts I wrote and quotations I chose would elucidate the basic meanings of the various myths I used. Excited, Marian described my concept to the Bollingen Foundation, which provided a grant: "The Heroic Encounter" was launched in 1958. The American Federation of Arts became enthusiastic and offered to send it around the country for two years.

Natacha Rambova was the first to arouse my interest in myth, but I stayed far away from her while preparing my material; I had to create the show on my own. Once it was completed and hung, I invited her to view it. If she found it inaccurate or uninspiring, I would know I had failed.

She walked around, carefully scrutinizing every panel. My heart beat fast; had I made inexcusable errors? She examined each plaque and then, with tears in her eyes, embraced me. "I didn't think it possible to achieve such a compelling exhibition about so complicated a subject." I was relieved and overjoyed by her approval, even more than by the critics' positive reviews.

East Hampton becomes the haven in which I also finish my two volumes on Jawaharlal Nehru. The idea for the publication had come to me in New Delhi on my first visit to India, as Nehru and I strolled on the lawn of his residence. Here, I mused, is one of the most magnificent authors of our time who, while in prison, has written a history of the world quite different from any Western account. Many of his books are out of print. Some of his most important occasional writings have never been collected or are printed only in partial or distorted form. His early articles against Fascism and the Nazis lie hidden in small, unavailable magazines or in volumes published abroad and not obtainable in America.

Nehru has described eloquently events in his life, but his autobiography, *Toward Freedom*, lacks chronological form. No truly adequate picture of the sequence of his entire career and writings exists. I am eager to select and organize the most significant material; to provide a record of a unique personality and the historical background against which he must be viewed.

I broach the subject to him and he gives me full permission to publish and edit any of his publications and letters. Many early speeches were taken down in sometimes imperfect English; he suggests I use my judgment in correcting them. His American publisher, the John Day Company, is delighted with the project, as is the Bodley Head Press, which will print it in London. The final member of the triumvirate, Asia Publishing House, will distribute it in India.

At first I had no notion that Nehru's works are so extensive and some so difficult to find. Limiting the scope to his first sixty years, I track down his words in print or even in typescript with the zeal of a detective, through a mass of libraries, archives, Congress Party records, and the British Information Service. He and his staff occasionally send me a rare document from his files that all had forgotten existed. I write to India for every available copy of speeches and anything else of interest. In London I find much material still in the possession of the British Government and obtain permission to use it.

The project grows and develops from a multitude of sources, and becomes so extensive that it must be published, to my amazement, in two volumes. Nehru tells me he had no conception how arduous the undertaking would be; that, as a result of it, he has rediscovered many experiences from his past. Writing and inserting brief background summaries throughout the text for the reader's convenience gives me an illuminating self-education in Indian history and the complex interplay of imperialism with a huge colony's desire for independence.

At last the complicated typescript, complete with annotations, emendations, glossary, notes, bibliography, is ready for the publisher in England in 1964. It is packed with loving care into an enormous suitcase and travels to and from London with other first-class luggage, especially cared for, via Air India.

Indira Gandhi and I have maintained our warm relationship established in 1949, when she first came to the United States with Nehru. Our tastes in art, architecture, and music have been similar: we love the primitive and modern; the extraordinary crafts of India and its traditional dance; nature and good films. And we adore our children.

I am aware of an underlying loneliness in Indira and a deep-seated sense of duty toward the poor and oppressed. She is quick and observant, like Nehru, but veils herself behind a shyness that both protects her from and deprives her of easy communication with others. Sometimes I sense a deceptive aloofness, at other times a submerged volcano of impatience with stupidity and insensitivity. Her life is that of a princess on the surface, but underneath she is enslaved by her public position as Nehru's daughter, living in a glass bowl at all times, and carrying out endless responsibilities that permit little time for private life. Often ill, she has developed enormous resilience.

After my first visit to India, she writes from a house called "The Retreat" in Simla:

October 13, 1950

I carry on in Delhi until I feel that I am on the verge of collapse and then I dash off. This time, on top of everything, Sanjay (my youngest) had mumps and the woman who looks after the children is also ill, so I had just about enough. Specially as I was head of a committee for collecting funds for the Earthquake relief.

I have brought the children up here—we are living in what is called The President's cottage but actually it is a huge house with 10 or 11 bedrooms. Very English country house in style and simply impossible to keep warm. And it gets quite cold in the evenings. Much much colder than Delhi in winter. The garden is rather lovely. . . .

I am full of ideas but I haven't the driving force and energy to execute them. One has to fight so much for every little thing. I was born bone lazy, so I have developed a system of dividing things into most important, important, less important and I fight only for the first, sometimes if I am very fit and energetic for the second as well.

What complicates life is our entanglement with other people. There is so much inter-dependence and so little understanding. And then growth. Every new experience brings its own maturity and a greater clarity of vision. Some people keep up to one, others get left behind—or else are able to share only a part of one's life. Do you think it is possible to have several sets of friends, each set moving in its own world and having no point of contact with the others? What else can you do if you are deeply interested in a large number of entirely different things and cannot find a single other person who shares all those interests? However, I do wish I were more interested in people as such. They amuse me and they irritate me and sometimes I find myself observing them as if I were not of the same species at all. Isn't that an awful thought?

It is late at night, the fire is out and my hand nearly frozen—so I shall close with my love.

The letters continue after Indira returns to New Delhi:

December 5, 1950

You were so anxious that [the film] *All the King's Men* [based on Robert Penn Warren's novel] should come to Delhi. Well, it has, finally. I went to see it a couple of days ago and I must say it is really good. Forceful and forthright and the acting superb, specially the supporting actress's. I wouldn't have missed it for anything.

But ever since I saw it I have been thinking of you and missing you. I like to see a good film with someone who would enjoy it in the same way but most people here seem to have missed the point of the whole thing, which irritates me intensely. It is silly to be irritated at such trifles, I keep telling myself—but all the same, not having anyone with similar tastes gives one a sense of loneliness and isolation which is not at all pleasant.

From one of her trips to South India:

I sent those few things—they are hand-blocked and printed old village designs from three quite different parts of India: the silk from Gujarat, the scarf from Kalimpong in the north-east, the handkerchiefs from Bengal—because I thought they would amuse you and also to tell you that you are very much in my thoughts. I haven't been able to write as I have been in a madder rush than usual, constantly travelling. . . .

If someone asks me at the end of the week what I have been doing, I can't really answer but moment by moment the odd jobs seem important and urgent. On the whole it is a frustrating life. Long ago when I was a student in England, I went to Harold Laski for advice about my studies. He said, "Young woman, if you want to amount to something you had better start on your own life right now—if you tag along with your father you won't be able to do anything else." But there doesn't seem to be any choice, in the sense that I *felt* my father's loneliness so intensely, and I felt also that whatever I amounted to, or whatever satisfaction I got from my own work, would not, from a wide perspective, be so useful as my "tagging" along, smoothing the corners and dealing with the many details, small but necessary, which in my absence he has to tackle himself with consequent loss of patience and temper! I'm not complaining. There has been the sharing of good things and bad. I am fortunate in having got just enough humour to tide me over the worst situations and enough love of nature to find beauty and delight in the most unexpected places. And there are so many other things—people and books, music and pictures and, above all else, my own children and the fascination of watching them grow and develop into two such very different persons.

However, now I must do something else as well. Write? But what about? I have such definite ideas about everything but they are all jumbled together. Perhaps writing would bring some kind of order and clear the path to future thought and work. The only other thing (or is it an aspect of the same?) that I could do or feel readily attracted to, is some kind of literary or historical research.

What amazes me is the way I can write to you about myself—I haven't done this to anyone ever.

You have done such wonderful work for us on the Food Bill. I don't quite know how to thank you. One says those two words so many times a day and so automatically that when one really means them from the heart, they somehow do not seem to be adequately expressive. And yet there are no other words. . . .

P.S. What an enchanting name Woods Hole is!

From my reply:

August 1, 1951

Queer how space plays no role whatever when one feels concern. . . . (Except that it can become a maddening barrier by way of separating—not by way of lessening caring.)

You say now you must do something by way of utilizing your creative or productive side. But you can't do that if you merely continue to push down all the other sides. . . . As for your keeping everything under such perfect control: I think of that in you so often. I am glad you feel free to talk to me, at least somewhat without reserve. How one longs always to be open and honest. Only honesty and the feeling that one *can* be honest with another can possibly satisfy. I have often thought how badly you need to be loved and to be able to love to your full capacity. To be honest and open about the most delicate things. There is so much of the artist in you—in your search for form and line and color, in the way you dress, and in your use of flowers—in every way. And in the way in which you look at things. . . .

Meanwhile—I am glad you like the name Woods Hole. And I am glad you exist.

Later Indira wrote:

December 10, 1953

I think I have changed since we met. Or grown. Certainly I look older and I feel more positive somehow. This trip abroad—my first extensive travel alone—has done me an enormous amount of good. I put on some weight and had fun wherever I went. Even in the U.S.S.R. But the place I liked best of all was Norway. I love its rugged beauty and the frankness and forthrightness of its people. The govt. seemed to me to be the most truly democratic and least encumbered with bureaucracy of all the countries I have visited. It may be, of course, that I was lucky enough to meet the right people and the right ministers!

May 31, 1955

What a life I have made for myself! Often I seem to be standing outside myself, watching and wondering if it's all worth the trouble. One acts the way one is made and it is only once in a lifetime that opportunity comes our way. I cannot say whether I have made good use of it or not.

It's certainly true that I have grown enormously since you saw me last. I am confident of myself but still humble enough to feel acutely embarrassed when all kinds of V.I.P.s come for advice and even help in their projects, as is increasingly happening. I still haven't gotten used to being on the Working Committee of the A.I.C.C. [All India Congress Committee]! (It is something like the National Executive of your political [parties].) Can you imagine me being an "elder statesman"?

My duties and responsibilities have also grown enormously. I have my finger in so many pies that it would take too long even to list them. And if you remember me and what a perfect tyrant of a conscience I have got, you will understand that this does *not* mean merely the lending of my name to some association or the attendance at committee meetings. It means hard work, planning, organizing, directing, scouting for new helpers, humouring the old and so on, in several fields—political, social welfare and cultural. Not to mention the visiting dignitaries—what a spate of them we have had this year!—and the constant entertaining and being entertained that it entails. The touring and public speaking. Besides all this, I have become almost a professional shoulder to lay upon for all those who are in trouble—the latest are two rather young widows whose husbands have died suddenly and very tragically. One of them (the husbands) was shot down by the Pakistanis in our latest "border incident." His widow is 26 and has three small daughters.

My first favourite—folk dancing—is merrily on its way and able to fend for itself. The current favourite—"community singing." As known in Europe and America this just does not exist in India, although we have folk songs that are sung by small groups, mostly women, at festival times. But this will soon be independent too. The "pet baby" is a recreation centre for 500 poor children. This is still at the plan stage and is going to shock a lot of people when it comes into being. I have "discovered" a young architect who has studied under Frank Lloyd Wright; even so it took a lot of doing to get him to plan something which is of no known shape or design and yet is practical and functional, with every room just where it is needed. We feel that it will be rather lovely when complete but most people do hate the new and unusual, so we are prepared for all kinds of criticism too.

As a trial, I have been running such a recreation centre on a small scale (70 children, all varieties belonging to sweepers, M.P.s and govt. officials) in my own garden. It's a stupendous success. So much so that we have been forced to start a club for their fathers (not the officials!) and a welfare centre for the mothers! So you see the more one does, the more one can do and the more there is to be done.

I have been and am deeply unhappy in my domestic life. Now, the hurt and the unpleasantness don't seem to matter so much. I am sorry, though, to have missed the most wonderful thing in life, having a complete and perfect relationship with another human being: for only thus, I feel, can one's personality fully develop and blossom. However, and perhaps as compensation, I am more at peace with myself. One of our 17th century poets has said "Go where thou wilt . . . if thy soul is a stranger to thee, this whole world is unhomely." I think I have come to a stage where home is wherever I go.

The boys are growing fast. They are in boarding school. I often go to see them at weekends and never cease to be surprised at the amount of ice cream they can consume at a sitting!

February 23, 1956

Bulganin and Khrushchev got a tremendous welcome here. There are many reasons for this but the main one was that they had accorded us a very wonderful welcome when we went to their country, and every

Indian felt that we should repay their hospitality. At no time did anyone think that we were growing nearer to the communists, neither did Bulganin and Khrushchev think so. On the contrary my father availed himself of every opportunity to make our standpoint clear.

All those of us who have the opportunity of visiting the communist countries are very clear in our minds that we should not follow that path and we realise that we can only avoid this by strengthening our own organisation and trying to prove to the people that ours is the better way.

March 26, 1956

Here in India the situation is . . . difficult. You must have read of Pakistan's increasingly belligerent attitude and the raids on our border areas. This has evoked such strong feelings all over the country that I doubt if people will listen even to my father on this issue. On my recent tour of Central India (I returned two days ago) everywhere I was asked why America was giving so much military aid to Pakistan. . . .

On these tours of mine at first I used to get physically exhausted, now I have got used to the physical strain but I still find it an emotional strain and I have a feeling of being drained out—as if I had given of my strength to people. The only thing that helps when I come back home is music and I have been listening to some of the lovely records you have sent me.

September 20, 1957

If you believe in telepathy, you will know that I have been thinking a great deal of you these last months. Many a time I wanted to write but I was so depressed that I felt I would be bound to convey some of it in my letters!

Apart from the mental depression there was a physical one too. I lost a lot of weight and have been quite shaky on my feet, fainting off a couple of times and so on. However, I'm better now. I'd better be as I'm off at the crack of dawn to Calcutta on my way to Bangkok.

I'm really writing to thank you for the wonderful records—all through this dark period, the only thing that seemed to help was music and poetry. Some of my loveliest ones are from you.

Do you know Dylan Thomas' *Under Milk Wood*? An English friend sent it to me some time ago but I only got time to listen to it recently. Isn't it simply wonderful.

Pupul [Jayakar] was here this afternoon. She's a stimulating person. I feel I know myself better after a talk with her. Are most people not just a split personality but several personalities? I feel I am and I have learnt to make all the separate personalities quite friendly with each other. But I still don't know how to present them to the world. Different people see different mes!

April 17, 1958

This last year has been rather a gruesome one—busy of course but full of disaster, for our country.

I myself am feeling very unsettled—is it age, do you think? Ever since I was a small girl, there seemed to be some force driving me on—as if there were a debt to pay. But suddenly the debt seems to be paid—anyhow I get a tremendous urge to leave everything and retire to a far far place high in the mountains! Not caring if I never did a stroke of work. Through the winter I felt carefree and light. Several people remarked that I looked "lit up from inside." As suddenly as it came that excellent mood has passed off. The heat may have had something to do with it.

It is 6 a.m. now but too hot to sleep. The temp. yesterday was around 104° F. A pall of dust is hanging over us, so that it is difficult to breathe.

I get up early these days to do a special set of exercises. It is a system (part of Yoga) that was taught us by an exceedingly good-looking Yogi. In fact, it was his looks, especially his magnificent body, which attracts everyone to his system, which is easy and practical. He is, however, exasperating to talk to—so full of superstition.

. . . We have had two very interesting Americans—Charles Eames and Buckminster Fuller. The latter was only passing through but managed to give me nearly five hours of higher mathematics. Quite exhausting but so stimulating.

In 1958 Indira and I visited Mrs. Pandit, India's High Commissioner in London. We then went to the Brussels Fair together. After her return to New Delhi, Indira wrote:

August 26, 1958

It is such a bore not being able to express one's feelings. As you know I am quite exasperatingly inarticulate. So I cannot even begin to tell you what a joy it was to have you around and to talk to you. Somehow I can tell you things which I wouldn't dream of telling anyone. Each time I meet you, it helps me to sort myself out a little more.

The trip to Europe was exhilarating and I enjoyed every minute of it—again thanks largely to you. Even though we were not always together, I felt your presence and your support. Even though the return journey was tedious and tiring, I got off the plane fresh and exuberant.

People here don't like exuberance. Even at the airport I felt "different" and as if I did not fit in. People's glances were suspicious and just a shade disapproving. What can one do but withdraw into oneself, in these circumstances? I really felt as if I had two wet blankets. Not only was this psychologically dampening but physically also, for I caught a bad cold!!

But seriously, I was in quite a turmoil and haven't got adjusted even now.

July 21, 1959

I wish telepathy were more advanced and I could convey my thoughts to you without having to write a letter.

A veritable sea of trouble is engulfing me. On the domestic front— F. has always resented my very existence, but since I have become President [of the Congress Party] he exudes such hostility that it seems to poison the air! Just to make things difficult for me, he is sabotaging my efforts to strengthen the Congress. Unfortunately he and his friends are friendly with some of our ministers and an impossible situation is being created.

. . . I cannot write much in a letter but you would be surprised that some of the ministers whom we had considered the most anti-Communist are now supporting the Communist government of [the state of] Kerela. My father cannot go against the wishes of the Home Minister, for instance. It is a very ticklish situation.

[My father] has given a very good lead from the beginning but he is incapable of dictatorship or of roughshodding over the views of his senior colleagues. More and more I find that he is almost the only one who thinks in terms of ideology rather than personality.

. . . Most American newsmen suffer from such Nehru-phobia that they are unable to gauge the situation and are therefore indirectly helping the Communists, since any weakening of the Congress organization can only advance the cause of Communism in India.

November 5, 1959

All sections in India, with the solitary exception of the Communists, feel that I have done a good job [as Congress Party President] and there is tremendous pressure on me to continue for another term. It has been tough work—sometimes exhausting, but always a worthwhile experience. I have gained tremendously in self-confidence. But I do not wish to continue for many reasons. The routine part of the work takes too much time and is too confining. I have felt like a bird in a too-small cage. Also I feel that I have now established myself and will be able to do quite a lot even from outside, besides being free to take up any particular project—there are some which are urgent.

16

In 1959 I was asked to go to New Delhi for a Planned Parenthood Conference, and then hoped to continue on a journey around the world. Seeing Nehru again was exhilarating. Indira Gandhi and Pupul Jayakar were, as always, warm, interesting, and hospitable. Once again the country's glorious arts and crafts held me spellbound. I noted many signs of progress, but mostly the ghastly, ever-present poverty.

I move on to Burma, where I am handsomely taken care of in Rangoon. U Pau Tin, whom I knew at home as consul general, is now high up in the Department of External Affairs and generously accompanies me wherever I wish to go. U Nu, for whom I was asked to have a gathering in New York, is no longer Prime Minister. His handsome appearance, exquisite Buddhist garb, and beguiling manner had made a most favorable impression on all who met him, although his official talk about Buddhism—a copy of which he was kind enough to send me—was so complex I couldn't understand a word.

The political situation in Burma has radically changed. The new Prime Minister, Ne Win, has cleaned up the marketplace in two weeks. "It was a horrible mess before." I have no doubt it has been improved, but it doesn't tempt me to buy or photograph a single thing.

In the Golden Pagoda priests sit on the floor smoking what look like cheroots. This seems odd; I question U Pau Tin about the Buddhists in Burma. A quizzical look. "Don't you know about our priests?" "No." "They do not serve; they are served." The voice is cutting.

I ask various Burmese about U Nu, but receive mixed reactions. Rumor has it that he is in retreat in a Buddhist monastery. Even those who had admired him complain he did too little for the country's poor. His passion for building a large and garish Palace of Peace, which I find uninspired and ugly, strikes the Burmese as wasteful and meaningless. Its interior looks more like a convention hall than a holy place. Outside priests squat, surrounded by paraphernalia designed to lure the superstitious. "Blood," or a red liquid resembling it, is contained in slabs of translucent rock purported to be sacred relics that will cure diseases. A hard white substance in the shape of kidneys and livers—meant to be placed on the corresponding ailing organs—is also for sale.

Even though U Nu has sequestered himself in a Buddhist monastery, I wonder whether it would be possible to visit him. I am met with a baffled stare. U Pau Tin: "I really don't know where he is, but I will do my best to find out." A little later, in an outlying section of the city, we note that building is going on. U Pau Tin: "My hunch is that a home is being constructed here for U Nu. Let us go and investigate."

We drive along a dusty road and stop before an unfinished house. A beautifully robed man, whose face resembles that of India's Krishna Menon, emerges. U Nu, he announces, is upstairs sleeping; could we come back at five o'clock? The discrepancy between expecting the ex–Prime Minister to be in a Buddhist retreat and finding him asleep in a half-built house amuses me. U Pau Tin tells me the man who greeted us had been Burma's Ambassador to Moscow under U Nu. I ask if his attitude resembles that of the pro-Soviet Krishna Menon. I am told it most emphatically does.

U Nu welcomes us warmly later. We discuss Buddhism and politics. I tell him I have seen the Peace Palace and the Golden Pagoda, and inquire about the cheroots. U Nu assures me no priest would ever smoke. What led him to become a Buddhist, I ask, since he so clearly has been a highly successful political figure?

Silence. U Nu: "I shall confess something to you. As a young man, I drank a lot and lived a most disreputable life. I conjugated a great deal. You do say 'conjugate,' do you not?" I nod my head affirmatively, knowing I must remain expressionless. "I realized I must stop my bad habits, so I became a Buddhist." "And it doesn't interfere with your politics?" I am answered only by a smile.

It is growing late; to drive over the back roads in the dark will be difficult. I thank U Nu warmly for our visit and say farewell.

After our talk I understand why Ne Win has displaced U Nu as Prime Minister. But I feel Burma is in for a difficult time.

Singapore: beautiful, a painting executed by an expert artist, using delicate brush strokes and the finest pigment. I stay at the Raffles Hotel and am invited by Lady Go Khee, whom I met in Delhi, to a dinner in honor of British diplomats and professional men whose time is up in Singapore.

Lady Go Khee's house is elegant, surrounded by jasmin and other plants laden with subtle scents. The dinner is sumptuous, prepared by a Cantonese chef who in her cooking combines the finest delicacies of India, Singapore, China, Indonesia. The atmosphere is warm and friendly; the special evening is festive with an undercurrent of sadness. The English are glad to be going home, but confess how much they will miss the colleagues they are leaving. It is the end of Empire, the birth of a new era. Those who live permanently in Singapore are glad to gain independence, but are also unhappy that personal ties with the English are being broken.

Before I left America, Henri Cartier-Bresson told me his lovely Indonesian wife, Elli, was on her way to Jakarta. She would be in Singapore at just the time of my arrival. Elli—who had been a dancer until an accident ended her career—and I had spent a good deal of time together in New York; I had often photographed her classic beauty. This would be our first encounter in Asia.

Now, at the Raffles Hotel, looking forward to seeing Elli again, I ask for her, only to be informed she departed the day before, leaving no forwarding address. I feel desolate; how can I possibly find her?

At the airport in Jakarta Mr. M., an Indonesian Cabinet Minister whom I have known in New York, greets me, accompanied by his young daughter. I am about to tell him I have made a reservation at the Hôtel des Indes, when he says he is taking me to a government guest house. I hadn't wished to become a "guest of the government" because, from everything I've heard, Sukarno has been behaving in dictatorial fashion, but I mustn't reveal my distaste to Mr. M.

The door of the car closes and I am driven through the twilight for many miles into a remote suburb. At last we stop at a rather small building that seems to be the equivalent of an American Y.W.C.A. hostel. A large room on the ground floor contains several tables piled with magazines. Upstairs, beyond a similar lobby, we walk through a common bathroom (in which a tub is half-full of gray water); it is also a passageway to my bedroom, where a washstand—but no other toilet facilities—stares at me. The walls do not reach to the ceiling. Mr. M., his daughter, and I return to the common room; no one else is present.

A "boy" appears who does not speak English but who will go down the street and bring back a delicious meal. I accept Mr. M.'s suggestions; the only word I recognize is rice. As the boy is going down the steps, the telephone rings. Mr. M. answers and, to my amazement, the call is for me. I hear, as though an angel were speaking, the familiar, comforting voice of Elli Cartier-Bresson. I say a delirious, "Hello! How are you? How wonderful to hear your voice!" She is curt, gruff: "Don't talk. Don't unpack. Don't do anything until a friend of mine and I call for you. We have managed to have the owner of the Hôtel des Indes move out of his suite so that you may have it. Don't worry. Just stay where you are; we'll be there soon." I utter a weak "thank you" and hang up. I explain that an old friend who is Indonesian is on her way to see me; she has arranged for me to stay at the Hôtel des Indes. I apologize for having caused so much trouble. But I have no clue as to what is happening.

In a short time Elli arrives with an older woman in a chauffeur-driven limousine. Elli throws her arms around me and whispers, "Don't say a word. Just let me arrange everything." I take her to my room. On the way, she turns on the faucet of the half-filled bathtub: no water. She tries the faucet of the bedroom washstand: no water. She points, without a word, to the space between walls and ceiling. Back in the lobby, she states in a firm, authoritative voice that my bags should be taken down to the car at once. I repeat my apologies to Mr. M. and his daughter, who are silent, kind, and ask no questions.

In the car Elli introduces me to the Indonesian lady and then is silent. I follow her lead. I want to hug her, but something warns me not to react or show emotion of any kind. At the front desk of the hotel, no one is in sight except the clerk.

Elli: "Mrs. Norman is to have the owner's suite. Would you kindly have her baggage brought in from the car?" (Elli's friend has remained in the automobile with the bags.)

No one responds to the clerk's call. Elli and I climb back into the limousine and drive through a short lane of two-story, shoddily built structures attached to the hotel. On the veranda of each, men are sitting, staring at the road, gazing at I don't know what. In front of a low building at the end, our chauffeur stops and takes out my baggage. There is no one to help him.

My "suite" consists of a large foyer, an enormous bedroom enclosed by screens, and behind it a bathroom. Elli doesn't waste a moment. She goes directly to the doors. No keys. She turns on the faucets in the tub and washstand: no water. She tries to flush the toilet: it won't. She goes to the telephone: no answer. Only the front door has a key. We lock it and drive back to the office. Elli tells the clerk about the situation in the owner's suite. He can do nothing about it; no one will be on duty until six in the morning. Elli is furious. We return to the suite. She and her friend block one door with a heavy potted plant, another with bulky furniture. We drive off to a restaurant for dinner. I am unnerved and exhausted. Are we in a police state?

I still don't dare ask questions. After dinner Elli checks everything in my rooms meticulously and decides, since it is so beastly hot, she will turn on the ceiling fan; it doesn't work. With a tall stick she pokes the blades and by some miracle they revolve. She tells me to brace the stick in front of my screened bedroom door for further protection.

She and her friend promise to call for me late in the morning, then leave. In spite of the barricaded doors, I feel terrified. I take a sleeping pill but have a sinking feeling that rest is not for me tonight. After thrashing about, I finally doze off, only to wake up in daylight, sensing that someone is in the room outside the screens. Without my hearing him, a smiling youth has put back the potted plant and the heavy furniture.

On a table is a tray of breakfast. My watch shows 6:00 A.M. I cannot speak with the boy but stupidly smile at him. Beyond my cage, the rest of the space feels almost icy by contrast. I eat my breakfast, praying that water for the tea has been boiled.

The thought of leaving my room to pass before the men who stare from their verandas is horrifying, but I run to the office to confirm my tickets for Bali and Japan. A clerk says I must give them to an airline attendant who is waiting there. I don't want to give up my tickets; I simply need to have them confirmed. The clerk insists; the young lady will bring them back to me. I have no choice: hand them over. Doubtless they will be sold to someone else at a higher rate.

My room is now open to anyone who may wish to enter. I phone Mr. M.; his daughter will take me wherever I wish. There is no way to take a bath. A slight amount of dirty water trickles into the wash basin. Nothing else works.

A knock at my door; I don't open it. A male voice, unconvincing and insidious, calls out that he knows I write for a newspaper; so does he. He needs money for a scholarship. I reply that I cannot help him and would he please go away. The voice persists. I scream at him that I will phone the office. Finally my shouting is so loud that he disappears.

Miss M. arrives; I want to visit museums and search for old Indonesian fabrics, which I greatly admire. On our way to a nearby shop I ask if Miss M. goes to college. She states, starry-eyed, that she does. "Is there any subject that specially interests you?" "Oh, yes—rock-and-roll."

Miss M. stays in the car while I enter the small shop, empty except for the owner and his wife, who speak no English. In a few moments a young man appears outside and, in a threatening manner, demands money. Obviously he is the one who came to my hotel door and is following me. I cannot reach the car, the chauffeur, or the daughter without running into him. Again I scream, "Go away," and finally he disappears.

I rush out to the waiting car. Miss M., who has been standing on the pavement, has just had her purse snatched, even though her chauffeur was sitting in the car close by. Trembling, the two of us phone her father.

I tell about the young man and the purse-snatching, and report that my tickets for Bali and Japan have been taken from me at the hotel. Mr. M. explains that President Sukarno is planning to escort a number of United States Senators now in Jakarta to Bali as his guests, so all plane and hotel reservations have been confiscated. He promises to get me other tickets, then consoles his daughter.

At the hotel, Elli and her friend are waiting for me. We immediately reexamine my suite and Elli decides I cannot remain there. Next to her friend's house, where she is staying, is a U.S. Embassy building being re-modeled for future American officials. She has already arranged for me to occupy one of the rooms. I will be much safer and quite close to her. At the Embassy annex I find myself in a large complex of empty quarters, but at least I have running water, a toilet, and a telephone—the latter miles away in another part of the bizarre building. The lock on my door works—at times.

President Sukarno invites me to his great White Palace. He is a different man from the one I met in New Delhi less than a decade ago. Now he is dressed in a sumptuous white uniform, as he was during his 1956 United States visit. On that spectacular trip he even had aides turn pages for him when he read his speech at the United Nations, and was accompanied by an enormous retinue. He made a vivid impression with his overelaborate uniforms and his dashing manner.

After a few pleasantries Sukarno takes me to task because our mutual friend, Louis Fischer, who recently visited Indonesia (he sent me a postcard: "Went swimming with Sukarno") and wrote a book about him, has been advocating birth control. "I want you to get him to stop!" snaps the imperious voice. "And another thing you must do is to make your government demand that our claim to West Irian [West New Guinea] be honored." I can just see myself marching to Washington and telling President Eisenhower what to do.

My eyes keep wandering to the huge, uninspired academic oil paintings —big ships and poor landscapes, nineteenth-century Western style—lining the vast walls. The lovely butterfly of New Delhi is no longer Sukarno's wife. His entire demeanor has changed. He asks cordially, nonetheless, if he can do anything for me. What I really want is to have him make certain that my reservations are returned and ensure my safe departure; I long to blurt out that he should be less oppressive, obliterate the country's corruption, and stop the warfare between the Celebes and Sumatra. He might also see that the best craftsmen are encouraged, the condition of the poor is alleviated, and get me some ancient fabrics I can buy. I remain speechless.

It rains steadily in steaming, hot, penetratingly damp Jakarta. I brought no umbrella and often lack transport. There is no way to have my drenched clothes washed or pressed. If I catch cold, I'll have to go to bed. I must leave Indonesia at once.

My tickets for Japan have never been returned. A travel agent tells me not a single seat on any flight out of Jakarta is available. Tired and disgruntled, I refused to tip him or to move from the counter; someone is sure to return a ticket. At last a man does; I ask to buy it. What day and where is it for? I almost don't care, but by the greatest stroke of luck, it is for a plane bound the next day for Hong Kong.

Having thanked Elli profusely, I tell her a long story about being afraid of catching cold; about being expected in Japan; about having to meet someone in Hawaii to discuss important plans; about my mother not being very well . . . Elli laughs heartily. "Spare your energy, Dorothy—everyone leaves Jakarta early!"

17

Tokyo: I arrive in time for the opening meeting of the Buddhist *Jayanti*, the 2500th anniversary of the birth of the Buddha. As planned, Dr. Suzuki and Mihoko Okamura greet me and take me to a large auditorium where ceremonies are being held.

Suzuki introduces me to a Zen Buddhist in a handsome suit decorated with an extraordinary piece of brocade. Abbot of Kamakura's Zen Temple, he invites me to see him on my visit there.

His temple is the oldest Zen Buddhist shrine in the country; the massive Amitaba Buddha statue stands before it. The day is dreary, the windowpanes spattered with the driving rain. I sit silent in front of the Master; finally my turn to speak comes. Our eyes meet. I lean over to Mihoko and plead, "Please apologize for me and explain I seem to have come to the end of my journey—my journey of search. As I sit here, I have no questions to ask and nothing to say."

Mihoko communicates my message. The Master throws back his head and laughs heartily. "Tell her," he replies, "congratulations." He continues to gaze into my eyes and I into his.

I had traveled long and far and was full of a thousand queries at every point along the way. I had learned much during my travels, but had sought always to learn more. Had my search truly come to an end? Impossible. I would go on as before, but now perhaps the quest would be concentrated even more intensely within.

Back from Japan, I no longer feel the need to wrestle with metaphysical questions which cannot be resolved in any event. Efforts of the East to achieve self-realization are not identical with but complement those of the West. Their interplay has consistently preoccupied me. I exult in having been exposed to the disciplines and insights of both worlds. Now to enjoy a moment of spiritual equilibrium brings release.

In New York, the image of my father suddenly becomes a symbol for me of modern America. He and those like him, coming from Europe without the privilege of having been molded by its great traditions, through their energy, strength of character, and determination helped build the world that has nourished me.

I bless the man for his integrity, caring, sense of responsibility; for his refusal to be imprisoned by narrow dogmas and confining labels. I could never thank him enough, nor give him all the love and affection he craved and deserved.

As the years have passed, my mother required ever more attention. Both my brothers died; I alone was left to take care of all her needs and affairs; I visited her in Philadelphia often. To move her to New York became impossible —her friends were her life. I learned to admire much in her I had once decried, but no matter how greatly I respected her, I couldn't feel really close; we never talked about anything that deeply mattered.

Staying with Mother now, I have the impression that she looks thinner, more fragile. I dare not leave her, must not be out of reach.

Her doctor recommends that she have a trained nurse on constant duty. I remain at her apartment. She sleeps late one morning; when she awakens, she calls my name. I go to her at once and sit next to her, but she falls asleep again. I lie down on the bed in the next room and cry. My mother is dying. All the pent-up love I have never been able to express rises within me and overflows into tears.

The nurse comes out of Mother's room. She scolds, "Don't cry." As though I could stop! I go and stay quietly by Mother's side again. She sits bolt upright, stares before her, reaches out her arms. She utters words she never has spoken to me: "Come here. Hold me close. Let me hold you. Hold me close, closer. Closer." She pulls me to her. Her grasp, around my neck, my shoulder, my back, is so tight I can scarcely breathe. As she clings to me, she says what she has never been able to express before and what I never knew she really felt. Her voice is strong. "I want to tell you how much I love you. More than anyone in the world. You have always been there. Every time I have needed you, you have been there. You have done everything for me. You and no one else. How can I ever thank you? Or tell you how proud I am of you? I love you. I love you. You have always been there. Hold me! Hold me closer!" Her arms tighten even more passionately. My tears run over the shoulder of my mother as hers are shed over me. The hold loosens; she falls back; her eyes close. I cannot stem my tears, but hers have stopped. The nurse sends me out of the room. My mother is dead, but the miracle we had both secretly wanted has taken place.

Funeral services are held. I sit frozen, surrounded by Nancy, Andrew, Mother's friends, a few relatives. I am remote, alone, yet curiously quiet. My mother's peace, I know, is as great as my own. And then, without prelude, I see her miraculously one with the Great Mother statues of all time: elements of a single, interwoven hymn to fertility and faith.

The forms—reassuring yet challenging since time immemorial—speak to me with new clarity and at a personal level. In my mind's eye I see two awkward, angular, ageless figures locked in a symbol of love beyond love—treasure bestowed and received with an embrace that throbs through my being.

I feel myself in tune with—enveloped by—the nameless, infinite mysteries in their primordial, light-giving forms.

Man's core and conscience: the Great Mother who sets the limitless problems that we must solve, that are indeed ourselves. The vast and colossal image mirrors the sacred secret of life itself, its continuity and glow, reaching forever toward the marvelous Yes.

1983